This Is Delicious!
What Is It?

This Is Delicious! What Is It?

An Eclectic Collection of International Comfort Foods

Robert Meyers-Lussier

iUniverse, Inc.
New York Lincoln Shanghai

This Is Delicious! What Is It?
An Eclectic Collection of International Comfort Foods

iUniverse, Inc.

For information address:
iUniverse, Inc.
2021 Pine Lake Road, Suite 100
Lincoln, NE 68512
www.iuniverse.com

Front Cover
Cat and Canary
Copyright © John Lund

ISBN: 0-595-30505-9

Printed in the United States of America

Dedicated to all those with whom I have broken bread

CONTENTS

LIST OF PHOTOGRAPHS

ACKNOWLEDGEMENTS

I have so very many persons to thank for their help over the years! Thank you to:

Those brave souls who have been taste testers at my experimental dinner parties.

Those braver souls who have hosted some of my experimental dinner parties, especially Doug Courson and Grant Dunmire, Radleigh Valentine, Christine Chalstrom, my old Pannekoeken Huis friends, my barracks 'family' when I lived in Augsburg, West Germany, as well as the ultimate experimentees—my family.

Those that helped with my television show, *Talking With Your Mouth Full*, especially Susan Peck, who was crazy enough to let me produce it at Bloomington (MN) Public Television. Thanks also to Mary Carl-Ramirez and Cheri Maxwell for their help with hosting duties.

Those that have invited me to cook in a professional manner. This includes Hopkins School District (MN), who allowed me to teach and further my knowledge in international recipe development by helping others prepare fun foods.

Stephen Rocheford, publisher of *Lavender Magazine*, and Heather Henderson, former editor. Heather passed away from the debilitating disease of anorexia she so desperately tried to battle. She even went so far as to try to help others with the disease. She allowed me wide control when writing restaurant reviews for *Lavender Magazine*. She was a truly wonderful person. We will remember you.

Susan Malmstein (my sister) and Susan Shangle for their help with various aspects of the preparation and coordination for taking some of the photographs for the cookbook.

Lastly, what started it all: *Babette's Feast,* a movie inspired by a story by Danish author Isak Dineson. One lonely winter eve while stationed in Germany I watched this amazing movie and it changed my life. I had a reason for cooking, other than simply sustenance. Whether you see the movie or read the short story, it's an awfully good tale.

INTRODUCTION

What you will see in the pages that follow are over 250 recipes for your consideration. Simple black text on white paper peppered with photographs. What you won't see are the endless hours of laughter, lively conversation, professions of love and friendship that occurred before, during or after their presentation. Nor will you see the blood, sweat and tears involved in their preparation. There are countless stories yet to be told with each and every recipe in this cookbook. You hold within your hands the very tools to create your own novel of culinary experiences. Just as I write poetry inspired by moments in time, food represents poetry personified. Add friends and family and poems lift off the page and into our collective experience.

Cooking and its related chores have played such an integral part of my life for one reason. I had a revelation. On a cold winter night while stationed with the U.S. Army in West Germany, the wind howled outside. It was a weekend and there was not a thing to do. I was alone in my barracks room, watching a movie just rented called *Babette's Feast*. I hadn't a clue what it was about, other than it somehow involved food. I had had an affair with food since I could remember, but it mostly involved consumption. This movie changed that.

The story is of a French-woman, Babette, who arrives at the doorstep of two women in a small Danish village. The woman needs a job, so the two women consent to let her cook for them, against their better judgment. They are daughters of a minister of a frugal religious sect, thus eat very plain, simple foods. Babette herself was a chef in the French imperial court, used to preparing some of the most sumptuous feasts imaginable. Yet she prepares their simple meals with a simple pleasure, happy for having escaped the French revolutionary uprising from where she fled. In the meantime, she becomes ingratiated into the small community.

One day, out of nowhere, Babette is informed she has won the French lottery (yes, they had them even way back then!). What she decides to do with her winnings is literary and cinematic magic. She spends all of her money on preparing a feast to surpass all feasts. To the dinner are invited village people she has come to know have feelings for one another, but can't act on them due to social and religious constraints. During the course of the dinner the guests, pleasantly surprised by some of the courses and subdued by wines, drop their defenses. They see not only each other, but for the first time what is in their hearts. Babette is again

1

broke, having spent every last cent on the dinner. But what she achieves is worth more than anything money could buy.

That's the story. I wanted to cook so badly after watching the movie I pulled together five nights of feasting for my fellow soldiers. I assembled different dinners from countries that fascinated me—France, Greece, Italy, Mexico and China. With five courses each night, never having cooked much more than macaroni and cheese (from the box, no less!), everyone had such fun. I knew I wanted to explore this cooking thing more.

I left the military soon after, with the world as my oyster. Intent on becoming a diplomat, I enrolled in the University of Minnesota as a Political Science major. I also began to cater to make a few extra dollars to get me through school. *The World On A Platter* was my first venture providing culinary services professionally. While I loved the end products of my jobs, I hated the process—cooking became a chore. I wanted it to be fun, but on my own terms. I would have to determine my own special path, in the *spirit* of *Babette's Feast*.

I determined political science classes were not for me, but found I loved immersing myself in the political process. Eventually I ran for public office in the great state of Minnesota, for State Representative. I ran against one of the most entrenched (but beloved) public servants in the state. I lost. In the process, I made several television debate appearances and became familiar with the woman who ran the station. After the race, we had lunch and talked about what the station was looking for in terms of programming. I mentioned a cooking show. Susan Peck was so enchanted with the idea, within weeks I was producing and hosting a cooking show for Bloomington Public Television, *Talking With Your Mouth Full*. The show had a variety of chefs cook different dishes, after which we sat down to eat the meal with a local personality. The very first person I invited to join us was my former political opponent, who graciously accepted. It was my first (surreal) chance to test those waters of bringing people together with food. Kathleen Blatz went on to become the Chief Justice of the Minnesota Supreme Court, where she still presides!

For two years I televised the program until I moved out of the community. About the same time, I finished college with a major in Russian Area Studies (if you'd like to fill in the blanks of this crazy timeline, feel free to log on to www.bobmeyers.com where you'll find additional autobiographical information). I thought perhaps I might go into the legal field. In typical fashion, I jumped in with both feet. While testing the legal waters, I was hired as a cooking instructor for the Minnetonka/Hopkins community (western suburbs of Minneapolis). Rather than entertain and inform as on TV, I took this craft to a new level. I conducted considerable research on the topics I was to teach. This is where I began to truly learn the techniques of other nation's culinary traditions.

Two years of teaching later I again moved on. Teaching had become less fun as more and more students attending classes were of a snootier nature (my next book of poetry has a poem reflecting this experience). Also by this time I had begun writing poetry. I thought I'd see if I couldn't convince someone to let me write about food. Thus I was introduced to Heather Henderson, the editor of a fairly new publication for the GLBT community in Minneapolis, *Lavender Magazine*. She originally hired me to do a sports column with the intention that I eventually do restaurant reviews. It only took one issue of sports writing before she asked if I'd also do the restaurant review column. It was with great gusto I accepted. For two years I wrote reviews of restaurants in the Twin Cities area. To dine at fabulous restaurants and write about (mostly) great food and get paid for it—is there really anything better?

****

I can't tell you when it was I decided to pull all my recipes together from over the years. There was no defining moment. However, after I physically bound my recipes together, I presented them to a group of fellow colleagues in the litigation support industry. Much to my surprise they encouraged me to publish it. That was over three years ago!

Thus with these last few words I complete the cycle. The cycle of an inspired moment, the years of interpreting and following through with the inspiration, the presentation of recipes for the next cycle of inspirations—my gifts to you—as you now create the next generation of stories, of poems, for your own tales of culinary and human experience.

HORS D'ŒUVRES

Cheesy Pepper and Olive Squares

I first made this bite-size snack for a dinner party with friends. They have since become a last-second host/hostess gift for many parties I've attended over the years. They are simple to make and serve many!

Makes 48 servings
Prep Time: 30 minutes

½ cup all-purpose flour
1 teaspoon baking powder
½ teaspoon salt
8 eggs
12 ounces Monterey Jack cheese, shredded
1 ½ cups cottage cheese
2 tablespoons jalapeno peppers, minced
2 tablespoons black olives, chopped fine

Preheat oven to 350 degrees. Grease a 13x9x2-inch baking dish.

1) In a small mixing bowl, stir together flour, baking powder and salt. Set aside.
2) In a large mixing bowl, beat eggs until well combined. Stir flour mixture into beaten eggs and mix well.
3) Fold in Monterey Jack cheese, cottage cheese, jalapeno peppers and black olives.
4) Pour into prepared baking dish.
5) Bake in oven about 40 minutes until the overall surface is golden brown or a toothpick inserted near the middle pulls out clean.
6) Let stand 10 minutes. Cut into 1 ½-inch squares.

Per serving (approximate values): 38 Calories; 2.3g Fat (55.5% calories from fat); 2.9g Protein; 1.4g Carbohydrate; 7mg Cholesterol; 100mg Sodium

PROSCIUTTO AND PEAR ROLLUPS

I first made these for a wedding and they were a big hit. Fairly simple to prepare, you can make a lot of them, then wrap them in plastic until ready to serve later the same day.

Makes 6 servings
Prep Time: 30 minutes

2 ounces ricotta cheese
2 ounces Stilton cheese, crumbled
1 tablespoon sour cream
12 slices prosciutto, thinly sliced
1 whole pear
Lemon juice, fresh or bottled

1) In a small bowl, thoroughly blend ricotta, Stilton and sour cream.
2) Spread evenly on prosciutto, spreading mixture almost to edges.
3) Peel and quarter the pear, then cut each quarter in half. Place pear pieces into medium bowl of cold water with a capful of lemon juice added.
4) To assemble, quickly dry pear slice on a paper towel. Place pear slice at the end of a slice of prosciutto. Roll up prosciutto to the other end, so it is completely wrapped around pear slice. Insert toothpick to make sure prosciutto doesn't unravel and to make it easier for guests to pick up the roulades.
5) Cover and refrigerate until ready to serve.

Per serving (approximate values): 122 Calories; 4.6g Fat (40.1% calories from fat); 3.3g Protein; 5.9g Carbohydrate; 323mg Cholesterol; 124mg Sodium

LOMI LOMI SALMON

Hawaii is not only one of the most beautiful places on Earth, it is also home to some of the most delicious foods as well! Lomi Lomi Salmon is a traditional luau staple, but is also a wonderful treat at your own table.

Makes 8 servings
Prep Time: 15 minutes

1 pound fresh salmon
1 tablespoon olive oil
3 whole fresh tomatoes, diced
⅓ cup green onions, thinly sliced
½ cup onion, finely chopped
2 tablespoons water
1 cup crushed ice

Preheat oven to 350 degrees.

1) Brush salmon with olive oil. Place salmon, skin side down, on baking sheet or dish so salmon lays flat. Roast salmon for about 20 minutes or until salmon flakes easily. Cool completely. Remove skin.
2) In medium bowl, shred salmon.
3) Combine remaining ingredients with shredded salmon, except ice. Cover and chill several hours or overnight.
4) Right before serving, add crushed ice, distributing evenly.

Per serving (approximate values): 93 Calories; 3.6g Fat (34.9% calories from fat); 11.8g Protein; 3.3g Carbohydrate; 31 mg Cholesterol; 320mg Sodium

TRI-OLIVES WITH FENNEL AND ORANGE

My sister about fainted the first time I made this dish, olives being one of her favorite foods. The citrus cuts the saltiness of the olives; fennel and red pepper add complexity. This dish doesn't encourage guests to overeat before the main meal, yet satisfies the need to munch.

Makes 12 servings
Prep Time: 30 minutes

2 cups Kalamata olives, pitted
2 cups black olives, pitted
2 cups green olives, pimento-stuffed
¼ cup olive oil
¼ cup fresh lemon juice
¼ cup fresh orange juice
2 tablespoons orange peel, grated
1 tablespoon fennel seed
½ teaspoon crushed red pepper

1) Combine all ingredients in a medium non-metal bowl until evenly distributed.
2) Cover in a non-metal container or pour into gallon-size resealable plastic bag. Chill at least one full day before serving. Stir or shake periodically to distribute flavors.

Per serving (approximate values): 123 Calories; 12.1g Fat (83.1% calories from fat); 0.9g Protein; 4.6g Carbohydrate; 0mg Cholesterol; 931 mg Sodium

Basic Fresh Tomato Salsa

Makes 6 servings
Prep Time: 20 minutes

2 tablespoons onion, minced
1 pound Roma tomatoes, diced
2 tablespoons cilantro, chopped fine
2 whole Serrano peppers, minced
1 teaspoon salt
1 tablespoon lime juice

1)   Place onion in a strainer. Rinse with hot water and drain.
2)   Thoroughly combine all ingredients in a medium mixing bowl. Cover and chill in the refrigerator for at least 30 minutes. Shake or mix the ingredients to evenly marinate until serving time.

Per serving (approximate values): 28 Calories; 0.3g Fat (8.6% calories from fat); 1.3g Protein; 6.4g Carbohydrate; 0mg Cholesterol; 365mg Sodium

CRAB AND CORN SALSA

I created this dish to compliment another salsa I was serving for an event I was catering. It had an egg-like odor to it, so I was a bit afraid of guest's reactions. It turned out to be a huge hit paired with corn tortilla chips. Just don't offer guests a whiff as you're preparing it!

Makes 6 servings
Prep Time: 30 minutes

1 cup corn, canned, crispy
1 whole pasilla chile, diced, size of corn
4 ounces crab meat, canned or fresh
½ whole red bell pepper, diced, size of corn
2 whole Serrano peppers, minced
½ teaspoon dried marjoram
2 tablespoons lime juice

1) Add all ingredients to medium mixing bowl. Combine thoroughly.
2) Scoop into a coverable container that you can shake. Shake periodically to ensure all ingredients are being marinated evenly.

Per serving (approximate values): 54 Calories; 0.6g Fat (9.1 % calories from fat); 5.3g Protein; 8.1 g Carbohydrate; 17mg Cholesterol; 69mg Sodium

ORANGE PAPAYA SALSA

I do not consider this a great salsa for chip dipping. This salsa is awesome when served as a side to a roast or grilled chicken, however. Beware the habanera chile when handling. It is the hottest chile on earth!

Makes 6 servings
Prep Time: 20 minutes

1 whole habanera chile, seeded, stemmed
1 whole tomato, yellow, roughly chopped
3 whole papayas, peeled, seeded, roughly chopped
¾ cup orange juice
2 tablespoons lime juice
1 tablespoon rice wine vinegar
1 tablespoon water
1 teaspoon sugar
¼ teaspoon salt

1) Place all ingredients in a food processor or blender and purée.
2) Pour into container and serve. Refrigerate covered for up to three days.

Per serving (approximate values): 82 Calories; 0.4g Fat (3.6% calories from fat); 1.4g Protein; 20.5g Carbohydrate; 0mg Cholesterol; 96mg Sodium

BLACK BEAN AND MANGO SALSA

Makes 6 servings
Prep Time: 30 minutes

14 ounces black beans, canned
½ teaspoon salt
1 large mango, peeled, diced
3 tablespoons red bell pepper, diced
1 teaspoon hot pepper sauce
1 tablespoon lime juice

1) Drain beans in a strainer, rinse in cool water, then drain again. Transfer beans to a medium mixing bowl.
2) Add remaining ingredients and mix thoroughly.
3) Place the finished salsa into a sealable container. Refrigerate and shake or stir periodically to evenly distribute ingredients.

Per serving (approximate values): 249 Calories; 1g Fat (3.6% calories from fat); 14.5g Protein; 47.6g Carbohydrate; 0mg Cholesterol; 202mg Sodium

BANANA SALSA

This salsa is another failed attempt at an interesting chip salsa. I don't like it with chips, perhaps you will. I loved it when I paired it with a grilled tuna and have been serving it since with all sorts of white fish!

Makes 6 servings
Prep Time: 30 minutes

3 medium bananas, peeled and diced
½ medium red bell pepper, diced
½ medium green bell pepper, diced
1 medium jalapeno pepper, minced
1 tablespoon ginger, grated
3 whole green onions, chopped fine
¼ cup fresh mint, chopped
3 tablespoons lime juice
2 tablespoons light brown sugar
1 tablespoon olive oil
Salt and pepper, to taste

1)   Combine all of the ingredients in a mixing bowl and gently toss to mix.
2)   Correct the seasonings, adding salt, lime juice or sugar to taste.

Per serving (approximate values): 126 Calories; 2.8g Fat (17.9% calories from fat); 2.5g Protein; 26.58 Carbohydrate; 0mg Cholesterol; 8mg Sodium.

BOURSIN

This is one of those cheeses you might see in the specialty cheese section of your supermarket for upwards of $5 an ounce! It is a traditional French cheese spread that you can make for a fraction of the store price. Age it for at least a day to let the flavors of the herbs fully develop.

Makes 30 servings
Prep Time: 10 minutes

16 ounces cream cheese, softened
8 ounces whipped butter
4 cloves garlic, minced
1 teaspoon oregano, dried leaves
¼ teaspoon basil, dried leaves
¼ teaspoon marjoram, dried leaves
¼ teaspoon thyme, dried leaves
¼ teaspoon black pepper, freshly ground
Salt, as necessary

1) Place all ingredients in a medium mixing bowl and stir until all ingredients are completely distributed. If everything has been properly softened, use a hand mixer. If not, a wooden spoon will work, but it will require a lot of effort!
2) Pack into crocks or jars. Cover and chill.

Per serving (approximate values): 107 Calories; 11.5g Fat (93.3% calories from fat); 1.2g Protein; 0.6g Carbohydrate; 33mg Cholesterol; 107mg Sodium

HOLIDAY PÂTÉ

One of my very favorite foods is liver pâté. Growing up, I would dream of having vats of pâté, caviar and champagne flowing at all times. Thus it is the one of several recipes you will find throughout the book where I have tested dozens of variations until I found just the right combination of ingredients. This pâté is also one I have found that even liver haters might like.

Makes 10 servings
Prep Time: 30 minutes

1 cup butter, divided
1 pound chicken livers, coarsely chopped
4 shallots, minced
3 large hard-boiled eggs, chopped
½ teaspoon salt
⅛ teaspoon cloves
¼ teaspoon pepper
½ teaspoon thyme, dried leaves
½ teaspoon marjoram, dried leaves
¼ teaspoon ground ginger
¼ teaspoon cinnamon
1 tablespoon Madeira
2 tablespoons brandy
2 tablespoons cognac

1) In medium saucepan over medium heat, simmer the chicken livers and shallots slowly in one stick of butter (½ cup), being careful not to brown them. Remove saucepan from the heat when the livers are firm but still tender, about 10 to 15 minutes. Cool slightly.

2) In a food processor, cream the remaining stick of butter until smooth.

3) Add the cooked livers and shallots with juices, eggs, seasonings, Madeira, brandy and cognac to the creamed butter in the food processor. Pulse to mix everything well, scraping down the sides of the work bowl as necessary and process until the mixture is fully puréed.

4) At this stage the mixture will be quite fluid. Don't worry! It will solid-ify as it cools. Pack the pâté into crocks, cover and refrigerate until ready to serve.

Per serving (approximate values): 263 Calories; 21.6g Fat (77.4% calories from fat); 10.5g Protein; 3.7g Carbohydrate; 312mg Cholesterol; 348mg Sodium

HUMMUS

This Middle Eastern spread is great for vegetable dipping in addition to scooping up with pita bread. Tahini paste is actually ground sesame seeds with a consistency of peanut butter. It is indispensable to creating the unique taste to this spread. I like to make it when I know I have a vegetarian or two joining me for dinner.

Makes 12 servings
Prep Time: 20 minutes

15 ounces canned garbanzo beans, drained, rinsed
½ cup tahini paste
1 tablespoon water
½ teaspoon onion powder
4 tablespoons lemon juice
¼ cup plain yogurt
¼ teaspoon garlic powder
¼ teaspoon salt

1) In a food processor, combine all ingredients. Cover and process until smooth, scraping down sides of container as necessary.
2) Spoon into container, cover and refrigerate until ready to serve.

Per serving (approximate values): 106 Calories; 5.7g Fat (45.7% calories from fat); 3.8g Protein; 11.4g Carbohydrate; 1mg Cholesterol; 154mg Sodium

PURÉED WHITE BEAN DIP

Makes 10 servings
Prep Time: 45 minutes

6 slices bacon
1 medium onion, chopped
1 tablespoon garlic, minced
1 tablespoon cumin powder
1 tablespoon chili powder
38 ounces canned white beans, drained (also known as cannellini)
4 ounces Pepper Jack cheese, grated
½ cup sour cream
1 tablespoon lime juice
Cayenne pepper, to taste

1) In a large skillet, fry bacon over moderate heat until crisp. Transfer bacon to paper towels. Leave remaining bacon fat in skillet.

2) In bacon fat, sauté onion and garlic over moderate heat. Stir until softened and pale golden, about 5 minutes.

3) Add chili powder and cumin powder. Stir 1 minute. Add beans, stirring constantly an additional 5 minutes.

4) Remove mixture from heat and let cool. Place slightly cooled mixture in food processor. Add cheese, sour cream and lime juice and process until smooth. Transfer to a large bowl. Add cayenne to taste.

5) Crumble bacon into mixture and mix well. Cover and refrigerate until ready to serve.

Per serving (excluding unknown items): 228 Calories; 8.3g Fat (32.2% calories from fat); 12.6g Protein; 26.7g Carbohydrate; 18mg Cholesterol; 620mg Sodium

TZATZIKI

Ever wondered what the delicious sauce is when eating a Gyros sandwich? It's some variation of this dish. I like to serve it ice cold on a hot summer day with some crusty French bread. It also pairs well with roasted lamb and chicken!

Makes 4 servings
Prep Time: 20 minutes

1 medium cucumber
1 ½ cups plain yogurt
4 cloves garlic, minced
1 ½ tablespoons red wine vinegar
½ teaspoon salt
¼ teaspoon black pepper, freshly ground

1) Peel the cucumber, cut it in half and scrape out the seeds with a spoon.
2) Shred cucumber using large holes of a hand grater.
3) Place shredded cucumber in cheesecloth or two layers of paper towel and squeeze out as much moisture as possible.
4) In a medium bowl, whisk the yogurt until smooth.
5) Add cucumber, garlic, vinegar, salt and pepper to yogurt. Stir to blend. Serve immediately or store in covered container for use within one day. Tzatziki does not stay fresh long, but it will probably go fast anyway!

Per serving (approximate values): 81 Calories; 3.2g Fat (33.5% calories from fat); 4.4g Protein; 9.8g Carbohydrate; 12mg Cholesterol; 313mg Sodium

MUFFALETA SPREAD

For those of you who have been to New Orleans, no doubt you may have tried a Muffaleta sandwich. This is my homage to the spread that covers the bread. I like to serve it as an hors d'œuvre with French bread slices.

Makes 10 servings
Prep Time: 45 minutes

1 cup green olives
1 cup Kalamata olives, pitted
½ medium red onion, chopped
2 teaspoons basil, dried leaves
2 tablespoons lemon juice
1 tablespoon horseradish, grated
1 tablespoon garlic, minced
1 tablespoon Dijon-style mustard
¼ teaspoon hot sauce
¼ teaspoon Worcestershire sauce
¼ cup olive oil
Salt and pepper, to taste

1) Combine all ingredients except olive oil in a food processor. Pulse until mixture is minced and mixed well.
2) With pouring tube open, turn food processor on and gradually add oil. Process until well blended.
3) Transfer to a medium bowl. Season with salt and pepper to taste.
4) Cover and refrigerate at least one hour or up to one week. Flavors get better as they age.

Per serving (approximate values): 71 Calories; 7.1 g Fat (86.7% calories from fat); 0.5g Protein; 2 Carbohydrate; 0mg Cholesterol; 350mg Sodium

Three-Cheese Crab Dip

Makes 8 servings
Prep Time: 30 minutes

16 ounces cream cheese, softened
¼ cup plain yogurt
1 tablespoon prepared horseradish
½ teaspoon Worcestershire sauce
¼ teaspoon cayenne pepper
1 teaspoon hot sauce
3 tablespoons green onions, finely chopped
¾ cup water chestnuts, chopped
¼ cup Parmesan cheese, fresh ground
16 ounces crabmeat, shredded
1 cup Pepper-Jack cheese, shredded
Salt and pepper, to taste

1) With hand mixer, beat cream cheese in large mixing bowl until completely smooth.
2) Add yogurt through hot sauce to cream cheese. Mix until all ingredients are well combined.
3) Add green onion, chestnuts and crabmeat to cream cheese mixture. Mix until all ingredients are well combined.
4) Add Parmesan and Pepper-Jack cheeses and mix until all ingredients are well combined.
5) Place in container, cover and refrigerate for at least two hours. The flavors are better when served the next day, if you can wait that long!

Per serving (approximate values): 265 Calories; 21.4g Fat (72.4% calories from fat); 15.98 Protein; 2.4g Carbohydrate; 109mg Cholesterol; 404mg Sodium

CHICKEN-ARTICHOKE SPREAD

This is one of the few hot hors d'œurves I have found guests have loved. This is also one of those recipes that I definitely encourage others to adjust according to their tastes. The flavors before it is heated are close enough for you to judge its final taste. It's great served with crackers or lightly toasted French bread slices.

Makes 10 servings
Prep Time: 45 minutes

14 ounces artichoke hearts, marinated, drained
Non-stick cooking spray
8 ounces boneless skinless chicken breast
1 tablespoon olive oil
½ cup green onions, chopped
4 cloves garlic, minced
1 cup plain yogurt
2 tablespoons mayonnaise
¼ cup Parmesan cheese, fresh grated
2 teaspoons Worcestershire sauce
3 drops Tabasco sauce
⅛ teaspoon paprika

Preheat oven to 350 degrees. Apply a shallow 1 ½ quart baking dish with non-stick cooking spray.

1) Place artichoke hearts in food processor and process only until coarsely chopped. Spoon into a medium mixing bowl and set aside.

2) Coat a baking dish with non-stick cooking spray. Lightly coat chicken breasts with spray, then lightly coat with minced garlic and season very lightly with salt and pepper. Bake at 350 degrees until chicken is fully cooked, about 15 minutes each side, turning over once. Remove chicken from oven and let cool. Once cool, cut chicken into 1-inch pieces.

3) Add olive oil to medium skillet over medium-high heat. Add onions and garlic. Sauté about 10 minutes or until just tender. Let cool for 5 minutes.

4) Place chicken and onion mixture in food processor and process until all is just ground, making sure there are no chunks of chicken. The mixture should be *not* be completely smooth. Turn into a large mixing bowl.

5) Add yogurt, mayonnaise, cheese, Worcestershire and Tabasco to the chicken mixture and mix until well blended. Add artichokes to chicken mixture and stir well. The goal is to have the mixture moist but not at all soupy. Add salt and pepper to taste.

6) Spoon mixture into a 1½-quart baking dish which had been coated with cooking spray. Sprinkle with paprika. Cover with aluminum foil.

7) Bake mixture in 350 degree oven for 30 minutes or until heated through.

Per serving (approximate values): 105 Calories; 5.5g Fat (45.1 % calories from fat); 8.5g Protein; 6.6g Carbohydrate; 19mg Cholesterol; 128mg Sodium

MUSHROOM AND CRAB SAVORY CHEESECAKE

This cheesecake is unlike any other you might ever serve! No one expects a savory cheesecake, especially one served before the main course. You'll interest everyone with the concept, but you'll hook everyone with the flavors!

Makes 12 servings
Prep Time: 1 hour

<u>Crust:</u>

1 ¾ cups bread crumbs
1 cup Parmesan cheese, fresh grated
6 tablespoons butter
<u>Filling:</u>
1 tablespoon olive oil
½ large onion, chopped
1 medium red bell pepper, chopped
4 cups mushrooms, chopped, assorted (Cremini, Shiitake, Portobello or regular button)
28 ounces cream cheese, softened
1 teaspoon salt
½ teaspoon pepper
4 large eggs
½ cup heavy cream
10 ounces crab meat, canned, drained
4 ounces smoked gouda cheese, shredded
½ cup parsley, chopped

Preheat oven to 350 degrees.

For Crust:
1) Mix all crust ingredients in a medium bowl until well blended. Press mixture onto bottom (not sides) of 9-inch spring form pan.
2) Bake until crust is golden brown, about 15 minutes. Cool crust while preparing filling.

For Filling:
1) Heat olive oil in heavy large skillet over medium heat. Add chopped onion and red pepper and sauté 2 minutes.

2) Add mushrooms and sauté until liquid evaporates and mushrooms begin to brown, about 10 minutes.

3) In a large mixing bowl using an electric mixer, beat cream cheese, salt and pepper until mixture is fluffy.

4) Beat in eggs one at a time, then heavy cream.

5) Into cream cheese add mushroom mixture, crabmeat, smoked gouda and chopped parsley.

6) Pour filling over crust. Place cheesecake on baking sheet. Bake in 350 degree oven for 90 minutes or until cheesecake is puffed and brown on top, but shakes slightly in the center.

7) Remove from oven and let cool completely, about 2 hours.

8) Run sharp knife around pan sides to loosen cheesecake. Release pan sides. Slice and serve with large crackers or baguette slices.

Per serving (approximate values): 514 Calories; 41.3g Fat (71.6% calories from fat); 20g Protein; 16.8g Carbohydrate; 210mg Cholesterol; 877mg Sodium

SALMON TORTILLA APPETIZERS

This is the typical finger food great for serving at parties where a sit-down dinner doesn't follow. It's a little bit coastal, it's a little bit Southwestern…it's just plain fun!

Makes 48 servings
Prep Time: 30 minutes

15 ounces canned salmon, drained, flaked
8 ounces cream cheese, softened
4 tablespoons salsa, mild or medium
2 tablespoons fresh parsley, minced
1 teaspoon cilantro, minced
¼ teaspoon ground cumin
8 flour tortillas, 8-inch size

1) Drain salmon and remove any bones.
2) In a small bowl combine salmon, cream cheese, salsa, parsley and cilantro. Add cumin.
3) Spread about 2 tablespoons mixture over each tortilla to within an inch of the outer edge.
4) Roll each tortilla up tightly and wrap individually with plastic wrap.
5) Refrigerate 2-3 hours. Slice each tortilla into 1-inch bite-size pieces.

Per serving (approximate values): 48 Calories; 2.6g Fat (49.0% calories from fat); 2.6g Protein; 3.5g Carbohydrate; 10mg Cholesterol; 95mg Sodium

BASIL CRÊPES

Makes 12 servings
Prep Time: 45 minutes

½ cup flour
¼ teaspoon salt
¼ teaspoon pepper
¾ teaspoon basil, dried leaves
1 large egg
¼ cup milk

1) In medium bowl, combine flour, salt, pepper and basil.
2) Add egg and half of milk. Beat with whisk until mixture is smooth.
3) Add other half of milk, beat until blended. Add more milk if necessary. Mixture should be a bit runnier than normal pancake batter.
4) Brush 6 or 7-inch non-stick pan with olive oil. Pour enough batter in pan to just cover the entire bottom of pan. Swirl batter around bottom of pan to cover.
5) Cook until crêpe begins to bubble. Flip crêpe over and cook until just golden brown. Place on plastic wrap, making sure to separate each crêpe with wrap as you continue.

To make pinwheels. use one 8-ounce package whipped herbed cream cheese, fresh leaf spinach, and Prosciutto. Spread the cream cheese over crêpe, top with slice of Prosciutto, then spinach leaf. Roll it up, slice it, then cover and refrigerate until serving.

Per serving (approximate values): 28 Calories; 0.6g Fat (20.5% calories from fat); 1.2g Protein; 4.3g Carbohydrate; 18mg Cholesterol; 52mg Sodium

POTATO MUFFINS

Makes 12 servings
Prep Time: 30 minutes

1 cup all-purpose flour
1 cup potato flour
1 tablespoon baking powder
1 tablespoon sugar
1 teaspoon onion salt
1 teaspoon thyme, leaves
½ teaspoon garlic powder
¼ teaspoon black pepper
1 cup milk, skim
½ cup mashed potatoes
1 large egg
¼ cup butter, melted
1 cup Monterey Jack cheese, shredded

Preheat oven to 375 degrees. Spray standard muffin tin or mini muffin tin with non-stick spray.

1) In a large bowl, stir together the flour, potato flour, sugar, baking powder, thyme, garlic powder, onion salt and black pepper. Set aside.
2) In a medium bowl, whisk together the milk and mashed potatoes.
3) Add egg, melted butter and cheese to mashed potato mixture. Blend until well mixed.
4) Add to the dry ingredients and stir until just blended.
5) Spoon into prepared muffin tins, filling each at least three-quarters full. Bake until toothpick inserted in the center of center muffin comes out clean, about 20 minutes.
6) Cool muffins in tins about 5 minutes, then remove.

Per serving (excluding unknown items): 184 Calories; 7.4g Fat (35.8% calories from fat); 6.1 g Protein; 23.9g Carbohydrate; 37mg Cholesterol; 354mg Sodium

SUN-DRIED TOMATO MINI MUFFINS

Mini muffins are a great snack before a formal dinner. I like to pair this one with a nicely aged Boursin, although any cream cheese spread or flavored butter would be nice. I have served this at many different functions, formal and informal, with great success!

Makes 12 servings
Prep Time: 30 minutes

2 cups flour
1 tablespoon baking powder
½ teaspoon salt
¼ teaspoon pepper
1 cup milk
1 large egg
¼ cup olive oil
2 ounces Parmesan cheese, freshly grated
¼ cup sun-dried tomatoes, oil-packed, finely chopped
½ teaspoon thyme, leaves
½ teaspoon oregano, leaves

Preheat oven to 375 degrees. Spray standard muffin tin or mini muffin tin with non-stick cooking spray.

1) In a large bowl, stir together the flour, baking powder, salt and pepper. Set aside.
2) In a medium bowl, whisk together the milk, egg and oil until smooth.
3) Add the cheese, tomatoes, and herbs to the milk mixture and stir until blended.
4) Add wet ingredients to the dry ingredients and stir until just blended.
5) Spoon into prepared muffin tins, filling each cup about three-quarters full.
6) Bake until a toothpick inserted in the center of a muffin comes out clean, about 20 minutes.
7) Cool in the tins about 5 minutes, then remove.

Per serving (excluding unknown items): 161 Calories; 7.6g Fat (42.0% calories from fat); 5.5g Protein; 18g Carbohydrate; 24mg Cholesterol; 289mg Sodium

APPETIZERS

SAUSAGE WON-TON CUPS

It sounds very Asian, yet these little cups are very cross-cultural. I first made them for a small dinner party, but didn't discover their appeal until I made a large batch of them for a birthday party bash. They went like hot cakes!

Makes 12 servings
Prep Time: 25 minutes

1 pound Italian sausage
1 ½ cups Monterey Jack cheese, shredded
1 ½ cups red peppers, minced
2 tablespoons black olives, sliced
1 cup ranch salad dressing, bottled
1 package won-ton wrappers

Use mild or a combination of mild and hot Italian sausage. Preheat oven to 350 degrees. Grease one mini muffin tin with non-stick cooking spray.

1) Brown sausage in medium skillet. Drain thoroughly.
2) In a large bowl, combine sausage with remaining ingredients except won-ton wrappers.
3) Place won-ton wrappers inside each muffin cup, pressing with fingers to form the shape of muffin cups. Brush wrappers lightly with vegetable oil.
4) Place in oven and bake wrappers 5 to 10 minutes or until lightly browned.
5) Fill the muffin cups with sausage mixture and bake 5-6 minutes longer until cheese is melted. Serve immediately!

Per serving (approximate values): 293 Calories; 27g Fat (82.2% calories from fat); 10g Protein; 3.1 g Carbohydrate; 45mg Cholesterol; 591 mg Sodium.

RAISIN-OLIVE EMPANADITAS

Makes 12 servings
Prep Time: 30 minutes

½ pound lean ground beef
¼ cup minced onion
2 tablespoons raisins, chopped
2 tablespoons green olives, chopped
¼ teaspoon salt
⅛ teaspoon black pepper
¼ cup cottage cheese
1 hard-boiled egg, chopped
1 large egg, separated
1 teaspoon water
1 batch ready-made refrigerated pastry/pie dough
2 teaspoons milk

Preheat oven to 375 degrees.

1) Sauté ground beef and onion in large skillet until beef is browned.
2) Drain and add to the beef the raisins, olives, salt and pepper.
3) Cook over low heat for 5 minutes. Remove from heat.
4) Stir in cottage cheese and chopped hard cooked egg. Set aside.
5) Prepare pastry according to directions on container or make your own recipe. Roll out the dough in two large circles (for easier handling). Cut about 12 circles total, each about 3 ½ inches in diameter.
6) Onto each circle place 2 teaspoons of filling.
7) Whisk egg white with 1teaspoon water. Brush edges of dough circles.
8) Fold edges over to make half-moon shape and seal with fork dipped in flour.
9) Place Empanaditas on ungreased cookie sheet.
10) Blend the egg yolk with the milk and brush this mixture on the tops of the Empanaditas. Bake in preheated oven until golden brown, about 15-18 minutes.

Per serving (approximate values): 130 Calories; 8.6g Fat (59.6% calories from fat); 5.9g Protein; 7.1 g Carbohydrate; 58mg Cholesterol; 142mg Sodium.

Quiche Lorraine

This is one of the very first dishes I ever made. With an ancient Betty Crocker cookbook by my side, my mom let me try this very traditional French treat. I had no idea what it was at the time, but it sounded so interesting, I had to try it. I have since developed my own variation. It's a perfect light brunch snack!

Makes 6 servings
Prep Time: 30 minutes

1 9-inch ready-made frozen pie crust
¼ pound bacon, cut into 1-inch pieces
2 cups half and half
3 large eggs
¼ teaspoon salt
⅛ teaspoon white pepper
1 dash ground nutmeg
1 teaspoon chives, chopped
4 ounces Swiss cheese, shredded

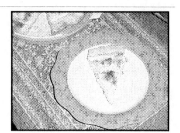

Preheat oven to 375 degrees.

1) Prick bottom and sides of pie shell with fork.
2) Cook bacon in skillet, stirring constantly until fat is completely rendered from the bacon (bacon is crisp). Drain bacon pieces on absorbent toweling.
3) In a medium mixing bowl, combine half and half, eggs, salt, pepper, nutmeg and chives.
4) Sprinkle bacon over bottom of crust, then sprinkle Swiss cheese over bacon. Pour egg mixture over bacon and cheese.
5) Bake 35 to 40 minutes until set in center and golden brown on the top. When a knife inserted in the center comes out clean the quiche is done. Remove from oven and let cool for at least 10 minutes before serving.

Per serving (approximate values): 456 Calories; 34.4g Fat (68% calories from fat); 18.5g Protein; 18g Carbohydrate; 171 mg Cholesterol; 699mg Sodium.

HERBED SEAFOOD TART

This recipe has served me well for catering several social functions. People love seafood and don't always have to know the seafood isn't the real thing! Please be sure to serve the tart fairly soon after preparation, as it tends to get a bit soggy after sitting any length of time.

Makes 8 servings
Prep Time: 30 minutes

10 ounces refrigerated ready-made pizza dough
3 medium Roma tomatoes, diced
½ medium green pepper, chopped
½ medium onion, chopped
½ cup Parmesan cheese, grated
8 ounces artificial seafood chunks, broken up
8 large eggs
8 tablespoons water
5 teaspoons Dijon mustard
1 ¼ teaspoons Italian seasoning

Preheat oven to 375 degrees. Coat 15x10-inch baking pan with non-stick cooking spray.

1) Spread dough over the entire bottom of baking pan, crimping the edges to form a border. Top the dough with the tomato, green pepper, onion, Parmesan cheese and imitation seafood chunks.
2) In a medium mixing bowl combine eggs, water, mustard and seasoning until well combined.
3) Pour evenly over vegetable mixture.
4) Bake for 30-40 minutes until mixture is set and puffed in the center. Let stand 10-15 minutes before cutting.

Per serving (approximate values): 220 Calories; 8g Fat (32.9% calories from fat); 15.5g Protein; 21.2g Carbohydrate; 228mg Cholesterol; 242mg Sodium.

SAVORY SPINACH RICOTTA PIE

Makes 6 servings
Prep Time: 30 minutes

Crust:
2 cups flour
½ teaspoon dried thyme leaves
⅛ teaspoon salt
⅔ cup butter
¼ cup cold water

Filling:
¾ cup Parmesan cheese, freshly grated
8 ounces ricotta cheese
3 large eggs
10 ounces spinach, frozen, chopped, thawed, well drained
1 medium onion, chopped
½ pound prosciutto, chopped
½ teaspoon dried thyme
¼ teaspoon ground pepper, fresh
2 tablespoons milk

Preheat oven to 350 degrees.

Crust:
1) In a large bowl stir together flour, thyme and salt.
2) Cut in butter until crumbly.
3) Mix in water with fork until flour is moistened and forms a ball.
4) Divide dough into ⅔ and ⅓ portions. Set aside ⅓ portion.
5) On lightly floured surface, roll out ⅔ dough portion to 14-inch circle, ⅛-inch thick. Gently fit into 9 or 10-inch deep dish pie pan, then set aside.

Filling:
1) In large bowl stir together Parmesan cheese, ricotta cheese and eggs.
2) Gently stir in all remaining filling ingredients except milk. Spoon into prepared crust.

Top crust:

1) Roll reserved ⅓ dough into 10-inch circle, ⅛-inch thick.
2) Place on top of pie. Crimp or flute edges. Make three small slits in top crust
3) Lightly brush crust with milk.
4) Bake 60 minutes or until crust is golden brown.

Per serving (approximate values): 576 Calories; 34.5g Fat (53.9% calories from fat); 28.4g Protein; 38.2g Carbohydrate; 216mg Cholesterol; 1559mg Sodium.

Sourdough Bread and Pumpkin Purée Strata

A strata is an Italian layered egg-and-bread casserole, traditionally served for brunch or sometimes breakfast. You might think of it as a savory bread pudding. I adore stratas, yet have had a hard time winning over family and friends with them. Thus I included only one recipe, one of my favorites.

Makes 6 servings
Prep Time: 45 minutes

1 pound sourdough bread, cut into 1 ¼-inch slices
Non-stick cooking spray
6 ounces sharp cheddar cheese, shredded
1 medium onion, chopped
4 ½ ounces canned green chiles, chopped
1 ⅔ cups skim milk
½ teaspoon thyme
½ teaspoon sage, rubbed
¼ teaspoon salt
¼ teaspoon pepper
15 ounces pumpkin, canned
2 large eggs
2 tablespoons pumpkin seeds, roasted, shelled

1) Arrange 2 bread slices in a single layer in a 2-quart soufflé dish coated with non-stick cooking spray.
2) Sprinkle with ½ cup cheese, ⅓ of onion and ⅓ of chiles. Repeat with bread, cheese, onion and chiles layers two more times.
3) Combine milk and next six ingredients though eggs. Mix with a wooden spoon in medium mixing bowl or in blender until smooth. Pour over layers. Cover with plastic wrap and refrigerate up to 8 hours.
4) Preheat oven to 350 degrees.
5) Uncover. Sprinkle strata with pumpkin seeds. Bake at 350 degrees for 1 hour or until a knife inserted comes out clean.
6) Let strata stand 10 minutes before serving.

Per serving (approximate values): 422 Calories; 13.9g Fat (29.5% calories from fat); 20g Protein; 54.9g Carbohydrate; 103mg Cholesterol; 763mg Sodium.

GREAT NORTHERN BEAN AND CHICKEN PIZZA

While I love traditional pizza (pepperoni and green olives gets me every time), I wanted to create something fun and unusual with 'pizza' in the title. While it may sound a bit bland at first glance, the flavors all really come together in the end.

Makes 6 servings
Prep Time: 30 minutes

16 ounces canned great northern beans
1 teaspoon lemon juice
¼ teaspoon garlic powder
⅛ teaspoon pepper
½ pound chicken, precooked, cut into
1-inch cubes
¼ teaspoon rosemary, crushed
10 ounces refrigerated ready-made pizza dough
1 cup fresh spinach, thinly sliced
4 ounces provolone cheese, shredded

Preheat oven to 425 degrees.

1) Place canned great northern beans through pepper in a blender or food processor and process until smooth. Set aside.
2) Combine chicken and rosemary in a large bowl and toss well.
3) Roll out pizza dough to desired dimensions on pizza stone or pan. Spread bean mixture evenly over crust leaving a ¼-inch border. Top with all of chicken, then spinach, then cheese.
4) Place pizza in oven and bake for about 10 minutes or until crust is golden.

Per serving (approximate values): 307 Calories; 9.8g Fat (28.9% calories from fat); 17.7g Protein; 36.8g Carbohydrate; 29mg Cholesterol; 193mg Sodium.

VEGETARIAN TORTA

I made this spectacular-looking appetizer specifically to entice one of the guests I had invited on my cooking show to appear. Appear she did, then went on to become the Chief Justice of the Minnesota Supreme Court!

Makes 12 servings
Prep Time: 1 hour

8 ounces fresh mushrooms, sliced thin
1 medium onion, chopped
3 tablespoons olive oil
20 ounces frozen spinach, thawed, chopped
¼ cup parsley, chopped
1 teaspoon dried basil
½ teaspoon black pepper, freshly ground
12 large eggs, beaten
½ cup sun-dried tomato paste
2 packages refrigerated ready-made pizza dough
8 ounces Parmesan cheese, freshly grated
1 pound provolone cheese, sliced thin
1 large egg yolk, mixed with 1 T. milk, for glaze

Preheat oven to 350 degrees. Grease a 9-inch spring form pan.

Spinach mixture:
1) In a large skillet over medium heat, sauté mushroom and onion in olive oil until vegetables are tender.
2) Turn up the heat a little and add spinach (make sure all moisture has been squeezed out of it). Heat to a simmer and continue cooking until most of the liquid has boiled away.
3) Set skillet aside. Add chopped parsley, basil, pepper and salt.

Egg mixture:
1) In a medium mixing bowl whisk together eggs and tomato paste.
2) In a 9-inch non-stick skillet, add 1 tablespoon olive oil over medium heat.
3) Pour half of this mixture into the skillet and cover, turning heat to low. Let cook until completely solid, but still soft. Turn omelet out onto plate.
4) Add a little more oil to skillet and repeat with remaining egg mixture.

To assemble:

1) Open one package of ready made pizza dough and carefully unroll. Stretch dough out with hands to fit bottom and sides of pan. Carefully lay dough into pan. Dough will be difficult to work with so be patient. Because the dough is meant to fit a rectangular pan, the corners will spill over the sides of the pan. Save and use the excess to form petals as a decoration for the top of the torta.

2) Cover the bottom layer of the pan and dough with half of the provolone, working in a circular manner. Sprinkle half of the fresh Parmesan evenly over the provolone. Cover the cheese with half of the spinach mixture. Top with one of the omelets.

3) Cover with remaining spinach mixture. Top with the second omelet. Cover omelet with remaining Parmesan, then provolone as in step (2).

4) Open the second roll of pizza dough, and in the same careful manner as before, lay it over the last layer of cheese. Since there is less area to cover, there will be more excess dough to use for decoration. Make sure to pinch the two crusts together all along where they meet.

5) Take the extra dough, most of which should be somewhat triangular in shape and form little leaves by pulling two of the corners together. Place on top layer of dough in a way that pleases the eye. Taking a very sharp knife, pierce dough, making five 1-inch slits in a circular manner on top crust for steam to vent.

6) Take a pastry brush and brush all exposed dough with the egg/milk glaze. Do not skip this step!! It will give the torta a very professional appearance.

7) Bake for 1 hour, checking periodically for crust color. If the crust gets too dark, cover it with foil. Remove from oven and let cool for at least 1 hour.

8) With a sharp knife, slide it around the outside of the torta. Carefully take the side off the pan. Cut into wedges.

Per serving (approximate values): 485 Calories; 26.4g Fat (48.7% calories from fat); 30g Protein; 32.5g Carbohydrate; 274mg Cholesterol; 834mg Sodium.

TOMATO QUICHE

Makes 4 servings
Prep Time: 45 minutes

1 9-inch ready-made frozen pie crust
2 tablespoons olive oil
½ cup chopped onions
½ cup green bell peppers, chopped
1 garlic clove, minced
2 pounds tomatoes
½ teaspoon dried basil
½ teaspoon dried oregano leaves
½ teaspoon salt
3 tablespoons tomato paste
3 tablespoons fresh parsley, chopped
⅛ teaspoon black pepper
4 large eggs, (1 whole egg and 3 egg yolks)
12 black olives, sliced
⅓ cup grated Parmesan cheese

Preheat oven to 350 degrees.

1) Bake pie crust in preheated oven about 4-7 minutes, until golden. Let cool about 5 minutes before filling with mixture to continue baking.

2) Sauté onions, green pepper and garlic in 2 tablespoons oil in a heavy skillet.

3) Add tomatoes that have been chopped and seeded. Add the basil, oregano, salt, green pepper and parsley. Cover and cook over low heat for 5 minutes.

4) Remove cover and raise heat so liquid evaporates. Do not let mixture scorch. Remove from heat.

5) Put 1 egg and 3 egg yolks along with tomato paste into a bowl and mix well. Combine with tomato mixture, then pour into pie crust.

6) Top with olives, grated cheese and anchovies, if you are using them.

7) Bake about 30 minutes or until firm and golden brown.

Per serving (approximate values): 483 Calories; 29.2g Fat (53.0% calories from fat); 17.6g Protein; 40.5g Carbohydrate; 229mg Cholesterol; 1305mg Sodium.

MUSSELS IN COCONUT MILK AND LIME BROTH

I love all sorts of shellfish: clams, mussels, oysters. They're all good in all their varia-
tions. This is a great appetizer or even a nice light supper. Make sure to have fresh
crusty bread handy to sop up the tasty juices.

Makes 4 servings
Prep Time: 30 minutes

1 tablespoon olive oil
½ medium onion, chopped
1 tablespoon ginger, grated
1 teaspoon turmeric
¼ teaspoon cumin seed
2 ½ pounds mussels, scrubbed
1 ½ cups clam broth (bottled clam juice)
1 cup unsweetened canned coconut milk
1 cup tomato, diced
1 whole jalapeno pepper, chopped fine
1 teaspoon lime peel, grated fresh
3 tablespoons fresh lime juice
2 whole green onions, sliced

1) Heat oil in large Dutch oven over medium heat. Add chopped onion and sauté until tender.
2) Add ginger, turmeric and cumin seed and stir 1 minute.
3) Add clam juice, coconut milk, tomato, jalapeno and lime peel and bring to a boil.
4) Add mussels. Bring back to a boil, cover and reduce heat. Let simmer until clams fully open, about 7 minutes. Discard any that do not open.
5) Stir in lime juice and green onions. Season to taste with salt and freshly ground pepper and serve.

Per serving (approximate values): 484 Calories; 24.6g Fat (44.9% calories from fat); 39.7g Protein; 28.4g Carbohydrate; 79mg Cholesterol; 830mg Sodium.

Roasted Red Pepper and Green Pea Purée Quesadillas

Makes 10 servings
Prep Time: 30 minutes

16 ounces canned green peas
1 small onion, finely chopped
1 tablespoon lemon juice
1 small jalapeno pepper, finely chopped
½ teaspoon cumin
7 ounces roasted red peppers, water-packed in a jar
8 ounces Monterey Jack cheese, shredded
5 8-inch flour tortillas
¼ cup melted butter or margarine

1) Combine green peas, onion, lemon juice, jalapeno and cumin in food processor. Process until coarsely chopped. You may need to stop several times to push mixture down the sides of the bowl.

2) Cut roasted peppers into thin strips. What doesn't get used can be diced for garnish.

3) Microwave tortillas as you need them for 20 seconds on high power, per side. Place two tortillas on a work surface. Spread a heaping tablespoon of green pea purée on tortilla, spreading to within ½-inch of edge of tortilla. Place enough roasted red pepper across half of tortilla to make three rows across. Sprinkle the same half with about 2 tablespoons cheese. Fold empty half of tortilla over loaded half of tortilla, pressing down to make as compact as possible. Don't press too hard, or you will lose some of the filling. Do the same with the second tortilla.

4) With a pastry brush, spread melted butter or margarine over surface of both tortilla halves. Place buttered side down in large skillet, which has been heated over a medium heat for about 1 minute. Cook tortillas until evenly browned. While first side of quesadilla cooks, brush side facing up with more melted butter or margarine. Flip over with a wide spatula. When the other side is nicely browned, remove from pan. Immediately cut quesadilla into thirds (wedges). Serve with salsa and sour cream!

Per serving (approximate values): 134 Calories; 7.1 g Fat (46.7% calories from fat); 8.5g Protein; 9.9g Carbohydrate; 20mg Cholesterol; 125mg Sodium.

SPICY THAI CRAB CAKES WITH TANGY SAUCE

During my teaching stint, I became very interested in all things Southeast-Asian, particularly Thai and Vietnamese. I decided to teach a class to introduce the community to this region's flavors with what I learned. This was one of the dishes I have since prepared many times.

Makes 4 servings
Prep Time: 30 minutes

<u>Crab Cakes:</u>
12 ounces crab meat, canned or fresh
¼ cup red onion, minced
2 tablespoons red bell pepper, minced
1 large egg white, beaten to blend
1 ½ teaspoons sesame seeds
¼ teaspoon allspice
¼ teaspoon white pepper
¼ teaspoon Tabasco sauce
1 cup bread crumbs
Vegetable oil

<u>Sauce:</u>
½ cup rice vinegar
5 tablespoons sugar
2 tablespoons lime juice
1 tablespoon bell pepper, minced
1 teaspoon garlic, minced
1 teaspoon sesame seeds
½ medium cucumber, peeled, halved, seeded, finely grated

Crab Cakes:
1) Mix all ingredients except bread crumbs in a large bowl until well combined.
2) Gradually add enough bread crumbs to form a stiff mixture. Shape into 12 patties.

Sauce:

1) Combine all sauce ingredients in a small bowl. Whisk until sugar is dissolved. Let stand at least 30 minutes to let flavors blend.
2) While sauce is blending, fry crab cakes.
3) In a large skillet, brush small amount of vegetable oil to cover bottom. Working in batches, fry patties until nicely browned on both sides. If desired, place finished crab cakes in ovenproof dish in 250 degree oven until all crab cakes are finished.

To finish:

1) Place 3 cakes on plate. Spoon sauce around cakes and serve!

Per serving (approximate values): 294 Calories; 3.9g Fat (11.9% calories from fat); 22.7g Protein; 42.5g Carbohydrate; 76mg Cholesterol; 534mg Sodium.

CHICKEN AND MANDARIN ORANGE BURRITOS

I first served this dish at one of my formal experimental dinner parties and to my surprise, it was well received. It is a fairly hearty appetizer, so you might want to follow it immediately with the main course or a very light salad.

Makes 6 servings
Prep Time: 30 minutes

2 tablespoons orange juice
½ teaspoon salt
½ teaspoon pepper
1 teaspoon cinnamon
Dash ground nutmeg
1 pound ground chicken
¼ cup almonds, sliced or chopped
10 ounces mandarin oranges
6 8-inch flour tortillas

Preheat oven to 250 degrees.

1) Place tortillas in an ovenproof dish, cover and place in 250 degree oven.
2) In a large mixing bowl, combine orange juice, salt, pepper, cinnamon and nutmeg. Add ground chicken and mix well.
3) Cook immediately and proceed to step 4 or refrigerate for several hours.
4) In a large skillet, cook chicken mixture. When the meat has lost its pinkness add nuts and well-drained orange segments. Cook over low heat until all ingredients are just warmed.
5) Remove tortillas from oven. Spoon 2 tablespoons of chicken mixture into a warmed tortilla. Fold tortilla burrito-style.
6) Turn oven temperature to 325 degrees. Place burritos in an ovenproof dish and bake in oven for 15-20 minutes until warmed through.

Drizzle hot burritos with Citrus Sour Cream and serve!

Per serving (approximate values): 333 Calories; 12.6g Fat (34.2% calories from fat); 27.6g Protein; 26.7g Carbohydrate; 71 mg Cholesterol; 415mg Sodium.

CITRUS SOUR CREAM SAUCE

Makes 6 servings
Prep Time: 30 minutes

½ cup fresh orange juice
¼ cup fresh lemon juice
¼ cup fresh lime juice
1 cup sour cream
Salt and pepper to taste
Pinch cayenne pepper to taste

1) Combine juices in heavy non-reactive saucepan. Boil the juice mixture until very reduced, about 2 tablespoons. Cool.
2) Whisk the juice reduction into the sour cream followed by salt, pepper and cayenne.
3) Serve at room temperature.

Serve with the Chicken and Mandarin Orange Burritos or any chicken or white fish recipe!

Per serving (approximate values): 97 Calories; 8.1g Fat (72% calories from fat); 1.5g Protein; 5.6g Carbohydrate; 17mg Cholesterol; 21mg Sodium.

THAI CHICKEN SATAY

Makes 6 servings
Prep Time: 30 minutes

½ cup lime juice
⅓ cup soy sauce
¼ cup brown sugar
4 cloves garlic
⅛ teaspoon red pepper
1 pound boneless skinless chicken or turkey breast
Wooden skewers, 4 to 6-inches in length

1) In medium glass bowl whisk the lime juice, soy sauce, brown sugar, garlic and red pepper until sugar dissolves. Set ⅓ cup marinade aside in cup or small bowl.

2) Slice chicken (or turkey) lengthwise into ⅓-inch thick strips. Add to marinade in medium glass bowl and stir evenly to coat. Alternatively, pour marinade into sealable plastic bag and add chicken. Make sure to squeeze out as much air as possible when sealing.

3) Cover and set aside at room temperature for about 30 minutes.

4) Cover wooden skewers with cold water, soaking for about 20 minutes. Drain water.

5) Drain chicken and discard marinade. Weave 1 or 2 slices chicken onto each skewer, making sure to weave chicken several times on the skewer.

6) Broil (or grill) 2-3 minutes per side or until chicken is no longer pink in center. Transfer to serving platter.

7) Serve immediately. Goes great with any Thai-style peanut sauce.

Per serving (approximate values): 228 Calories; 9.1 g Fat (34.9% calories from fat); 21.6g Protein; 16.6g Carbohydrate; 44mg Cholesterol; 1025mg Sodium.

THAI PEANUT SAUCE

While working at Williams-Sonoma, I was given a taste of a new peanut sauce we were just starting to sell. I bought several bottles for myself and set out to recreate it. In the process, I created something quite different than the bottled version, yet absolutely perfect when paired with any chicken satay recipe (or the Vietnamese meatballs that follow).

Makes 16 servings
Prep Time: 20 minutes

2 teaspoons vegetable oil
½ cup onion, finely chopped
3 cloves garlic, minced
½ cup peanut butter, chunky
3 tablespoons brown sugar
2 tablespoons fish sauce
1 teaspoon paprika
½ teaspoon cayenne pepper
1 cup coconut milk
1 tablespoon water
1 tablespoon cornstarch
2 tablespoons lime juice

1) Heat oil in medium saucepan over medium-high heat. Add onion and garlic and cook 2 to 3 minutes or until soft.

2) Reduce heat to medium-low. Add peanut butter, brown sugar, fish sauce, paprika and cayenne pepper. Stir until smooth.

3) Slowly stir in coconut milk. Mix until well blended.

4) Increase heat to medium and stir sauce constantly until bubbly. Reduce heat to low.

5) Combine water and cornstarch in small cup. Stir into sauce. Cook and stir 1 to 2 minutes or until sauce is thickened. Stir in lime juice. Serve!

Serve this peanut sauce with Thai Chicken Satays. It's also great with plain grilled chicken or turkey!

Per serving (approximate values): 106 Calories; 8.5g Fat (67.3% calories from fat); 2.4g Protein; 6.9g Carbohydrate; 0mg Cholesterol; 43mg Sodium.

VIETNAMESE MEATBALLS

Something about meatballs I have discovered make a nice appetizer. Portion size is easily controlled and several sauces can be prepared for guests to keep their interest. This recipe has a very intense flavor, with or without sauces!

Makes 6 servings
Prep Time: 20 minutes

1 ½ pounds ground beef
1 large egg
2 tablespoons soy sauce
2 tablespoons fish sauce
½ teaspoon salt
½ teaspoon white pepper
1 tablespoon sesame oil
2 cloves garlic, crushed
2 tablespoons brandy or sherry
½ teaspoon liquid smoke flavoring
1 teaspoon sugar
1 tablespoon cornstarch

Heat oven to 400 degrees.

1) Place all of ingredients in a large mixing bowl. Using clean hands, mix ingredients until well blended.
2) Clean hands again. Using a tablespoon, mold the meat mixture into little-larger-than walnut-sized meatballs. Place them in a baking dish, making sure they do not touch each other.
3) Place baking dish in hot oven and bake until meatballs are cooked through, about 15 minutes.
4) Place toothpick in each meatball and serve with favorite sauces such as the Thai peanut sauce.

Per serving (approximate values): 420 Calories; 34g Fat (75.7% calories from fat); 20.3g Protein; 4.2g Carbohydrate; 133mg Cholesterol; 61 0mg Sodium.

VIETNAMESE DIPPING SAUCE

Makes 6 servings
Prep Time: 15 minutes

½ cup water
¼ cup fish sauce
2 tablespoons lime juice
1 tablespoon sugar
1 clove garlic, minced
⅛ teaspoon crushed red pepper

1) Whisk together all ingredients in small bowl.
2) Refrigerate to let flavors meld, at least 30 minutes. Serve.

Serve this sauce with Vietnamese Meatballs or any dish requiring a dipping sauce, such as egg rolls.

Per serving (approximate values): 33 Calories; 1.5g Fat (38.6% calories from fat); 0.1 g Protein; 5.2g Carbohydrate; 1 mg Cholesterol; 1 mg Sodium.

GREEK MEATBALLS

Makes 4 servings
Prep Time: 45 minutes

1 pound ground beef, extra lean
½ cup bread crumbs
¼ cup parsley, chopped
¼ cup milk
1 large egg
1 medium onion, chopped
2 cloves garlic, crushed
1 teaspoon mint leaves, dried
1 teaspoon salt
½ teaspoon oregano, leaves, crushed
¼ teaspoon pepper

Preheat oven to 350 degrees.

1) In a large mixing bowl combine all ingredients. Use your freshly cleaned and dried hands to make sure all is well mixed. Shape into 1-inch balls.
2) Place meatballs in a large non-stick baking pan.
3) Bake for about 25 minutes until evenly brown all over.

Serve meatballs plain with mint or warmed hot pepper jelly.

Per serving (approximate values): 369 Calories; 22.2g Fat (54.7% calories from fat); 25.8g Protein; 15.4g Carbohydrate; 134mg Cholesterol; 755mg Sodium.

MOCK MEATBALLS

Not being a vegetarian myself, I have constantly challenged myself to create recipes specifically for vegetarians. I even went so far as to prepare a class to teach others about basic vegetarianism. Needless to say, I learned a lot. This is actually a very fun alternative!

Makes 6 servings
Prep Time: 30 minutes

3 large eggs, beaten
4 ounces Co-Jack (Colby/Monterey Jack) cheese, shredded
½ cup cottage cheese
½ cup onion, chopped
1 teaspoon basil
½ teaspoon salt
2 cups herb-seasoned stuffing cubes, crushed
1 cup walnuts, finely chopped
2 tablespoons vegetable oil

Preheat oven to 350 degrees.

1) In a large mixing bowl combine all ingredients. Shape into meatballs or small patties.
2) Pour a tablespoon of oil in a large skillet over medium heat and brown the meatballs. Repeat until all meatballs are browned. Place in baking dish until all meatballs are finished.
3) Cover with your favorite BBQ sauce or leave plain. Bake for approximately 20 minutes until warmed through.
4) Serve in a heated hoagie bun if shaped into meatballs or on hamburger buns if shaped into patties.

Per serving (approximate values): 256 Calories; 15.2g Fat (51.7% calories from fat); 13.7g Protein; 18.2g Carbohydrate; 11g Cholesterol; 790mg Sodium.

TUNA PUFFS

Makes 36 servings
Prep Time: 15 minutes

1 cup all-purpose flour
1 ½ teaspoons double-acting baking powder
1 teaspoon onion salt
½ teaspoon curry powder
1 dash cayenne pepper
¼ cup margarine
½ cup milk
7 ounces canned tuna, drained
1 cup cheddar cheese, shredded
1 tablespoon green bell pepper, minced
1 tablespoon black olives, chopped

Preheat oven to 450 degrees.

1) In large mixing bowl combine flour, baking powder, onion salt, curry powder and cayenne pepper.
2) Cut in margarine until mixture is size of small peas.
3) Add milk all at once and stir until well blended.
4) Add drained and flaked tuna, cheese, green pepper and olives. Blend well.
5) Drop by teaspoonfuls onto lightly greased cookie sheets.
6) Bake in preheated oven for 10-12 minutes until golden brown. Serve warm

Per serving (approximate values): 45 Calories; 2.5g Fat (50.2% calories from fat); 2.7g Protein; 3g Carbohydrate; 5mg Cholesterol; 121mg Sodium.

CANDY CHICKEN WINGS

This recipe is a dream to make! The first time I made a wing recipe in this manner, I had my doubts as to how it would turn out. Doubt not! If you follow this recipe, the meat will literally fall of the bones, with a gorgeous glaze your guests will clamor for!

Makes 4 servings
Prep Time: 15 minutes

1 cup soy sauce
1 cup lime juice
1 cup apricot preserves
⅔ cup sugar
3 pounds chicken wings, whole

Preheat oven to 400 degrees.

1) Mix all liquid ingredients in a quart measuring cup. If preparing sauce ahead of time, make sure all ingredients well mixed before the next step.
2) Take chicken wings and tuck tip under main portion of wing. Place in a broiler pan or any pan large enough to place all wings in one layer, but not any larger. Typically all the wings should fit tightly in a 15x10-inch baking pan.
3) Pour liquid over wings. Place in oven and bake for 40 minutes.
4) Remove baking pan from oven. It will seem like there is far too much liquid but all is OK! Turn wings over using tongs.
5) Place back in oven and bake for 40 more minutes.
6) Remove from oven. They should be perfectly glazed and falling off the bones. Serve!

Per serving (approximate values): 785 Calories; 29.6g Fat (33.1 % calories from fat); 38.3g Protein; 96.5g Carbohydrate; 142mg Cholesterol; 4282mg Sodium.

GLAZED CHICKEN WINGS

Makes 6 servings
Prep Time: 15 minutes

3 pounds chicken wings
1 cup soy sauce
½ cup red wine
½ cup sugar
¼ teaspoon ground ginger

Preheat oven to 400 degrees.

1) Take chicken wings and tuck tip under main portion of wing. Arrange wings in a roasting pan large enough to hold them in one layer. Typically all the wings should fit tightly in a 15x10-inch baking pan.

2) In a small saucepan, heat soy sauce, wine, sugar and ginger over moderate heat. Stir until sugar is dissolved.

3) Pour liquid evenly over wings.

4) Bake wings in middle of oven for 45 minutes. Remove from oven. It will seem like there is far too much liquid but all is OK! Turn wings over using tongs and bake until cooking liquid is thick, about 45 minutes to 1 hour more.

5) Transfer wings to serving plate and serve.

Per serving (approximate values): 467 Calories; 26.1 g Fat (52.3% calories from fat); 32.5 Protein; 21.1 g Carbohydrate; 126mg Cholesterol; 2875mg Sodium.

SALADS

ATHENIAN PASTA SALAD

I substituted for a cooking instructor whose job it was to show how to prepare several different salad types. As I was preparing this salad, I decided I had to make some changes on-the-fly while preparing it for the class. It was tasty with the changes, but with more fine tuning at home, even tastier!

Makes 12 servings
Prep Time: 30 minutes

Salad:
2 medium green peppers, ½-inch pieces
4 ounces pimentos, chopped
12 ounces rotini pasta, cooked
2 cups green olives, chopped
2 cups black olives, chopped
4 medium carrots, shredded
1 jar artichoke hearts, marinated, drained
12 ounces feta cheese, crumbled

Marinade:
1 cup red wine vinegar
½ cup lemon juice
1 tablespoon oregano
1 tablespoon basil
2 tablespoons garlic powder
½ cup olive oil
1 teaspoon sugar
1 teaspoon pepper

1)   Toss together all salad ingredients in a very large bowl.
2)   Mix together all marinade ingredients in a medium glass bowl. Pour over salad. Stir to completely coat salad ingredients and refrigerate no more than an hour.
3)   Drain well before serving.

Per serving (approximate values): 347 Calories; 20.8g Fat (51.9% calories from fat); 9.2g Protein; 34.1 g Carbohydrate; 25mg Cholesterol; 1073mg Sodium.

MEDITERRANEAN CHICKEN AND RICE SALAD

Makes 4 servings
Prep Time: 1 hour

4 tablespoons red wine vinegar
1 ½ tablespoons olive oil
½ teaspoon black pepper
4 cloves garlic, minced
3 cups cooked rice
6 ounces chicken breast, cooked, diced
½ cup roasted red peppers, bottled, diced
½ cup black olives, drained, halved
¼ cup chives, chopped
¼ cup fresh basil, chopped
¼ cup fresh oregano, chopped
14 ounces artichokes, canned, quartered, drained
1 small package feta cheese, crumbled

1) Combine vinegar, oil, pepper and garlic in a small bowl. Cover and set aside in refrigerator until ready to use.
2) Combine rice and remaining ingredients in a large bowl.
3) Add dressing and stir until well blended.
4) Refrigerate until well chilled.
5) Serve on a bed of romaine or other large, flat greens.

Per serving (approximate values): 438 Calories; 18.6g Fat (38.0% calories from fat); 18.2g Protein; 49.9g Carbohydrate; 55mg Cholesterol; 629mg Sodium.

SOUTHWESTERN POTATO SALAD

I love a good creamy potato salad, but it gets a little boring bringing to family events. I decided to incorporate Southwestern elements to jazz it up a bit. It's been a family get-together hit since!

Makes 4 servings
Prep Time: 30 minutes

2 pounds cooked red potatoes, cubed (6 cups)
8 ounces cheddar cheese, shredded
1 medium red bell pepper, chopped
1 cup black beans, canned, drained
½ cup celery, thinly sliced
⅓ cup green onions, sliced, with tops
2 tablespoons cilantro, chopped
½ teaspoon salt
¾ cup ranch salad dressing
½ cup salsa, chunky

1) In a large bowl combine potatoes, 1 ½ cups of cheese, red bell pepper, beans, celery, green onions, cilantro and salt.
2) In a small bowl combine dressing and salsa. Pour over potato mixture. Toss gently to coat.
3) Chill at least one hour before serving. Top with remaining cheese and serve!

Per serving (approximate values): 703 Calories; 29g Fat (39.4% calories from fat); 31g Protein; 69.88 Carbohydrate; 20mg Cholesterol; 1228mg Sodium.

WHITE CORN SALAD

Makes 6 servings
Prep Time: 15 minutes

2 cups white corn, frozen or canned, (thaw if frozen)
¾ cup chopped Roma tomatoes
½ cup cucumber, chopped
½ cup green bell pepper, chopped
3 tablespoons white wine vinegar
1 ½ teaspoons olive oil
2 teaspoons Dijon mustard
¼ teaspoon salt
⅛ teaspoon pepper
2 cloves garlic

1) Combine first 4 ingredients in a bowl and toss together.
2) Combine vinegar and remaining five ingredients in a jar. Cover and shake vigorously.
3) Pour over corn mixture and toss well.

Per serving (approximate values): 70 Calories; 1.7g Fat (19.4% calories from fat); 2.1 g Protein; 14.1 g Carbohydrate; 0mg Cholesterol; 114mg Sodium.

Marinated Mushrooms

Makes 16 servings
Prep Time: 24 hours

2 pounds button-type mushrooms
2 10-ounce jars artichoke hearts, drained
¾ cup water
¼ cup olive oil
1 clove garlic, chopped
¼ teaspoon peppercorns
¼ teaspoon ground thyme
¼ cup cider vinegar
2 tablespoons salt
¼ teaspoon dried basil
1 tablespoon bay leaf
¼ cup fresh lemon juice

1) Slice mushrooms in half through stems. Quarter artichoke hearts. Combine artichoke hearts and mushrooms in large non-metallic mixing bowl.

2) Combine remaining ingredients (water through lemon juice) into large skillet or Dutch oven over medium heat. Heat until the mixture just begins to boil. Pour over mushrooms and artichoke hearts.

3) Cover and refrigerate overnight. Remove peppercorns and bay leaf before serving.

Per serving (approximate values): 51 Calories; 3.7g Fat (57.7% calories from fat); 1.6g Protein; 4.5g Carbohydrate; 0mg Cholesterol; 812mg Sodium.

GRILLED PORTOBELLOS AND GOAT CHEESE SALAD WITH EARL GREY VINAIGRETTE

I had to prepare a northern Italian dinner for a client who decided to use my services for a cooking lesson dinner party. The dinner was quite complicated and I wanted something simple for at least one of the courses. This salad was the solution. If you make the dressing ahead of time, it's a fast yet really different salad to serve!

Makes 4 servings
Prep Time: 30 minutes

2 tablespoons Earl Grey tea, brewed strong
2 tablespoons olive oil
1 tablespoon balsamic vinegar
1 tablespoon parsley, chopped fine
4 cloves garlic, minced
1 teaspoon Dijon mustard
½ teaspoon marjoram
Salt and pepper, to taste
4 large Portobello mushrooms
6 cups lettuce leaves, washed, dried and torn
2 ounces goat cheese
1 large Roma tomato, diced

1) Place a broiler pan in the broiler about 6 inches from the heat source. Preheat the broiler.

2) In a large bowl whisk together tea, 1 tablespoon of the oil, vinegar, parsley, garlic, mustard and marjoram. Season with salt and pepper to taste.

3) Trim mushroom stems and reserve for another use (use in a soup stock). Wipe mushroom caps clean with a damp paper towel. Brush the mushrooms caps with the remaining oil and season lightly with salt and pepper. Place the caps, rounded side facing up, on the broiler pan and broil until tender and lightly browned, 2 to 4 minutes per side.

4) While the mushrooms broil, add salad greens to the dressing and toss. Arrange the greens on individual plates.

5) When the mushrooms are done, cut them into thick slices and set them on the greens. Crumble cheese over the mushrooms and scatter tomatoes over all. Add a grinding of black pepper and serve!

Per serving (approximate values): 179 Calories; 12.9g Fat (60.0% calories from fat); 8.5g Protein; 10.8g Carbohydrate; 15mg Cholesterol; 102mg Sodium.

SUNOMONO

My very first trip abroad was to Japan as an exchange student. The Japanese have some incredible delicacies, mostly centered around fish and vegetables. Funny enough, I do not include many recipes in this cookbook. The Japanese are as concerned about how food is presented as they are in flavors and preparation, thus I leave it to perhaps a future edition to tackle. In the meantime, this salad is super-yummy served on a hot summer day!

Makes 6 servings
Prep Time: 20 minutes

2 tablespoons white vinegar
1 tablespoon sugar
1 tablespoon mirin
½ teaspoon salt
2 teaspoons soy sauce
2 medium cucumbers

1) Combine vinegar through soy sauce in small bowl.
2) The key to making perfect Sunomono is very thinly sliced cucumbers. If you do not have a mandolin to help you achieve this, be patient when slicing by hand. Just make sure they are very thin slices! Pour sauce over cucumbers and cover. Refrigerate at least 2 hours.

Per serving (approximate values): 35 Calories; 0.3g Fat (5.8% calories from fat); 1.5g Protein; 8.1 g Carbohydrate; 0mg Cholesterol; 296mg Sodium.

Papaya Relish over Greens with Ginger and Sesame Vinaigrette

Makes 8 servings
Prep Time: 30 minutes

8 cups salad greens, gourmet (pre-packaged is great)
1 medium papaya, sliced, peeled
1 medium cucumber, peeled, seeded, sliced thin
½ medium red bell pepper, cut into strips
½ cup cilantro leaves, whole
½ cup rice vinegar, seasoned
1 tablespoon fresh ginger, peeled, grated
3 teaspoons sesame oil

1) Combine greens through cilantro leaves in a very large bowl.
2) In a cruet or other closeable jar combine vinegar, ginger and sesame oil. Shake vigorously.
3) Pour over salad and toss to coat.

Per serving (approximate values): 43Calories; 1.9g Fat (34.6% calories from fat); 0.8g Protein; 7.1 g Carbohydrate; 0mg Cholesterol; 3mg Sodium.

GRAPEFRUIT AND SHRIMP SALAD

This is a salad that could also double as an appetizer with the addition of shrimp. It's a little bitter, a little sweet and really sets up an appetite for whatever follows.

Makes 4 servings
Prep Time: 30 minutes

<u>Grapefruit Vinaigrette:</u>
2 tablespoons olive oil
3 tablespoons grapefruit juice
1 ½ tablespoons cider vinegar
1 teaspoon Dijon mustard
½ teaspoon sugar
½ teaspoon oregano leaves
<u>Salad:</u>
1 whole green onion
1 ½ pounds large shrimp, cooked, peeled
1 whole pink grapefruit, sectioned
1 head Boston lettuce
1 head radicchio
1 bunch fresh spinach

Grapefruit Vinaigrette:
1) In a container with a tight fitting lid combine olive oil through oregano leaves. Cover and shake until uniformly combined. Refrigerate until ready to serve.

Salad:
1) Dice green onion including most of the green portion.
2) In medium bowl, combine shrimp, green onion and grapefruit sections. Add 2 tablespoons of vinaigrette. Toss well to combine. Cover shrimp mixture and place in refrigerator for 1 hour.
3) When ready to serve, tear Boston lettuce, radicchio and spinach into bite-size pieces. Add shrimp mixture and toss once. Serve with remaining vinaigrette on the side.

Per serving (approximate values): 300 Calories; 10.28 Fat (30.3% calories from fat); 37.9g Protein; 14 9g Carbohydrate; 259mg Cholesterol; 292mg Sodium.

WARM SPINACH SALAD WITH CRANBERRY DRESSING

Makes 8 servings
Prep Time: 45 minutes

<u>Cranberry Relish:</u>
12 ounces cranberries, fresh or frozen
1 medium orange, quartered, with peel
2 tablespoons honey, to taste
<u>Dressing:</u>
1 ½ cups Cranberry Relish (above)
2 tablespoons honey, or to taste
¼ teaspoon salt
¼ teaspoon pepper
1 ½ tablespoons fresh ginger root, grated
1 pinch ground nutmeg
½ cup walnut oil
<u>Salad:</u>
1 pound spinach leaves, stemmed
½ cup walnuts, halves
8 ounces mandarin oranges in juice

Relish:
1) Place all relish ingredients in a food processor. Pulse until finely chopped, about 60 seconds.
2) Scoop out relish into large bowl. Measure 1 ½ cups cranberry relish and place back into food processor. Place remaining relish in covered container.

Dressing:
1) Place all dressing ingredients except oil in food processor with cranberry relish. Pulse a few times to blend.
2) With machine running slowly add oil until incorporated. Transfer the mixture to a medium saucepan.
3) Heat over low heat until ready to serve.
4) At serving time, turn up heat until sauce is quite hot.

Salad:

1) In a large salad bowl, toss together spinach and hot salad dressing two tablespoons at a time until it tastes just right.
2) Garnish with walnuts, orange sections and reserved cranberry relish.

Per serving (approximate values): 252 Calories; 18.4g Fat (61.4% calories from fat); 4.1 g Protein; 21.9g Carbohydrate; 0mg Cholesterol; 114mg Sodium.

CREAMY CRUNCHY BROCCOLI SALAD

Makes 12 servings
Prep Time: 30 minutes

<u>Dressing:</u>
1 cup mayonnaise, low-fat
3 teaspoons red wine vinegar
3 tablespoons sugar
<u>Salad</u>
4 cups broccoli flowerets, cut small
½ pound turkey bacon, cooked crisp, crumbled
½ cup raisins
½ cup sunflower seeds
½ cup onions, minced
Salt and pepper, to taste

1) Whisk all dressing ingredients in small bowl.
2) Combine all salad ingredients.
3) Add dressing to salad and toss well. Add salt and pepper as necessary. Refrigerate until ready to serve.

Per serving (approximate values): 182 Calories; 12.4g Fat (59.3% calories from fat); 8.1 g Protein; 11.0g Carbohydrate; 16mg Cholesterol; 309mg Sodium.

Tuna and Lemon Couscous Salad

I'm always a bit surprised when I find someone who has never heard of couscous. It's a wonderful staple from the Mediterranean region that takes an instant to prepare. It's also very versatile. Although I use it for the salad here, it's traditionally used like rice or pasta, with a topping.

Makes 8 servings
Prep Time: 30 minutes

1 large lemon
2 ¼ cups water
10 ounces couscous
2 tablespoons olive oil
1 tablespoon Dijon mustard
1 teaspoon dried dill weed
12 ounces canned tuna in water, drained
1 cup zucchini, diced
1 cup yellow squash, diced
4 medium Roma tomatoes, quartered

1) Remove rind from lemon using grater or zester.
2) In a medium saucepan add lemon rind and water. Bring to a boil.
3) Stir in couscous and cover. Remove from heat. Let stand for 5 minutes. Remove the lid and let cool at least 10 minutes.
4) Roll lemon on countertop to soften pulp. Cut lemon in half and squeeze to yield 2 to 3 tablespoons juice.
5) In a small bowl combine lemon juice, olive oil, mustard and dill. Stir with a fork until blended.
6) Combine lemon juice mixture and couscous in a large mixing bowl. Fluff couscous with a fork.
7) Add tuna, zucchini, yellow squash and tomatoes. Toss gently until dressing is well distributed. Chill at least two hours before serving.

Per serving (approximate values): 235 Calories; 4.3g Fat (16.4% calories from fat); 16.5g Protein; 33.1 g Carbohydrate; 13mg Cholesterol; 180mg Sodium.

ORANGE MARINATED VEGGIE SALAD

Makes 12 servings
Prep Time: 30 minutes

1 ½ cups broccoli flowerets, broken up
1 ½ cups cauliflower flowerets, broken up
1 cup carrots, cut into coins
1 medium onion, cut into 1-inch pieces
1 cup celery, cut, 1-inch pieces
1 cup cherry tomatoes, cut in half
1 medium green pepper, cut into 1-inch pieces
Orange Dressing/Marinade (recipe follows)

1) Combine all vegetables. Toss with Orange Dressing and marinate for up to 4 hours. Serve cold!

Per serving (approximate values): 20 Calories; 0.2g Fat (6.6°/a calories from fat); 1g Protein; 4.5g Carbohydrate; 0mg Cholesterol; 20mg Sodium.

ORANGE DRESSING/MARINADE

Makes 12 servings
Prep Time: 20 minutes

3 tablespoons safflower oil
2 cups orange juice
¾ cup red wine vinegar
½ cup sugar
1 ½ teaspoons salt
1 teaspoon garlic powder
¼ teaspoon pepper
1 teaspoon oregano
½ teaspoon seasoned salt
¾ teaspoon basil

1)   In a large mixing bowl, combine all ingredients. Use immediately or cover and place in refrigerator.

Per serving (approximate values): 84 Calories; 3.5g Fat (35.6% calories from fat); 0.4g Protein; 13.9g Carbohydrate; 0mg Cholesterol; 324mg Sodium.

FRUIT SPINACH SALAD WITH RASPBERRY JAM VINAIGRETTE

I love fruit in my salads! Especially after a hearty appetizer, it helps cleanse the palate in preparation for an even heartier main course. This recipe was first made for a friend's baby shower, a yummy springtime treat!

Makes 6 servings
Prep Time: 20 minutes

8 cups spinach leaves, washed and torn
2 cups cantaloupe, chunks
1 ½ cups strawberries, quartered
<u>Raspberry Vinaigrette</u>
2 tablespoons raspberry jam
2 tablespoons white wine vinegar
1 tablespoon honey
2 teaspoons olive oil
2 tablespoons sunflower seeds

1) Combine first three ingredients in a large bowl and toss gently.
2) For vinaigrette, combine jam and next three ingredients in a small bowl. Stir with a wire whisk until blended.
3) Just before serving drizzle dressing over salad and toss well. Sprinkle with sunflower seeds.

Per serving (approximate values): 104 Calories; 3.6g Fat (27.3% calories from fat); 3.6g Protein; 17.8g Carbohydrate; 0mg Cholesterol; 67mg Sodium.

TROPICAL FRUIT SALAD

Makes 8 servings
Prep Time: 45 minutes

1 large tomato, ¼-inch dice
1 large avocado, ¼-inch dice
¼ cup lime juice
1 cup cantaloupe, ¼-inch dice
1 cup pineapple, ¼-inch dice
¼ cup orange juice
4 cups salad greens
<u>Lime-Garlic Vinaigrette</u>
2 tablespoons red wine vinegar
2 tablespoons lime juice
2 cloves garlic
¼ teaspoon salt
3 tablespoons olive oil
1 teaspoon basil leaves
¼ cup fresh mint leaves, chopped
Crème frâiche, if desired

1) Toss the tomato and avocado with lime juice in a large bowl.
2) Add the cantaloupe, pineapple and orange juice and toss again.
3) Whisk all vinaigrette ingredients in a small bowl. Cover and refrigerate.
4) Just before serving toss the salad greens with the vinaigrette.
5) Add the chopped mint to the fruit mixture.
6) To serve, divide the salad greens to plates and spoon the fruit salad over the center. Place a dollop of crème frâiche on top, if desired.

Per serving (approximate values): 97 Calories; 6.7g Fat (55.7% calories from fat); 1.9g Protein; 10.1 g Carbohydrate; 0mg Cholesterol; 47mg Sodium.

SOUPS

CREAM OF GOUDA SOUP

I love Gouda cheese, therefore this soup was a dream to make! Inspired by my visit to Holland, it really is not as heavy as it might sound. I first made it for a holiday dinner for co-workers when I worked at Pannekoeken Huis, a Dutch-themed restaurant quite popular in Minneapolis.

Makes 8 servings
Prep Time: 45 minutes

3 ounces bacon, chopped
¼ cup butter
1 medium onion, chopped
2 tablespoons tomato paste
1 teaspoon Dijon mustard
1 teaspoon Worcestershire sauce
½ teaspoon paprika
Salt and pepper, to taste
4 cups chicken stock
½ pound Gouda cheese (2 cups), shredded
2 cups cream, heated in microwave for 2 minutes at high

1) In a large saucepan, fry bacon until very crisp.
2) Pour off fat and drop in butter. Let butter melt, then add onion. Sauté onion until soft and translucent.
3) Mix in the tomato paste, mustard, Worcestershire, paprika, salt and pepper. Stir to mix well.
4) Cook for 1 to 2 minutes to blend flavors.
5) Add chicken stock and bring to a boil over medium heat. Simmer slowly for 30 minutes over reduced heat.
6) Add cheese, stirring well to break apart the shreds. Simmer, not boil, for about 20 minutes. Add the heated cream. Remove from heat and serve immediately.

Per serving (approximate values): 381 Calories; 33.9g Fat (80.4% calories from fat); 12.7g Protein; 5.8g Carbohydrate; 109mg Cholesterol; 1603mg Sodium.

BORSCHT

*Russian cooking is so very hearty! This very traditional beet soup has as many varia-
tions as we do meatloaf. This is my favorite. I first tried it while living with my dad
after being (honorably) discharged from the military. He loved it served hot, I love it
served cold, just as the Russians do!*

Makes 6 servings
Prep Time: 1 hour

2 quarts beef stock
6 large beets, leaves trimmed to 1 inch above root
4 medium potatoes, peeled and halved
1 large onion, peeled and halved
2 stalks celery, cut into 1-inch pieces
1 large carrot, peeled, cut into 1-inch pieces
7 allspice berries
3 bay leaves
Salt and pepper, to taste
12 ounces kielbasa, cut into ½-inch pieces
¼ cup lemon juice
1 teaspoon sugar
Sour cream, if desired

1) Bake the whole unpeeled beets in a preheated 325 degree oven for about 40 minutes or until tender. Cool and peel them. Cut into juli-enne strips (my personal preference) or grate coarsely. Set aside.

2) To julienne—Slice beet in half, then the halves into no greater than ¼-inch thick slices. Lay beet slice so the flat portion is on the cutting sur-face. With a sharp knife, cut along the long edge of the beet slice to make very thin strips, like matches. If the strips are long, they will be difficult to eat, so cut the strips in half.

3) Beets are very slippery to deal with when peeling, so be very careful. Consider using gloves, as the juice will stain your hands a deep red.

4) Place the potatoes, onion, carrot, celery, allspice and bay leaves in a large Dutch oven. Add two quarts of beef stock. Bring to a boil. Simmer, par-tially covered, for about 30 minutes or until potatoes are tender.

5)   Drain the contents of the Dutch oven in a colander. Make sure to have a large bowl or another Dutch oven underneath to catch the liquid. Discard the onion, carrot, celery and allspice berries, saving only the potatoes.

6)   In a medium bowl mash the potatoes. Add mashed potatoes to stock and mix thoroughly.

7)   To the potato mixture add the beets, bay leaves and kielbasa.

8)   Bring to a boil, then add the lemon juice, sugar and if necessary, salt and pepper.

9)   Reduce the heat, partially cover and simmer for 30 minutes. Remove bay leaves and serve.

10) Alternatively, let soup cool, then refrigerate until cold. Serve cold with a dollop of sour cream.

Per serving (approximate values): 471 Calories; 16.8g Fat (32.1 % calories from fat); 16g Protein; 64.1 g Carbohydrate; 38mg Cholesterol; 3541 mg Sodium.

FRENCH ONION SOUP

I remember my first trip to a formal French restaurant as if it were yesterday. It was an evening field trip for my 9ᵗʰ grade French class, accompanied by my mom. The French onion soup was so delicious, the experience prompted me to buy my first French cookbook, by none other than Julia Childs! This is one of my core need-to-know recipes for those learning soup and stew basics.

Makes 4 servings
Prep Time: 45 minutes

4 medium onions, sliced
2 tablespoons butter
24 ounces beef broth
1 ½ cups water
1 whole bay leaf
1 pinch pepper
¼ teaspoon dried thyme leaves
4 whole French bread slices, ¾-inch thick
1 cup Swiss cheese, shredded
¼ cup Parmesan cheese, freshly grated

1) Heat butter in Dutch oven or stockpot over low heat. Add sliced onions, stirring occasionally until caramelized and tender, about 30 minutes. Onions should be a lovely caramel brown color.

2) Add beef broth, water, bay leaf, pepper and thyme. Increase heat to boiling, then reduce heat. Cover and simmer 15 minutes.

3) While soup is simmering, place French bread slices on cookie sheet. Place in oven heated to 400 degrees for about 10 minutes until quite dry. Remove from oven and let cool until hard.

4) Place a slice of French bread in four ovenproof bowls. Add broth and onions to bowl. Sprinkle liberally with Swiss cheese, then sprinkle with Parmesan cheese. Place bowls on cookie sheet. Turn oven temperature to broil. Place cookie sheet with bowls on it in oven at least 5 inches from heat, until cheese is melted, about 1 to 2 minutes. Serve hot!

Per serving (approximate values): 341 Calories; 16g Fat (41.8% calories from fat); 20.7g Protein; 29.48 Carbohydrate; 45mg Cholesterol; 1158mg Sodium.

SILKY GARLIC SOUP

This soup begs the question, can you ever have too much garlic? This is really an elegant soup that even my family loves. The boiling process is much like roasting the garlic. It also allows you to easily remove the peel from the garlic cloves.

Makes 4 servings
Prep Time: 30 minutes

2 heads garlic bulbs, large
4 cups water
2 medium onions, chopped fine
¼ cup olive oil
6 medium sage, leaves, fresh
3 ½ cups chicken stock
Salt and pepper, to taste
Croutons, store-bought or homemade
4 ounces Parmesan cheese, fresh grated

1) Separate the cloves from each head of garlic but do not peel them.

2) Bring the water to a rolling boil in a medium saucepan. Drop in all the cloves of garlic and boil 10 minutes. Drain them in a sieve and peel. The peels should slip off easily.

3) Return the garlic cloves to the saucepan and add the onion, olive oil, sage and chicken stock.

4) Bring to a lively boil over medium high heat. Partially cover and cook 5 minutes. Uncover and adjust the heat so the liquid bubbles slowly and cook another 5 minutes.

5) Place prepared croutons in each bowl. Remove all but one of the sage leaves from the soup and purée the soup in a blender or food processor.

6) Season with salt and pepper to taste. Pour the purée over the croutons. Sprinkle fresh ground Parmesan over the top of each bowl.

Per serving (approximate values): 206 Calories; 14.3g Fat (62.9% calories from fat); 3.3g Protein; 15.7g Carbohydrate; 0mg Cholesterol; 1892mg Sodium.

ORANGE-TOMATO SOUP WITH BASIL

Makes 8 servings
Prep Time: 45 minutes

¼ cup olive oil
1 ½ cups chopped onions
⅔ cup carrots, chopped
2 teaspoons garlic, chopped
2 teaspoons dried basil
½ teaspoon crushed red pepper
6 cups chicken stock
56 ounces Italian plum tomatoes, canned, drained, coarsely chopped
3 ½ teaspoons orange peel, grated
6 tablespoons orange juice, fresh-squeezed if possible
Salt and pepper, to taste

1) Heat oil in heavy Dutch oven or small stock pot over medium heat. Add onions and carrots. Stir until vegetables begin to soften, about 5 minutes.
2) Add garlic, dried basil and red pepper. Sauté 1 minute.
3) Add stock, tomatoes and orange peel. Simmer uncovered until vegetables are very tender, about 25 minutes.
4) Purée soup in batches in blender or food processor. Return soup to Dutch oven or stock pot. Stir in orange juice. Season with salt and freshly ground pepper, to taste. Serve hot!

Per serving (approximate values): 138 Calories; 7.6g Fat (49.4% calories from fat); 2.9g Protein; 14.7g Carbohydrate; 0mg Cholesterol; 1631 mg Sodium.

PUMPKIN RAVIOLI IN SAGE BROTH

Makes 4 servings
Prep Time: 45 minutes

1 cup pumpkin, cooked or canned
¼ cup ricotta cheese, part skim milk
¼ cup Parmesan cheese, fresh grated
⅛ teaspoon ground nutmeg
½ teaspoon salt
½ teaspoon pepper
30 whole round won-ton wrappers
4 cups vegetable broth
10 whole sage leaves, fresh, cut into thin strips

1) In a food processor or blender, purée pumpkin, ricotta, Parmesan, nutmeg, salt and pepper.

2) Place a generous tablespoon of pumpkin mixture in the center of each won-ton wrapper. Moisten the edges with water and cover with another wrapper. Press edges firmly to seal. Cut around edges with pizza cutter to within 1-2 inches of filling.

3) In a medium saucepan, bring vegetable stock to a boil. Reduce heat, then add sage. Cover and simmer for 10 minutes. Remove sage leaves and keep warm.

4) In a large pot, bring 4 quarts of water to a boil. Gently drop 3-4 ravioli into the boiling water and cook for about 4 minutes. Remove with a slotted spoon. Place on a serving dish, cover (with aluminum foil, if necessary) to keep moist.

5) When all ravioli are finished place ravioli in serving bowls. Ladle sage broth into bowls. Serve.

6) Serve with any leftover grated Parmesan and freshly ground nutmeg.

Per serving (approximate values): 408 Calories; 8.2g Fat (18.0% calories from fat); 16.6g Protein; 67.6g Carbohydrate; 17mg Cholesterol; 2375mg Sodium.

SEAFOOD CHOWDER

I was a nervous wreck when preparing this dish the first time. It was an experimental dinner I had decided to prepare for several of my political friends, and wouldn't you know, it also turned out to be the dinner my friends would invite soon-to-be governor of Minnesota, Jesse Ventura to attend, to entice him to run on the Independence Party ticket. It was a low-fat *experimental dinner, to boot! Needless to say, the dinner turned out fabulous, as did Jesse's run for the governorship!*

Makes 10 servings
Prep Time: 45 minutes

1 teaspoon olive oil
1 cup onion, chopped
1 cup celery, chopped
1 cup red bell pepper, chopped
4 cloves garlic, minced
½ cup flour
1 ½ cups water
3 cups chicken broth
3 cups red potatoes, unpeeled, diced
1 cup carrots, chopped
½ teaspoon thyme
½ teaspoon pepper
1 whole bay leaf
24 ounces evaporated skim milk
2 9-ounce cans creamed corn
½ teaspoon Tabasco sauce
1 ½ pounds medium shrimp, peeled
1 pound crabmeat, chopped or imitation crabmeat

1) Coat the inside of a large Dutch oven or stock pot with cooking spray, then add oil. Place over medium-high heat until oil is hot.
2) Add onion, celery, red pepper and garlic. Sauté 10 minutes or until crisp-tender.
3) Add flour and cook 1 minute more and stir constantly.

4) Gradually stir in water and broth and continue to stir vigorously until no lumps remain.

5) Add potato, carrots, thyme, pepper and bay leaf. Bring to a boil. Cover and reduce heat. Simmer 20 minutes or until potato is tender. Stir frequently.

6) Stir in milk, corn and Tabasco and return to a boil.

7) Reduce heat and add shrimp and crabmeat. Simmer 10 minutes or until shrimp is done. Stir constantly.

8) Discard bay leaves and serve immediately.

Per serving (approximate values): 269 Calories; 3.3g Fat (11.2% calories from fat); 32.6g Protein; 26.6g Carbohydrate; 142mg Cholesterol; 873mg Sodium.

SHRIMP BISQUE WITH SUMMER VEGETABLES

The first time I ever tasted a bisque, it was the lobster variety at the Hamburger Hamlet across from Mann's Chinese Theater in Hollywood. It was pure heaven! This is my shrimp version and it too is pretty darn good, although be prepared for a bit of work. I try to make recipes as quick and easy to prepare as possible, but the shrimp stock is crucial to this recipe.

Makes 8 servings
Prep Time: 1 hour 30 minutes

1 ½ pounds large cooked shrimp, with tails
<u>Shrimp Stock:</u>
7 tablespoons butter
1 medium yellow onion, chopped
3 stalks celery, chopped
3 cups cold water
2 cups bottled clam juice
1 cup dry white wine
2 sprigs parsley
1 sprig fresh thyme
¼ teaspoon whole black peppercorns
<u>Summer Vegetable Mix:</u>
1 medium zucchini, cubed
1 medium red bell pepper, cubed
¼ cup flour
¼ cup Madeira
3 tablespoons tomato paste
1 cup half and half
2 tablespoons Sherry
Salt and pepper, to taste

Shrimp stock:
1) Gently squeeze tails off shrimp. Reserve tails and bodies separately.
2) Melt 1 tablespoon butter in heavy medium saucepan. Add onion and celery. Cover and cook until tender. Stir occasionally, about 5 to 10 minutes.

3) Add shrimp tails, 3 cups cold water and next five ingredients. Bring liquid to a boil. Reduce heat to low and simmer uncovered for at least 30 minutes until liquid has reduced to about 5 cups.
4) Remove from heat and strain. Discard all solids.
5) In a heavy stockpot over medium heat, melt 4 tablespoons butter. Add flour and whisk until mixture begins to bubble. Do not let it turn brown.
6) Whisk in Madeira and tomato paste.
7) Slowly add in shrimp stock. Whisk vigorously until all liquid has been added.
8) Bring mixture to boil and cover. Reduce heat and simmer 30-45 minutes.

Summer Vegetables:
1) In a medium heavy skillet over medium-high heat, melt 2 tablespoons butter.
2) Add zucchini and red bell pepper. Sauté until just crisp tender.
3) Add to simmering shrimp stock.

15 minutes before serving:
1) Whisk in half and half. Cook until liquid begins to boil.
2) Add shrimp. Cook just until shrimp are just heated through. Add Sherry. Add salt and pepper to taste. Serve!

Per serving (approximate values): 318 Calories; 14.8g Fat (45.7% calories from fat); 21.6g Protein; 18.1g Carbohydrate; 204mg Cholesterol; 637mg Sodium.

CHICKEN CHILI WITH TEQUILA, LIME AND WHITE BEANS

I have been asked to prepare foods for all sorts of events, but food for 500 runners after they'd finished a 10K run in a Minnesota fall was a new one. What to prepare? A hearty chili with chicken instead of beef was just the right thing to get the runners warmed up inside and get their fuel reserves pumped back up!

Makes 6 servings
Prep Time: 45 minutes

2 tablespoons olive oil
4 cloves garlic, crushed
2 medium onions, finely chopped
1 tablespoon chili powder, medium-hot
1 tablespoon cumin seed
1 teaspoon crushed red pepper, or dried red chile flakes
1 teaspoon coriander, ground
1 ½ pounds ground chicken or turkey
28 ounces tomatoes, crushed
½ cup tequila
¼ cup lime juice
¼ cup cilantro, finely chopped
¼ cup fresh basil leaves, finely shredded
2 tablespoons tomato paste
1 tablespoon dried oregano, leaves
2 teaspoons dried basil
2 teaspoons dried summer savory
2 teaspoons salt
1 teaspoon white pepper
2 whole bay leaves
1 tablespoon sugar
15 ounces canned white beans
2 tablespoons masa harina

1) In a Dutch oven or stock pot, heat oil over medium heat. Add garlic, onions, chili powder, cumin seeds, chile flakes and coriander. Sauté for ten minutes or until onions are crisp tender.

2) Add chicken and sauté until no longer pink, about 10 minutes. Stir to break chicken into rough chunks.

3) Stir in remaining ingredients except masa. Bring mixture to a boil and reduce heat. Cover and simmer. Stir occasionally until mixture is fairly thick, but still slightly liquid, about 1 ½ hours.

4) Sprinkle in masa and stir. Simmer until thick, about 15 minutes more. Serve.

Per serving (approximate values): 512 Calories; 16.2g Fat (30.6% calories from fat); 43.1 g Protein; 39.9g Carbohydrate; 107mg Cholesterol; 1206mg Sodium.

VEGETARIAN BLACK BEAN CHILI

Makes 12 servings
Prep Time: 1 hour 30 minutes

¼ cup olive oil
2 whole Anaheim chile peppers, seeded and chopped
1 whole Pasilla green pepper, seeded and chopped
1 whole red Serrano chile peppers, seeded and chopped
2 medium onions, chopped
2 cloves garlic, chopped
1 tablespoon cumin seed
1 tablespoon caraway seed
5 cups water
1 pound dried black beans, soaked overnight, then drained
1 large red bell pepper, diced
1 small eggplant, diced
1 large green bell pepper, diced
1 medium yellow squash, summer, diced
1 medium zucchini, diced
4 medium tomatoes, diced
1 tablespoon sugar
2 teaspoons dried oregano, leaves
1 teaspoon dried basil, leaves
1 teaspoon dried savory, leaves
1 teaspoon salt
½ teaspoon white pepper
2 whole bay leaves
½ cup cilantro, chopped

1) In a large, heavy stock pot, heat oil over high heat. Add chiles, peppers, onions, garlic, cumin and caraway seeds. Sauté and stir briskly, about 10 minutes or until onion is crisp tender.
2) Add water, beans, half of the bell peppers, squash, zucchini and tomatoes.
3) Stir in the sugar, oregano, basil, savory, salt, pepper and bay leaves.

4) Bring to a boil and cover. Simmer, stirring occasionally. Add more water if necessary to keep beans covered. Cook until beans are tender, 1 ½ to 2 hours.

5) Stir in remaining vegetables and simmer until the just-added vegetables are crisp tender. Serve.

Per serving (approximate values): 227 Calories; 5.7g Fat (21.2% calories from fat): 10.5g Protein; 36.98 Carbohydrate; 0mg Cholesterol; 194mg Sodium.

SPICY-HOT BEANLESS BEEF CHILI

Living in West Germany was very different for Americans when I lived there. Pretty much everything closed at 5 or 6 p.m. and we were left to our own devices to come up with things to do. Thus I decided to try my first hand at making chili. I must have made over 20 variations of chili before I made this my final choice. Feel free to add beans, if you like, but I prefer it without!

Makes 12 servings
Prep Time: 1 hour

3 pounds ground beef, extra lean
2 large onions, chopped
2 cloves garlic
3 cups water
14 ½ ounces tomatoes, canned (do not drain)
8 ounces tomato sauce, canned
6 ounces tomato paste
4 tablespoons chili powder
8 whole jalapeno peppers, chopped fine
8 ounces green chiles, canned, diced
2 tablespoons Tabasco sauce
1 teaspoon cayenne
1 ½ teaspoons cumin
½ teaspoon oregano

1) In a large skillet, brown ground beef with onions and garlic. Drain.
2) Add all other ingredients to ground beef mixture. Salt to taste. Bring everything to a boil, cover and reduce heat to simmer. Cook at least an hour.
3) This chili is best when made the day before and refrigerated, then reheated the next day.

Per serving (approximate values): 327 Calories; 20.3g Fat (54.8°!o calories from fat); 23.9g Protein; 13.7g Carbohydrate; 78mg Cholesterol; 399mg Sodium.

BLACK BEAN SOUP WITH BANANAS

Makes 8 servings
Prep Time: 1 hour

5 cups black beans, precooked or canned, rinsed and drained
6 cups water
½ cup rice
½ pound pancetta
2 medium onions, diced medium
8 cloves garlic, minced
1 tablespoon herbes de Provence
1 tablespoon chili powder
14 ounces plum tomatoes, canned
Salt and pepper, to taste
2 tablespoons olive oil
2 tablespoons red wine vinegar
2 teaspoons Tabasco sauce
4 whole bananas
2 tablespoons lemon juice
½ teaspoon black pepper

1) In a large heavy saucepan, add black beans, water, rice and pancetta. Bring to a boil over high heat. Reduce heat. Cover and simmer for 1 hour. Stir occasionally to make sure beans don't stick to the bottom.
2) Stir in the onions, garlic, herbes de Provence, chili powder, tomatoes and salt. Bring to a boil. Cover, reduce heat and simmer for 1 hour longer.
3) In a small bowl combine olive oil, Tabasco and vinegar. Stir into soup.
4) Just before serving, slice bananas and toss in lemon juice and pepper. Add to soup. Serve!

Per serving (approximate values): 354 Calories; 7.1 g Fat (17.4% calories from fat); 20g Protein; 55.7g Carbohydrate; 20mg Cholesterol; 788mg Sodium.

BLACK BEANS WITH VINEGAR SOUP

Makes 8 servings
Prep Time: 45 minutes

1 tablespoon olive oil
3 medium onions, chopped
2 medium bay leaves
4 14-ounce cans black beans
4 cups vegetable broth
½ cup brown sugar
6 tablespoons cider vinegar
2 tablespoons dry mustard
1 teaspoon lime peel, grated
¼ cup parsley, chopped

1) Heat oil in a Dutch oven or medium stock pot over medium high heat. Add onions and bay leaves. Cook, stirring often, until onions are soft, about 10 minutes.

2) While the onions cook, empty two cans of beans and their liquid in a medium bowl. Mash with a potato masher until mostly smooth.

3) Add the black bean purée, the remaining black beans and their liquid, broth, brown sugar, vinegar, mustard and lime peel to onion mixture.

4) Increase heat to high. Cook, stirring often, until mixture begins to simmer.

5) Remove and discard bay leaves. Garnish each bowl with a little chopped parsley.

Per serving (approximate values): 511 Calories; 5.5g Fat (9.4% calories from fat); 25.1 g Protein; 93.6g Carbohydrate; 1 mg Cholesterol; 841 mg Sodium.

Brazilian Black Bean Soup (Feijoada)

I fell in love with this national dish of Brazil the very first time I made it. The combination of meats and flavors absolutely tickled my taste buds. After a few changes, I decided to include it as one of the soups I used in my soups and stews classes. While Brazilians may make it for special occasions, I like to make it for any occasion.

Makes 8 servings
Prep Time: 45 minutes

6 cups canned black beans
½ pound Italian sausage, spicy
½ pound spareribs, fat trimmed
4 cups beef stock
3 cups water
¼ pound ham, chopped
¼ pound pepperoni sausage, sliced thin
1 medium onion, sliced thin
2 medium green peppers, sliced
2 cloves garlic
1 teaspoon oregano
½ teaspoon crushed red pepper
½ teaspoon cumin
1 14-ounce can tomatoes, drained
1 cup red wine
2 medium oranges, peeled, sectioned

1) Brown the sausage and spareribs in a medium skillet over medium heat. Set aside meats and reserve fat in skillet.

2) Drain black beans and place in a Dutch oven or stock pot. Add the stock, water and all of the meats.

3) In the reserved fat in the skillet, sauté the onions, peppers, garlic, herbs and spices. Cook over medium-high heat until onion is translucent.

4) Add this to the Dutch oven or stock pot and stir to mix all ingredients. Bring to a boil. Cover, reduce heat and simmer until beans are soft, about 1 hour. Stir frequently so beans don't stick to the bottom.

5) Add tomatoes and wine and continue cooking for another 30 minutes. Stir in the oranges a few minutes before the stew is to be served. Serve immediately.

Per serving (approximate values): 480 Calories; 21.8g Fat (42.6% calories from fat); 25.4g Protein; 40.8g Carbohydrate; 55mg Cholesterol; 1786mg Sodium.

Bœuf Bourguignon (Beef Burgundy Stew)

Makes 8 servings
Prep Time: 45 minutes

6 slices bacon, cut into 1-inch pieces
2 pounds beef, bottom round roast, 1-inch cubes
½ cup flour
2 cups Burgundy wine
4 cloves garlic
1 whole bay leaf
1 cup beef broth
1 teaspoon dried thyme, leaves
¼ teaspoon pepper
8 ounces mushrooms, sliced
4 medium onions, sliced
2 tablespoons butter

1) Fry bacon in Dutch oven or stock pot over medium heat until crisp. Remove bacon and set aside. Reserve bacon fat in pan.
2) In a medium bowl, coat the beef with flour. Cook and stir beef in bacon fat over medium high heat until browned.
3) Drain pot of all fat. Add Burgundy to beef. Add just enough broth to make sure beef is completely covered with liquid.
4) Stir in remaining ingredients. Heat mixture to boiling. Reduce heat. Cover and simmer until beef is tender, about 1 ½ hours. Serve.

Per serving (approximate values): 454 Calories; 27.4g Fat (59.5% calories from fat); 26.1 g Protein; 15.9g Carbohydrate; 88mg Cholesterol; 338mg Sodium.

CARBONNADES (FLEMISH BEEF AND BEER STEW)

Some friends and I decided to participate in the street fair that takes place during the 100 mile march held every year in the city of Nijmegen, Holland. I was desperately hungry, so I stopped at the first vendor I saw, who just happened to be serving the most delicious beef dish. It was quite awhile before I determined what it was I had eaten that day. Once I did, I spent quite some time trying to recreate the experience.

Makes 6 servings
Prep Time: 45 minutes

---

2 pounds beef, top round, 1-inch cubes
1 pound bacon, cut into ½-inch pieces
4 medium onions, sliced
4 cloves garlic
6 tablespoons flour
36 ounces beer, light or dark
2 whole bay leaves
1 tablespoon brown sugar
1 teaspoon salt
1 teaspoon thyme
1 teaspoon pepper
2 cups beef stock
1 tablespoon cider vinegar

---

1) Fry bacon in Dutch oven or stock pot until crisp. Remove bacon with slotted spoon. Drain on paper towels.

2) Cook and stir onions and garlic in bacon fat until tender, about 10 minutes. Remove onions and set aside.

3) Add beef to the pot and brown on all sides, about 15 minutes. Stir in flour to coat beef. Gradually stir in beer until completely incorporated. Make sure mixture is free of lumps.

4) Add onions, bay leaves, brown sugar, salt, thyme and pepper. Add just enough beef stock to cover beef. Heat mixture to boiling. Reduce heat and cover. Simmer until beef is tender, 1 to 1 ½ hours.

5) Remove bay leaf. Stir in vinegar, then add bacon. Serve over mashed potatoes.

Per serving (approximate values): 966 Calories; 66.7g Fat (65.7% calories from fat); 53.4g. Protein; 25.1 g Carbohydrate; 166mg Cholesterol; 1661 mg Sodium.

RED WINE BEEF STEW WITH SHIITAKE MUSHROOMS

Makes 6 servings
Prep Time: 1 hour

1 cup all-purpose flour
Pinch salt and pepper
6 tablespoons butter, split
3 pounds beef chuck roast, boneless, cut into 1-inch cubes
2 large onions, chopped
¼ cup tomato paste
3 cups dry red wine
3 ½ cups beef broth
1 tablespoon dark brown sugar
1 ½ pounds small red skinned potatoes, quartered
30 small baby carrots, trimmed
1 pound baby zucchini, sliced ¾-inch thick
1 pound shiitake mushrooms, stemmed, thickly sliced
1 tablespoon dried marjoram, or 3 T. fresh chopped
Salt and pepper, to taste

1) Place flour in medium or large mixing bowl. Season with salt and pepper.

2) Melt 4 tablespoons butter in heavy large saucepan over medium-high heat. Working in batches, coat meat with flour, then add to saucepan. Brown on all sides. Using slotted spoon, transfer to a plate.

3) It is important the heat is fairly high and the amount of meat browned is small to ensure an evenly browned meat. Otherwise too much liquid will be released, resulting in mushy meat.

4) Melt remaining 2 tablespoons butter in the same saucepan over medium-high heat. Add onions. Sauté until tender, about 10 minutes.

5) Mix in tomato paste, then wine. Bring to a boil. Scrape up any browned bits from the bottom of the pan.

6) Add broth and sugar, then beef and any accumulated juices from the beef. Bring to boil. Reduce heat and cover partially. Simmer for 1 ½ hours.

7) Add potatoes and carrots. Simmer until meat and vegetables are almost tender, about 25 minutes.

8) Add zucchini. Simmer until almost tender, about 10 minutes.
9) Add mushrooms and 1 tablespoon dried marjoram. Simmer until mushrooms are tender, another 5 minutes.
10) Season with salt and pepper, to taste. Serve.

Per serving (approximate values): 1048 Calories; 48.4g Fat (43.0% calories from fat); 54.68 Protein; 89.6g Carbohydrate; 162mg Cholesterol; 1186mg Sodium.

CHICKEN WITH LEMONS AND OLIVES

Makes 12 servings
Prep Time: 45 minutes

8 pounds chicken, cut into a total of about sixteen pieces
4 large onions, chopped
1 bunch parsley, stemmed, chopped
1 bunch cilantro, stemmed, chopped
24 cloves garlic, chopped
8 medium lemons, quartered
6 tablespoons olive oil
8 teaspoons ground cumin
2 teaspoons ground ginger
1 ½ teaspoons black pepper
1 teaspoon saffron threads
3 cups chicken stock
24 Kalamata olives, pitted

1) Divide chicken, onions, parsley, cilantro, garlic, lemons, oil, cumin, ginger, pepper and saffron threads between two large Dutch ovens or large saucepans.

2) Add one cup chicken stock to each pot. Bring to a boil. Cover and simmer over medium-low heat until chicken is almost cooked through, about 45 minutes.

3) Add more chicken stock to each pot as necessary to prevent chicken from sticking.

4) Add half of olives to each pot. Cover and continue cooking about 10 minutes. Serve in large soup plates or bowls.

Per serving (approximate values): 605 Calories; 41.8g Fat (62.0% calories from fat); 42g Protein; 15.6g Carbohydrate; 158mg Cholesterol; 579mg Sodium.

VELVETY PEANUT SOUP

I don't recall the first time I made this soup, but I do recall the last. It was for friends in Maine specifically to take a photograph for this book. They enjoyed it so much, I think they licked their bowls. In any case, you'll never look at peanut butter quite the same after making this recipe.

Makes 8 servings
Prep Time: 45 minutes

2 tablespoons olive oil
1 medium onion, finely chopped
4 medium scallions, finely chopped
4 cloves garlic
2 teaspoons fresh ginger, grated
1 whole jalapeno pepper, minced
2 tablespoons flour
3 cups chicken stock
3 cups half and half
2 cups peanut butter
Salt and pepper, to taste
½ cup parsley, finely chopped
2 tablespoons lime juice, split

1) Heat the olive oil in a large saucepan over medium heat.
2) Add the onion, scallions, garlic, ginger and jalapeno. Cook until soft but not brown, about 10 minutes.
3) Stir in the flour and cook for 1 minute. Remove pan from heat.
4) Whisk in the chicken stock. Bring the soup to a boil.
5) Whisk in the half and half, peanut butter, salt, pepper, parsley and 1 tablespoon of the lime juice. Lower heat and gently simmer the soup, uncovered. Stir from time to time until creamy and well-flavored.
6) Add more salt or lime juice to taste. Add additional chicken stock if too thick. Serve immediately.

Per serving (approximate values): 563 Calories; 46.3g Fat (70.4% calories from fat); 20g Protein; 23.8g Carbohydrate; 33mg Cholesterol; 1159mg Sodium.

CIDER CHICKEN

Makes 4 servings
Prep Time: 45 minutes

4 whole bacon slices, cut into ½-inch pieces
1 tablespoon vegetable oil
3 pounds chicken, cut into 8 pieces, skin/fat removed
4 medium onions, sliced thin
4 cloves garlic, minced
2 ¾ cups hard apple cider
⅓ cup Calvados, or brandy
8 whole prunes, pitted
1 whole bouquet garni
Salt and pepper, to taste

Preheat oven to 325 degrees.

1) In a deep ovenproof skillet with a lid or a ovenproof Dutch oven, brown bacon over medium high heat, about 3 minutes. Transfer to paper towels to dry. Pour off any fat in the pan.

2) Add ½ tablespoon of vegetable oil to the pan and brown the chicken over high heat, about 3 minutes per side. Transfer chicken to a plate. Season with salt and pepper and set aside.

3) Add remaining oil to the pan. Reduce heat to low and add onions. Stir occasionally until the onions are very tender and golden, about 25 minutes.

4) Stir in garlic and cook for 1 minute.

5) Pour in cider and Calvados and bring to a boil.

6) Add prunes, bouquet garni, the reserved bacon and chicken.

7) Cover and place in preheated over. Bake until the chicken is very tender and no longer pink inside, 45 minutes to 1 hour. Remove the bouquet garni. Taste and adjust the seasonings.

Bouquet garni:

6 sprigs parsley
4 sprigs fresh thyme (½ tsp. dry leaves)
2 bay leaves

1) All should be tied together with kitchen string or put in a cheesecloth bag and tied.

Per serving (approximate values): 725 Calories; 36.8g Fat (49.2% calories from fat); 41.2g Protein; 44.2g Carbohydrate; 154mg Cholesterol; 250mg Sodium.

Coq Au Vin

Another sublime traditional French stew. This is the variation upon which I finally settled, after many attempts.

Makes 6 servings
Prep Time: 1 hour

¼ pound bacon, chopped coarsely
3 pounds chicken
2 tablespoons flour
3 cups red wine
2 tablespoons brandy
2 tablespoons parsley, chopped
1 teaspoon dried marjoram
1 teaspoon dried thyme leaves
2 whole bay leaves
2 bunches green onions, white portion only, sliced
1 pound mushrooms, sliced
2 large carrots, thinly sliced
4 cloves garlic
3 tablespoons flour
3 tablespoons butter

---

1) In a large saucepan or Dutch oven, cook bacon until very crisp. Remove from pan and drain bacon on paper towel. Leave bacon fat in pan.

2) Brown the chicken in the bacon fat over high heat. Turn as necessary to brown on all sides. Remove from the pan. Repeat until all chicken is browned. Set aside.

3) Stir 2 tablespoons flour and salt and pepper to taste into remaining drippings in the pan. Mix well.

4) Whisk in red wine and brandy and stir until thickened and bubbly. Cook and stir 1 to 2 minutes more.

5) Stir in parsley, marjoram, thyme and bay leaves.

6) Return chicken to the Dutch oven along with onions, mushrooms, carrot, garlic and bacon. Bring mixture to a boil. Reduce heat and cover. Simmer for 40 minutes or until chicken is done.

7) In a separate small sauté pan melt 3 tablespoons butter. Whisk 3 table-spoons flour into butter. Remove from heat.

8) Whisk ¼ cup liquid from chicken mixture to flour mixture. Slowly then add butter/flour mixture to the hot liquid. Stir until entire mixture is thick. Season with additional salt and pepper as necessary. Serve.

Per serving (approximate values): 619 Calories; 35.5g Fat (60.4% calories from fat); 34.3g Protein; 18.2g Carbohydrate; 130mg Cholesterol; 545mg Sodium.

HUNGARIAN GOULASH

Makes 6 servings
Prep Time: 1 hour

2 tablespoons canola oil
1 ½ pounds beef round, ½-inch cubes
2 cloves garlic
2 cups beef broth
1 cup red wine
15 ounces Italian tomatoes
1 pound Roma tomatoes, diced
1 tablespoon paprika
2 large onions, sliced
1 teaspoon caraway seed
2 medium potatoes, 1-inch pieces
1 medium green peppers, 1-inch pieces
1 medium yellow pepper, 1-inch pieces
1 small turnip, 1-inch pieces
2 medium carrots, sliced thin
½ cup red wine
Salt and pepper, to taste

1) Heat oil in large saucepan or Dutch oven over high heat until hot. Cook and stir beef and garlic until browned on all sides, about 15 minutes. Drain fat.

2) Add broth, red wine, tomatoes with liquid, onions, paprika, salt, pepper and caraway seed. Break tomatoes into smaller pieces. Heat to boiling. Cover and reduce heat. Simmer 1 hour.

3) Add all remaining vegetables. Cover and simmer until potatoes are tender, about 30 minutes. Check to make sure meat is tender. If not, continue to simmer until completely tender.

4) Add ½ cup red wine and simmer and additional 15 minutes. Serve.

Per serving (approximate values): 515 Calories; 20.1 g Fat (37.3% calories from fat); 32.5g Protein; 43.5g Carbohydrate; 72mg Cholesterol; 577mg Sodium.

SOLIANKA

With a background in the Russian language and culture, you'd think I would have more Russian-influenced recipes. I do very much understand the ingredients look rather bizarre, but they work! Russians use cucumbers in many of their dishes, and here it adds a nice texture, in addition to flavor. There is always the next cookbook for more recipes from Russia!

Makes 6 servings
Prep Time: 1 hour

4 cups beef stock
12 ounces dark beer
1 ½ pounds beef stew meat, 1-inch pieces
2 bay leaves
4 tablespoons butter
1 medium onion, chopped
3 medium tomatoes, chopped
2 tablespoons tomato paste
¾ pound kielbasa sausage, sliced ½-inch thick
4 medium cucumbers, peeled, seeded, sliced
10 prunes, pitted, soaked in hot water
12 Kalamata olives, pitted and sliced
2 teaspoons capers
Salt and pepper, to taste
½ cup sour cream

1) Bring the beef stock and beer to a boil in a large stock pot.
2) Add meat and bay leaves to beef stock mixture. Reduce the heat to a simmer and cook uncovered for 1 ½ hours.
3) While the beef cooks, heat the butter in a heavy skillet over medium heat and cook onions until soft. Add the tomatoes, tomato paste and sausage. Simmer for 10 minutes.
4) Drain liquids from skillet, then add skillet contents to the meat mixture along with the cucumbers, prunes, olives and capers.
5) Cook for 15 more minutes and adjust with salt and pepper. Serve hot with a dollop of sour cream.

Per serving (approximate values): 600 Calories; 34.6g Fat (53.3% calories from fat); 36.5g Protein; 31.7g Carbohydrate; 121 mg Cholesterol; 2317mg Sodium.

LAMB STEW

Makes 8 servings
Prep Time: 1 hour

¼ cup olive oil
1 ½ pounds lamb, 1 ½-inch cubes
1 medium onion, chopped
6 cups beef stock
1 large turnip, peeled, ½-inch dice
1 large zucchini, ½-inch dice
2 medium carrots, ½-inch dice
2 large green bell peppers, cored, seeded, cut into strips
1 ½ pounds plum tomatoes, coarsely chopped
1 ½ teaspoons cumin seed
2 small red chile peppers, dried
1 teaspoon coriander seeds
16 ounces canned chickpeas, drained
2 tablespoons white vinegar
Salt and pepper, to taste

1) Heat the oil in a large saucepan or Dutch oven over medium high heat. Add lamb and brown lightly, about 5 minutes.

2) Add the chopped onions and continue to cook until the lamb is thoroughly browned and the onions are softened and colored, about 10 minutes more.

3) Spoon or drain off all the fat from the pot. Add the stock and bring to a boil. Cover, and reduce the heat to low. Simmer until the lamb is tender, about 1 hour. Uncover and skin off as much fat as possible.

4) Add the turnip, zucchini, carrots, peppers, tomatoes, cumin seeds, chiles and coriander. Cook covered for about 20 minutes.

5) Add the chickpeas and cook for 10 minutes more.

6) Remove the dried red chiles from the soup and add salt, pepper and vinegar to taste. Let stand covered for 10 minutes more. Serve!

Per serving (approximate values): 308 Calories; 12.6g Fat (37.3% calories from fat); 22.6g Protein; 24.9g Carbohydrate; 55mg Cholesterol; 1845mg Sodium.

MULLIGATAWNY

Makes 6 servings
Prep Time: 1 hour

3 pounds broiler chicken, cut up
4 cups water
1 teaspoon salt
1 teaspoon curry powder
1 teaspoon lemon juice
⅛ teaspoon ground cloves
⅛ teaspoon ground mace
1 medium onion, chopped
3 tablespoons butter or margarine
3 tablespoons flour
1 medium potato, ½-inch dice
1 medium carrot, thinly sliced
1 medium apple, chopped
1 medium green pepper, ½-inch pieces
3 medium Roma tomatoes, chopped

1) Heat chicken, water, salt, curry powder, lemon juice, cloves and mace to boiling in large saucepan or Dutch oven. Reduce heat. Cover and simmer until thickest pieces of chicken are done, about 45 minutes.

2) Remove chicken from broth. Skim fat from broth if necessary.

3) Pour broth mixture into heat-proof bowl or large Pyrex measuring cup. Add enough water to broth to measure 4 cups.

4) After chicken has cooled, remove bones and skin from chicken. Cut chicken into pieces and set aside.

5) In same pan used for the chicken, add butter or margarine over medium-high heat. Add onions and cook until tender and translucent. Remove from heat. Whisk in the flour until mixture is smooth. Gradually whisk in broth.

6) Add reserved chicken, potato, carrot, apple, green pepper and tomatoes.

7) Heat to boiling. Reduce heat. Cover and simmer until vegetables are tender, about 15-20 minutes.

8) Serve immediately or cool slightly and refrigerate up to a week.

Per serving (approximate values): 491 Calories; 29.4g Fat (54.0% calories from fat); 31.5g Protein; 24.8g Carbohydrate; 111 mg Cholesterol; 551 mg Sodium.

RAKOTT KAPOSZTA

Hungary is represented here in what may very well be considered a casserole. I first served it as a 'thank you' to the studio personnel where my TV show was taped and it was a big hit. I most recently served it to my family and was again surprised at how much everyone loved it. It is what I affectionately call a 'putzy' dish, with all the steps involved. Trust me, it's worth every one of them!

Makes 6 servings
Prep Time: 1 hour

1 pound Polska kielbasa sausage, 1-inch pieces
2 tablespoons olive oil
2 medium onions, sliced thin
1 tablespoon garlic, chopped
1 medium yellow bell pepper, sliced thin
3 tablespoons paprika, Hungarian sweet
1 teaspoon caraway seed
1 teaspoon dried marjoram
2 cups cooked chicken breast, diced
1 cup beef stock
12 ounces beer, dark
27 ounces sauerkraut, drained
3 cups rice, cooked
2 cups sour cream

Preheat the oven to 350 degrees.

1) In a large skillet, fry the sausage in the olive oil over medium-high heat for 3 minutes. Remove with a slotted spoon and set aside.

2) In the remaining fat from the sausages, add garlic and onions. Cook onions until they just begin to brown.

3) Add the sliced pepper and cook 2 minutes. Sprinkle the vegetables with the paprika, caraway and marjoram. Cook for 1 minute until everything is well coated with spices and herbs.

4) Add the reserved sausage and cooked chicken.

5)   Slowly add the stock and beer to the chicken and sausage mixture and stir constantly. Bring to a boil. Make sure to scrape up any brown bits from the bottom of the pan. Boil for 15 minutes.

6)   To assemble: Spread half the sauerkraut on the bottom of a 2 quart casserole baking dish. Cover with half the chicken mixture. Cover the chicken mixture with all of the cooked rice, followed by the remaining chicken mixture and then the remaining sauerkraut.

7)   Cover the casserole and bake for 45 minutes.

8)   Remove from oven and spread the sour cream evenly over the top of the casserole. Sprinkle generously with paprika.

9)   Increase oven temperature to 425 degrees and bake for 15 minutes or until sour cream is firm, but not dried out. Serve immediately!

Per serving (approximate values): 750 Calories; 49.1 g Fat (59.9% calories from fat); 26.5g Protein; 47.5g Carbohydrate; 119mg Cholesterol; 2093mg Sodium.

SAUTÉED CHICKEN WITH TOMATOES

Makes 4 servings
Prep Time: 30 minutes

1 whole chicken, cut into pieces
Salt and pepper, to taste
3 tablespoons olive oil
8 ounces fresh mushrooms, sliced
2 whole bay leaves
½ teaspoon thyme leaves
2 tablespoons onion powder
4 cloves garlic, minced
2 tablespoons flour
1 cup white wine
1 28-ounce can whole tomatoes
1 cup chicken broth
24 whole green olives

Preheat oven to 350 degrees.

1) Sprinkle the chicken pieces with salt and pepper.
2) Heat the oil in a large skillet and add the chicken pieces, skin side down. Cook over moderately high heat until golden brown. Turn the pieces over and continue cooking until golden brown on the second side. Remove from skillet and set aside.
3) Add mushrooms to the skillet and sauté until most of the liquid has boiled away.
4) Add the bay leaves, thyme, onion and garlic. Shake the skillet and stir to evenly distribute everything.
5) Sprinkle the pan ingredients with flour. Stir to blend evenly.
6) Slowly add the wine, then the broth. Add the tomatoes. Stir and bring to a boil.
7) Place chicken in a 2-quart casserole with a cover, then ladle sauce evenly over chicken. Cover and bake for 50 minutes.
8) Remove dish from oven. Add olives and gently mix to blend. Bake 15 more minutes. Remove from oven and let cool for 10 minutes. Serve!

Per serving (approximate values): 977 Calories; 65.6g Fat (64.3% calories from fat); 68.8g Protein; 13.1 g Carbohydrate; 255mg Cholesterol; 1273mg Sodium.

CHILLED CREAM OF BLACK OLIVE SOUP

I have had much resistance over the years to chilled soups, even though I adore them. This is one I love to make to help change attitudes. You have the option of not chilling it after you make it, but the flavors become so much more intense when chilled.

Makes 6 servings
Prep Time: 30 minutes

3 cups chicken stock
1 cup black olives
1 tablespoon onion, grated
2 cloves garlic, crushed
2 large eggs, beaten
2 cups heavy cream
⅓ cup sauterne wine
1 tablespoon Worcestershire sauce
Salt and pepper, to taste

1) In a medium saucepan, combine chicken stock, olives, onion, and garlic. Bring to a boil. Cover and reduce heat. Simmer for 15 minutes.

2) In a medium bowl, beat eggs with cream. Very gradually whisk in some of the hot chicken stock mixture. Remove chicken stock mixture from the stove. Add egg mixture to main chicken mixture in a slow stream, whisking constantly until all is combined.

3) Place saucepan back on heat and cook on low heat until mixture just begins to thicken. Remove from heat.

4) Add sauterne and Worcestershire. Adjust flavors with additional Worcestershire, salt and pepper to taste.

5) Pour mixture into blender in batches. Purée until smooth.

6) Pour soup into a covered container and refrigerate. Serve cold.

Per serving (approximate values): 348 Calories; 33.5g Fat (88.5% calories from fat); 4.5g Protein; 5.3g Carbohydrate; 181mg Cholesterol; 1347mg Sodium.

CHILLED CREAM OF TOMATO-BASIL SOUP

Makes 4 servings
Prep Time: 30 minutes

2 pounds tomatoes, chopped
1 small cucumber, peeled, seeded, chopped
1 cup chicken broth
½ teaspoon celery salt
Dash hot pepper sauce
¼ cup sour cream
¼ cup whipping cream
3 teaspoons dried basil leaves
Salt and pepper, to taste
Fresh basil

1) Purée tomatoes, cucumber and chicken stock in batches in blender until smooth. Transfer to large bowl.
2) Mix in celery salt and hot pepper sauce. Season soup with salt and pepper.
3) Refrigerate until cold, at least 3 hours or overnight.
4) Mix sour cream and whipping cream together in small bowl to blend.
5) Stir basil into sour cream mixture, then stir into soup to blend.
6) Add fresh ground pepper to taste. This seems to bring out the flavors best. Serve with fresh basil leaves.

Per serving (approximate values): 176 Calories; 9.8g Fat (46.5% calories from fat); 6.4g Protein; 18.9g Carbohydrate; 27mg Cholesterol; 624mg Sodium.

CHILLED YELLOW BELL PEPPER SOUP

Makes 4 servings
Prep Time: 45 minutes

1 pound yellow bell peppers, coarsely chopped
2 tablespoons olive oil
1 medium onion, chopped
2 cloves garlic, chopped
1 teaspoon dried thyme, crumbled
1 bay leaf
⅓ cup dry white wine
Pinch turmeric
3 cups chicken stock
Salt and pepper, to taste

1) Heat oil in heavy large skillet or Dutch oven over medium heat. Add bell peppers, onion, garlic, thyme and bay leaf. Sauté until vegetables are tender, about 15 to 20 minutes.
2) Add wine and turmeric and bring to boil. Boil 2 minutes.
3) Add 3 cups chicken stock and reduce heat. Simmer until vegetables are very tender, stirring occasionally, about 15 minutes. Discard bay leaf.
4) Purée soup in batches. Season to taste with salt and pepper. Cover and refrigerate soup until cold.

DO NOT use any other color pepper! Yellow bell peppers are incredibly sweet!

Per serving (approximate values): 133 Calories; 7.2g Fat (55.3% calories from fat); 2.2g Protein; 11.0g Carbohydrate; 0mg Cholesterol; 1615mg Sodium.

ZUCCHINI VICHYSSOISE

Makes 8 servings
Prep Time: 30 minutes

3 tablespoons vegetable oil
1 large onion, chopped
2 pounds zucchini
3 cups vegetable broth
1 ½ teaspoons dried basil leaves
¼ teaspoon ground nutmeg
¼ teaspoon white pepper
1 cup half and half

1) Heat oil in a 3 quart saucepan over medium heat. Add the onion and cook, stirring often, until soft but not browned, about 7 minutes.
2) Meanwhile, slice zucchini about ¼ inch thick.
3) Add zucchini, broth, basil, nutmeg and pepper to pan. Bring to a boil. Cover and reduce heat. Simmer until zucchini is tender.
4) Transfer mixture to blender or food processor and in batches process until smooth.
5) Pour into large bowl and stir in half and half.
6) Cover and refrigerate at least 2 hours or until thoroughly chilled. Serve!

Per serving (approximate values): 170 Calories; 10.38 Fat (52.1 % calories from fat); 4.8g Protein; 16.5g Carbohydrate; 12mg Cholesterol; 636mg Sodium.

VICHYSSOISE

I think this may be one the very first soups I ever made from scratch. It sounded so exotic in the recipe, as well as simple, that my mom was more than willing to let me try it. We were on welfare at the time, so this was really a treat. We were so very tired of canned soup! Needless to say, my mom was also a welfare success story. Sometimes the system does really work the way it's supposed to!

Makes 6 servings
Prep Time: 45 minutes

3 medium onions, sliced thin
2 tablespoons butter
4 large potatoes, sliced thin
4 cups chicken stock
1 ½ cups heavy cream
Salt and pepper, to taste

1) Heat 2 tablespoons butter in a Dutch oven or large saucepan over medium heat. Add onions and sauté until soft and translucent, about 10 minutes.
2) Add chicken stock to onions. Turn up heat to medium-high and add potatoes.
3) Bring mixture to boil. Cover and reduce heat. Simmer until potatoes are completely tender, about 15-20 minutes. Remove from heat and cool slightly, about 15 minutes.
4) In batches, place potato mixture in blender and blend until smooth. Pour puréed soup into heatproof bowl. When all potato mixture has been puréed, pour back into pan over low heat.
5) Add cream ½ cup at a time to your taste. Add salt and pepper after each addition to taste.
6) This soup is traditionally then refrigerated until completely cold, then re-seasoned. However, our American palates seem to enjoy it served piping hot!

Per serving (approximate values): 469 Calories; 26.38 Fat (50% calories from fat); 7.7g Protein; 51.5g Carbohydrate; 92mg Cholesterol; 1509mg Sodium.

STRAWBERRY SOUP

Northern Europeans make incredible chilled fruit soups. This is a delicious addition to a hot summer menu! You might be tempted to pour it in a glass and drink it, but do as the Europeans, sip it with a spoon.

Makes 6 servings
Prep Time: 30 minutes

4 cups strawberries, fresh or frozen
4 cups buttermilk
¾ cup sugar
1 ½ cups sour cream, split
¼ cup orange juice
1 tablespoon lemon juice

1) Purée berries, 1 cup of buttermilk and sugar in a blender.
2) In a large bowl combine remaining buttermilk (3 cups), 1 cup sour cream, orange and lemon juice. Blend well.
3) Add the strawberry purée and mix well. Refrigerate until well chilled.
4) Serve in chilled bowls and add a dollop of sour cream.

Per serving (approximate values): 280 Calories; 9.9g Fat (30.7% calories from fat); 7.3g Protein; 42.7g Carbohydrate; 23mg Cholesterol; 193mg Sodium.

BREADS

Hot Pepper Beer-Cheese Bread

This is a fun bread to make when you don't want to mess with the whole 'rise-and-knead dough' ordeal. It's made more like a fruit bread. Thus its crumb is moister than a yeast bread, but equally as tasty.

Makes 12 servings
Prep Time: 15 minutes

1 cup all-purpose flour
1 cup whole-wheat flour
6 ounces Monterey Jack cheese, hot pepper-type, shredded
1 teaspoon sugar
¾ teaspoon baking powder
½ teaspoon baking soda
½ teaspoon salt
⅓ cup butter, melted
1 cup beer, warm
2 large eggs, slightly beaten

Heat oven to 350 degrees.

1) In medium bowl stir together flour, whole wheat flour, 1 cup cheese, sugar, baking powder, baking soda and salt.
2) Stir in butter, beer and eggs until just moistened.
3) Spoon batter into greased 9x5-inch loaf pan. Sprinkle remaining ½ cup cheese over top of batter.
4) Bake for 45 to 55 minutes or until wooden toothpick inserted comes out clean. Remove from pan. Cool on wire rack 10 minutes. Serve warm.

Per serving (approximate values): 191.4 Calories; 10.5g Fat (49.9% calories from fat); 7.1 g Protein; 16.6g Carbohydrate; 62mg Cholesterol; 304mg Sodium.

PORTUGUESE CORN BREAD

I love traditional corn bread, so it's a logical step to try a yeast-leavened corn bread. I can thank the influence of the Portuguese for this recipe. It's very dense, so you'll want to slice the bread thin!

Makes 6 servings
Prep Time: 45 minutes

1 ½ cups yellow cornmeal
1 ½ teaspoons salt
1 ¼ cups boiling water
1 tablespoon olive oil
2 packages dry yeast
2 cups bread flour

Preheat oven to 350 degrees. Grease a baking sheet.

1) Pulverize cornmeal in blender or food processor, ¼ cup at a time, until it is fine and powdery. The bread can be made skipping this step, but the texture will be nowhere near as smooth.

2) In a large mixing bowl combine 1 cup of the powdered cornmeal, salt and boiling water. Stir until smooth.

3) Stir in the olive oil and cool mixture until it is lukewarm. Blend in yeast.

4) Gradually add in the rest of the cornmeal and 1 cup flour, stirring constantly by hand. Work the dough until it is a mass. Add more flour as necessary to overcome the stickiness.

5) Place plastic wrap tightly over bowl and leave at room temperature until dough has doubled in volume, about 30 minutes.

6) Turn the dough onto a floured work surface and knead for about 8 minutes. Add flour as necessary. Shape it as you like, but a simple round shape is most traditional.

7) Place dough on baking sheet. Cover with waxed paper and leave until it doubles in bulk, about 30 minutes.

8) Place in preheated oven and bake until loaf is golden and the bottom crust sounds hard and hollow when tapped, about 40 minutes. Remove from oven and place on a rack to cool.

Per serving (approximate values): 322.8 Calories; 3.8g Fat (10.6% calories from fat); 9.9g Protein; 61.5g Carbohydrate; 0mg Cholesterol; 538mg Sodium.

ENGLISH MUFFIN BREAD

Makes 6 servings
Prep Time: 45 minutes

1 package dry yeast
½ cup milk, hot (120–130 degrees)
2 teaspoons salt
4 cups bread flour
½ teaspoon baking soda, dissolved in 1 T. warm water

Grease two medium (8 ½x4 ½-inch) loaf pans. Preheat oven to 325 degrees.

1) In a large bowl combine yeast, salt and 2 cups of the flour.
2) Pour in the hot milk and stir to blend thoroughly.
3) Stir in additional flour ½ cup at a time until batter is thick. Stir the batter about 200 strokes by hand until dough pulls away from the sides of the bowl in thick ribbons.
4) Cover the bowl with plastic wrap and put in a warm place for about an hour or until batter has doubled in volume. It will be quite bubbly.
5) Stir down the batter-like dough and add the dissolved baking powder. Be certain to make sure the dough is well blended. This step is the key to this very special bread.
6) Spoon or pour into the pans. Push the dough into the corners with a spatula. The pans will be about two-thirds full.
7) Lay plastic wrap over the pans and return to a warm place. Let dough rise to the edge of the pans, about 1 hour.
8) Bake the loaves for about 1 hour. The loaves will be well browned and pulled away from the sides of the pan when done.
9) Turn the bread out of the pans. Allow to cool on a wire rack before cutting.

Per serving (approximate values): 348.1 Calories; 2.3g Fat (6.0% calories from fat); 12.4g Protein; 68g Carbohydrate; 3mg Cholesterol; 828mg Sodium.

OREGANO AND ONION BREAD

Since I haven't made many breads over the years, the few I have included tend to be a bit more unusual than your plain white bread. The inclusion of oregano and onion in this recipe will add flavor to any meal of your favorite comfort foods.

Makes 6 servings
Prep Time: 1 hour

2 tablespoons olive oil
½ cup chopped onion
1 ½ cups water, warm (105 to 115 degrees)
1 package dry yeast
1 teaspoon sugar
4 ½ cups all-purpose flour
2 ½ teaspoons salt
3 teaspoons dried oregano leaves

Preheat oven to 350 degrees.

1) Heat oil in heavy skillet over medium heat.
2) Add chopped onion and sauté until translucent, about 5 minutes. Remove from heat. Cool.
3) Pour 1 ½ cups warm water into small bowl. Stir in yeast and sugar. Let stand until foamy, about 10 minutes.
4) Mix 4 cups flour and salt in very large bowl. Stir in onion and any remaining oil from skillet.
5) Add yeast mixture and oregano and mix well.
6) Knead briefly in bowl just until dough comes together. Turn dough out onto generously floured surface. Knead dough until smooth and elastic. Add more flour by tablespoonfuls as necessary to keep dough from sticking, about 10 minutes.
7) Oil large bowl. Add dough to bowl, turning to coat. Cover bowl with kitchen towel and let dough rise in warm area until double in volume, about 1 hour.
8) Oil heavy large baking sheet. Punch down dough. Turn out onto floured surface and knead briefly. Divide into 2 equal parts.

9) Shape each piece into a 6-inch round. Place loaves on prepared sheet and cover loosely with greased plastic wrap. Let rise in warm area until doubled in volume, about 45 minutes.

10) Place in oven and bake for about 45 minutes or until golden brown in color. Transfer loaves to rack and cool.

Per serving (approximate values): 397 Calories; 5.6g Fat (12.9% calories from fat); 10.7g Protein; 74.6g Carbohydrate; 0mg Cholesterol; 893mg Sodium.

SPICY RYE BREAD

Makes 6 servings
Prep Time: 45 minutes

2 teaspoons salt
½ teaspoon ground cloves
½ teaspoon allspice
1 teaspoon caraway seed
2 tablespoons brown sugar
3 tablespoons light molasses
1 ¾ cups water, hot (120-130 degrees)
2 packages dry yeast
2 tablespoons shortening
2 ½ cups rye flour
3 cups bread flour

Preheat oven to 375 degrees. Grease baking sheet and sprinkle with cornmeal.

1) In a large mixing bowl measure salt, cloves, allspice, caraway seeds, sugar, molasses and hot water.
2) Add the yeast. Stir to blend. Add the shortening.
3) Measure the rye flour and 1 cup of the bread flour into the bowl. Beat with a wooden spoon until smooth, about 100 strokes.
4) Add flour as necessary until dough begins to clean the sides of the bowl. The dough will be a bit sticky, but firm. Turn out onto floured surface.
5) Knead by hand until dough is smooth and elastic to the touch. Place the dough into a greased bowl. Turn once to coat all sides. Cover with plastic wrap and leave to rise until double in volume, about 1 hour.
6) Divide the dough into two parts. Form each part into a ball or oblong loaf and place onto opposite ends of the cookie sheet. Cover loosely with wax paper. Leave until loaves double in bulk, about 45 minutes.
7) Uncover the loaves. Make slashes on top of loaves diagonally. Bake until loaves are brown, about 45 minutes. Remove and cool.

Per serving (approximate values): 491.8 Calories; 6.4g Fat (11.7% calories from fat); 13.8g Protein; 95.5g Carbohydrate; 0mg Cholesterol; 721mg Sodium.

SWEDISH ORANGE-CARAWAY BREAD

I first made this bread for a wedding party, where it made a very nice compliment to a beef main course. Use it with your leftover beef roast for a yummy sandwich!

Makes 6 servings
Prep Time: 45 minutes

¾ cup water
2 tablespoons brown sugar
1 medium orange, zested
1 tablespoon butter
1 teaspoon caraway seed
1 teaspoon salt
1 package dry yeast
2 cups bread flour

Grease medium (8 ½x4 ½-inch) loaf pan. Preheat oven to 350 degrees.

1) In a small saucepan boil the water, brown sugar, orange zest, butter and caraway seed for 3 minutes. Pour into large mixing bowl. Cool to luke-warm (105-115 degrees).

2) When cooled add the salt, yeast and 1 cup flour. Stir together for about 2 minutes. More flour will be added later.

3) Scrape down the sides of the bowl and cover with plastic wrap. Put in a warm place for 1 ½ hours.

4) Stir down the raised batter-like dough with a wooden spoon. Add the remaining flour ½ cup at a time. Begin to blend first with the spoon, then by hand as the dough becomes more difficult to work with. The dough will be a shaggy mass that will clean the sides of the bowl. If it does not and is sticky, sprinkle with additional flour.

5) Turn the dough onto a lightly floured work surface and knead with a rhythmic motion of push-turn-fold. The dough will become smooth and elastic and bubbles will rise beneath the surface. Knead by hand about 8 minutes.

6) Shape the dough into a ball and let rest on a work surface for 3 or 4 minutes. Form a loaf and place in the pan. Cover pan with plastic wrap and leave in warm place for 1 hour or until dough has doubled in bulk.

7) Place in oven and bake about 1 hour or until loaf is brown and crusty. Remove from the pan and place on a metal rack to cool before slicing.

Per serving (approximate values): 216.2 Calories; 2.8g Fat (11.8% calories from fat); 6.5g Protein; 41.1g Carbohydrate; 5mg Cholesterol; 379mg Sodium.

GARLIC BREAD

The French really know garlic! If you like to make garlic bread the traditional way, however that might be, you may want to give this recipe a go. The flavor of garlic is completely infused in every bite

Makes 6 servings
Prep Time: 45 minutes

1 ½ teaspoons garlic powder
¼ cup butter, softened
5 cups bread flour
2 packages dry yeast
2 teaspoons salt
1 tablespoon sugar
2 ¼ cups hot milk, 120-130 degrees

Preheat oven to 375 degrees. Grease 2 medium (8 ½x4 ½-inch) loaf pans.

1) In a small bowl blend garlic powder with butter. Set aside.
2) Blend 3 cups flour into large mixing bowl and add salt, yeast and sugar.
3) Pour milk into flour and stir vigorously with wooden spoon to blend thoroughly. Drop in butter mixture and mix into batter.
4) Add flour ¼ cup at a time until a shaggy dough mass develops. Knead to create a dough that is soft and elastic. Sprinkle with flour if sticky.
5) Place the dough in a greased bowl and cover tightly with plastic wrap. Put aside to double in volume, about 1 hour.
6) Turn the dough onto work surface and knead briefly to push out air bubbles and divide in half. Form into loaves and place into pans.
7) Cover pans with wax paper and let rise until the dough has doubled in volume, about 1 inch above the rim, about 45 minutes. Place loaves in the oven and bake until light brown, about 40 minutes. Turn loaves out from the pans to cool.

Per serving (approximate values): 278.7 Calories; 6.4g Fat (20.7% calories from fat); 9.2g Protein; 45.6g Carbohydrate; 16mg Cholesterol; 419mg Sodium.

FRESH PLUM PUMPKIN QUICK BREAD

You'll see pumpkin as an ingredient in all sorts of recipes throughout this book. It's a very versatile ingredient. In this instance, the pumpkin adds a moist element. Plums add tartness and quick is just, well, quick.

Makes 12 servings
Prep Time: 30 minutes

½ cup sugar
½ cup canned pumpkin
⅓ cup skim milk
1 tablespoon oil
1 large egg
1 ¼ cups all-purpose flour
2 teaspoons baking powder
½ teaspoon ginger
½ teaspoon cinnamon
2 medium purple plums, chopped

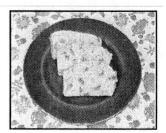

Heat oven to 350 degrees. Spray 8x4-inch loaf pan with non-stick cooking spray.

1) In a large bowl combine sugar, pumpkin, milk, oil and egg. Mix well.
2) In a medium bowl combine all remaining dry ingredients.
3) Add flour mixture into pumpkin mixture. Stir until just combined.
4) Add fresh chopped plums. Spoon batter into pan.
5) Bake for 20-25 minutes or until toothpick inserted comes out clean.

Per serving (approximate values): 113.4 Calories; 1.9g Fat (14.4% calories from fat); 2.4g Protein; 22.3g Carbohydrate; 18mg Cholesterol; 70mg Sodium.

SIDE DISHES

DRIED APRICOT CHUTNEY

Chutneys make a great addition to any type of roasted meat, such as pork, chicken, even beef. This particular chutney pairs well with pork or poultry. I happen to like it with Cumin Pork Tenderloin, although even pan-fried or roasted pork chops would even work great.

Makes 4 servings
Prep Time: 30 minutes

1 cup water, divided
1 cup dried apricot halves, chopped
1 cup onion, chopped
⅓ cup cider vinegar
⅓ cup raisins
1 ¼ teaspoons pumpkin-pie spice
1 teaspoon dry mustard
⅛ teaspoon crushed red pepper
1 cup Golden Delicious apples, chopped coarsely

1) Combine ½ cup water, apricot and next 6 ingredients (onion through red pepper) in a medium saucepan and stir well.

2) Bring to a boil. Cover and reduce heat. Simmer 20 minutes, stirring occasionally.

3) Add ½ cup water and apples. Cover and cook an additional 15 minutes or until apple is tender.

4) Remove from heat and uncover. Let stand 5 minutes before serving.

Per serving (approximate values): 145 Calories; 0.4g Fat (2.4% calories from fat); 2.3g Protein; 37.3g Carbohydrate; 0mg Cholesterol; 9mg Sodium.

CHEDDAR CORN CAKES

While I included this as a side, this is another dish that could be used for a nice brunch item. Buttered or slathered with something sweet (like the compote that follows), as a side or as a course, these cakes will delight even picky eaters.

Makes 8 servings
Prep Time: 20 minutes

¼ cup butter
1 ¼ cups all-purpose flour
4 teaspoons baking powder
1 tablespoon sugar
1 teaspoon salt
2 large eggs
1 cup whole milk
14 ounces canned corn, drained
8 ounces cheddar cheese, shredded finely

Preheat oven to 200 degrees.

1) Melt butter in microwave and cool slightly
2) In a large bowl sift or mix together flour, baking powder, sugar and salt.
3) In a medium bowl mix together whole milk, eggs and melted butter.
4) Whisk milk mixture into flour mixture. Add milk as necessary (1 tablespoon at a time) to make mixture easy to pour.
5) Make sure corn has all liquid drained from it. Pat it dry if necessary. Stir corn into batter.
6) Heat large griddle or heavy skillet over moderate heat until hot enough to make a drop of water scatter over surface.
7) Butter skillet. Either take a cold stick of butter and quickly running it over the surface of the pan or melt a little butter in a small dish and brush butter over surface with a heatproof pastry brush.
8) Working in batches, drop ¼-cup of batter onto griddle or skillet. Sprinkle cheddar cheese over surface of each cake. Cook until bubbles appear on surface. Flip cakes with a spatula and cook until pancakes are cooked through. They should be golden brown on both sides.
9) Transfer pancakes to an oven-proof dish. Cover and place in oven.
10) Continue until all batter is used.

Per serving (approximate values): 322 Calories; 18.1 g Fat (49.5% calories from fat); 13.3g Protein; 28.4g, Carbohydrate; 103mg Cholesterol; 720mg Sodium.

CRANBERRY, TANGERINE AND BLUEBERRY COMPOTE

More than simply a fruit sauce, this compote packs a punch. I typically serve it with the Cheddar Corn Cakes recipe preceding. It also goes nicely with plain pancakes or even over ice cream.

Makes 8 servings
Prep Time: 30 minutes

6 large tangerines
1 cup golden brown sugar, packed
1 tablespoon fresh ginger, peeled, grated
⅛ teaspoon ground cloves
6 cups cranberries, fresh or frozen (18 oz.)
2 cups blueberries, frozen, thawed

1) Finely grate enough peel from tangerines to measure 2 ½ tablespoons.
2) Squeeze enough juice from all of the tangerines to measure 1 ½ cups.
3) In a heavy large saucepan, combine peel, juice, brown sugar, ginger and cloves. Bring to a boil. Stir constantly until sugar dissolves. Reduce heat and simmer for 5 minutes.
4) Add cranberries and cook until cranberries pop and juices thicken, about 15–20 minutes.
5) Add blueberries. Stir until blueberries are heated through.
6) Serve immediately!

Per serving (approximate values): 192 Calories; 0.4g Fat (1.9% calories from fat); 1g Protein; 49.5g Carbohydrate; 0mg Cholesterol; 15mg Sodium.

RED CABBAGE WITH FRUIT AND ONIONS

Makes 8 servings
Prep Time: 45 minutes

½ cup butter
⅔ cup shallots, chopped
2 ½ pounds red cabbage, sliced thin
1 large onion, sliced
2 large tart green apples, cored, sliced thin
¾ cup raspberry vinegar
½ cup sugar
2 cups frozen raspberries or blackberries, thawed
Salt and pepper, to taste

1) Melt butter in large heavy skillet over medium heat. Add shallots and sauté until tender, about 10 minutes.
2) Add cabbage, onions, apples, vinegar and sugar to skillet. Cook until cabbage is limp, stirring frequently, about 15 minutes.
3) Add raspberries. Cook until most of the liquid has evaporated, about 25 more minutes.
4) Season to taste with salt and pepper.

Per serving (approximate values): 284 Calories; 11.9g Fat (35.3% calories from fat); 3.1 g Protein; 46.1 g Carbohydrate; 31 mg Cholesterol; 135mg Sodium.

LEMON AND SWEET ONION MARMALADE

Please don't substitute this for your favorite orange marmalade! This is a savory marmalade used in the same vain as a chutney. Serve alongside any of your favorite roasted cuts of meat.

Makes 4 servings
Prep Time: 1 hour

2 tablespoons olive oil
2 large sweet onions, coarsely chopped
1 medium lemon, coarsely chopped
4 teaspoons sugar
4 teaspoons balsamic vinegar

1) Heat oil in heavy saucepan over medium-high heat. Add onion and lemon and cook 10 minutes, stirring constantly.
2) Sprinkle sugar on top. Mix thoroughly.
3) Reduce heat to low and cover partially so steam can escape. Cook 30 minutes, stirring occasionally.
4) Add vinegar. Combine completely and continue cooking until mixture is thickened. Serve.

Per serving (approximate values): 105 Calories; 7g Fat (51.9% calories from fat); 1.7g Protein; 12.9g Carbohydrate; 0mg Cholesterol; 3mg Sodium.

CLASSIC CRANBERRY CUMBERLAND SAUCE

Makes 6 servings
Prep Time: 1 hour

8 ounces cranberries, frozen or fresh
¾ cup Tawny Port wine
½ cup sugar
3 tablespoons fresh orange juice
¾ teaspoon cornstarch
½ teaspoon dry mustard
½ teaspoon fresh lemon juice
Pinch ground cloves
Pinch ground ginger
¼ cup golden raisins
1 tablespoon orange peel, grated
½ teaspoon lemon peel, grated

1)   Combine cranberries and Port in heavy large saucepan over medium-high heat. Cook until berries burst, stirring occasionally, about 10 minutes.
2)   Add ½ cup sugar. Stir one minute.
3)   Combine juices, cornstarch, mustard and spices in bowl. Whisk until smooth. Stir into berry mixture.
4)   Add raisins and peels. Simmer until thickened, stirring occasionally, about 5 minutes. Season with more sugar if desired.
5)   Cool, cover and chill.

Per serving (approximate values): 156 Calories; 0.2g Fat (1.2% calories from fat); 0.5g Protein; 31.9g Carbohydrate; 0mg Cholesterol; 3mg Sodium.

COCONUT MILK AND GINGER RICE

With all the Southeast Asian main courses I've included, it's only appropriate I have at least one rice dish that pairs well with many of them. A nice jasmine-style rice is great too, but this makes it even more special.

Makes 8 servings
Prep Time: 25 minutes

3 cups water
2 cups long-grain rice
1 cup coconut milk
2 tablespoons sugar
2 teaspoons fresh ginger, peeled and grated

1) Bring water, rice, coconut milk, sugar and ginger to a boil in medium saucepan over high heat.
2) Reduce heat to low. Cover and simmer 25 minutes or until liquid has been absorbed.
3) Let rest about 5 minutes covered. Uncover and serve.

Per serving (approximate values): 245 Calories; 7.5g Fat (26.8% calories from fat); 4g Protein; 42.1 g Carbohydrate; 0mg Cholesterol; 12mg Sodium.

CURRIED RICE

Makes 6 servings
Prep Time: 45 minutes

1 cup medium grain rice, uncooked
1 small apple, peeled and cored
3 tablespoons butter
½ cup onion, finely chopped
2 cloves garlic
1 tablespoon curry powder
½ bay leaf
1 ½ cups chicken broth

1) Dice apple into ¼-inch cubes. Set aside
2) Heat 2 tablespoons butter in a saucepan. Add the onion and garlic. Cook until onion wilts.
3) Add the apple and curry and stir.
4) Add the rice, bay leaf and chicken broth. Bring mixture to a boil. Cover and reduce heat to low. Simmer 17-18 minutes.
5) Remove from heat. Let stand 10 minutes. Uncover and add the remaining tablespoon butter and fluff. Serve.

Per serving (approximate values): 206 Calories; 6.8g Fat (29.7% calories from fat); 5.4g Protein; 30.8g Carbohydrate; 16mg Cholesterol; 452mg Sodium.

CUBAN RED BEANS AND RICE

Red beans and rice is a very common combination south of our borders. While this recipe tips its hat to Cuba, there are an endless array of variations to these common ingredients.

Makes 8 servings
Prep Time: 45 minutes

1 cup dried pinto beans
Water to cover
1 whole bay leaf
1 small whole onion
4 cloves garlic, minced
2 whole cloves
1 ½ cups long-grain rice
3 tablespoons olive oil
1 medium onion, chopped fine
Salt and pepper, to taste

1) In a large saucepan add dry beans and cover completely with water. Soak beans overnight.

2) Drain beans and place in large saucepan or stock pot with 2 quarts of water. Place bay leave in pot. Stick cloves into sides of onion and add to beans. Add garlic. Turn heat to medium high and bring water to a boil.

3) Reduce the heat and simmer the beans uncovered until tender, about 1 hour. Drain the bean mixture in a colander. Discard bay leaf and onion. Set aside.

4) Bring 2 ½ cups of water to a boil in a medium saucepan. Add the rice and bring back to boil. Cover and reduce heat. Gently simmer until rice is done, about 18 minutes. Let the rice sit covered for about 5 minutes. Fluff rice with a fork and again cover.

5) Heat the oil in a large frying pan. Add chopped onion and cook until soft, about 2-3 minutes.

6) Add beans and rice and cook over medium heat until the mixture is well mixed. Season with salt and pepper and serve.

Per serving (approximate values): 270 Calories; 6g Fat (19.4% calories from fat); 8.1 g Protein; 47.9g Carbohydrate; 0mg Cholesterol; 11 mg Sodium.

RICE PILAF WITH DRIED CHERRIES

This recipe had its roots in an attempt to develop some fun ideas for giving the gift of food. All the ingredients can be mixed together, packaged in a container, tagged with cooking instructions and given to someone special. Since I have had the chance to serve it at several parties, I decided to go ahead and include as the side dish it is, with a plain roasted chicken or other poultry.

Makes 6 servings
Prep Time: 20 minutes

1 ½ cups brown rice, long-grain
¼ cup dried onions, chopped
½ teaspoon salt
½ teaspoon ground allspice
½ teaspoon turmeric
¼ teaspoon curry powder
Freshly ground pepper
½ cup dried tart cherries, chopped
¼ cup slivered almonds
3 ½ cups chicken stock

Preheat oven to 350 degrees.

1)   Heat 2 tablespoons olives oil in a 3 to 4-quart saucepan (that can also be placed in the oven) over medium high heat. Add all ingredients and sauté gently in the oil until the rice is opaque, about 5 to 7 minutes.

2)   Add 3 ½ cups chicken stock and bring to a rolling boil. Cover the dish and remove from the heat.

3)   Place in the oven and bake for 60 to 70 minutes until rice is done. Once rice is cooked, cover and place back in oven. Turn oven off and let pilaf sit for 10 minutes. Remove from oven, fluff and serve.

Per serving (approximate values): 215 Calories; 4g Fat (16.4% calories from fat); 5g Protein; 40.9g Carbohydrate; 0mg Cholesterol; 182mg Sodium.

MAIN DISHES

Pastitsa

If I had a dime for every time my family requested I make this, well, it would be a good thing. This is my Dad's very favorite dish, as it is in the country of origin, Greece. I have taken a few liberties from the original preparation, especially with the use of American cheeses. Velveeta makes a very smooth dish, although hard to work with due to its softness. I place a block of Velveeta in the freezer for about 15 minutes, which helps firm the cheese up a bit.

Makes 6 servings
Prep Time: 45 minutes

2 cups elbow macaroni, uncooked
1 pound ground beef
1 medium onion, chopped
15 ounces tomato sauce
1 teaspoon salt
2 cups American cheese, grated or Velveeta, refrigerated, diced
½ teaspoon cinnamon
1 ¼ cups milk
3 tablespoons butter
2 large eggs, beaten
⅛ teaspoon ground nutmeg

Preheat oven to 325 degrees.

1) Cook macaroni as directed on package. Drain. Cover and set aside until ready to use.
2) Cook and stir beef and onion in a large skillet until beef is light brown. Drain. Stir in tomato sauce and salt.
3) Spread half the macaroni in greased 2 ½-quart baking dish. Cover with beef mixture.
4) In a medium bowl mix all of cheese with the cinnamon. Sprinkle half of cheese over beef mixture. Cover with remaining macaroni.
5) Cook and stir milk, nutmeg and butter in medium saucepan until butter is melted. Remove from heat. Stir half of milk mixture into beaten eggs to warm them. Gradually blend egg mixture back into remaining milk in saucepan. Pour over macaroni.

6) Sprinkle with remaining cheese. Cook uncovered in oven until brown and center is set, about 50 minutes.

Per serving (approximate values): 643 Calories; 41.7g Fat (58.3% calories from fat); 30.5g Protein; 36.7g Carbohydrate; 194mg Cholesterol; 1188mg Sodium.

RENAISSANCE LASAGNA

I came up with this nutty idea to try my hand at something completely new. It was right after I had completed two years of cooking on TV and I was looking for something to keep my interest. 'Cooking lesson dinner party' was the name I on which I settled. The concept was to see if anyone was interested in having me prepare a menu, shop for it, then have the host or hostess invite four or six of their closest friends and have me teach them how to prepare the dishes, then eat them. A good friend of mine encouraged me by being the guinea pig and I decided that this would be the main course. Talk about ambitious! It is indeed a lot of work, but you will never taste a more scrumptious lasagna ever.

Makes 8 servings
Prep Time: 45 minutes

6 tablespoons golden raisins
1 cup hot water
10 quarts water
1 pound lasagna noodles
2 tablespoons butter
1 recipe Renaissance Ragu (recipe follows)
1 cup heavy cream
⅓ pound prosciutto, very thinly sliced
8 ounces Parmesan cheese, grated
6 tablespoons pine nuts, lightly toasted
1 pinch cinnamon
Nonstick cooking spray

Preheat the oven to 350 degrees.

1) Soak the raisins in the hot water about 30 minutes while the other ingredients are prepared.
2) In stock pot bring the 10 quarts of water to a boil. Drop in 4 pieces of lasagna noodles. Cook about 4 minutes until barely tender. Remove from boiling water and immediately plunge into cold water to stop the cooking process. Drain on wax paper with paper towels underneath. Continue until all the noodles are cooked.

3) Use the 2 tablespoons butter to coat the bottom of a 3-quart baking dish, which is at least 2 inches deep.

4) Spread 3 to 4 tablespoons of the Ragu (recipe follows) over the bottom. Cover this mixture with sheets of cooked lasagna noodles, placing them side by side. Spread about ⅓ of the Ragu over the noodles. Top with another layer of noodles.

5) Spread over the noodles 3 tablespoons of heavy cream. Sprinkle with half of the prosciutto, 6 tablespoons of the Parmesan, 2 tablespoons raisins (which have been drained) and 3 tablespoons of the pine nuts. Sprinkle lightly with a pinch of cinnamon.

6) Cover this with another layer of pasta. Spread ⅓ Ragu over the pasta. Again spread 3 tablespoons cream, remaining prosciutto, 6 tablespoons Parmesan, 2 tablespoons raisins, and remaining pine nuts. Dust with a pinch of cinnamon.

7) Cover with a final layer of noodles. Cover with remaining ⅓ of Ragu.

8) In a medium bowl blend the remaining cheese, cream and raisins. Stir in a pinch of cinnamon. Spoon this evenly over the Ragu.

9) Spray the bottom side of a sheet of aluminum foil with nonstick cooking spray and fold tightly over cooking dish. Place into the oven and bake 45 to 50 minutes. Uncover and bake another 5 minutes. The top should be bubbly and creamy, not dried out and brown.

10) Let the lasagna rest in the turned off oven for 10 minutes. Remove from oven and serve.

Per serving (approximate values): 566 Calories; 28.6g Fat (45.1 % calories from fat); 27g Protein; 51.6g Carbohydrate; 84mg Cholesterol; 1119mg Sodium.

RENAISSANCE RAGU

Makes 8 servings
Prep Time: 45 minutes

8 ounces mild Italian sausage
1 pound chicken thighs without skin, boneless, minced
8 ounces ground pork
8 ounces ground beef, extra lean
2 tablespoons olive oil
1 tablespoon butter
1 small carrot, minced
1 stalk celery, minced
1 small onion, minced
3 ounces pancetta, minced
1 whole bay leaf
1 cup white wine
1 pinch cloves
2 cups chicken stock
4 cloves garlic, crushed
3 tablespoons tomato paste
½ cup cream
Salt and pepper, to taste

1) Mince and combine the meats by hand. Avoid using a food processor.

2) In a large sauté pan heat the oil and butter over medium heat. Add the vegetables through the pancetta. Cook and stir often until they begin to color, about 8 minutes.

3) Add the sausage, chicken, pork, beef and bay leaf. Cook over high heat 8 more minutes or until the meats begin to brown.

4) Lower the heat to medium and continue sautéing. Stir often with wooden spoon for 10 minutes or until the meat is rich dark brown. It should sizzle quietly in the pan, not violently pop and sputter. Slow browning protects the brown glaze that will develop on the bottom of the pan.

5) Drain the fat and return to a medium heat. Add the wine and pinch of cloves. Cook at a lively bubble 3 minutes or until the wine has evaporated. As the wine bubbles use the wooden spoon to scrape up the brown glaze from the bottom of the pan.

6) Reduce the heat to medium and add ½ cup of the stock. Simmer about 3 minutes until almost all liquid is gone.

7) Stir in the garlic, tomato paste and another ½ cup of the stock. Cook until almost no liquid is left.

8) Add the remaining stock to the saucepan and let it simmer slowly uncovered, about 30 to 40 minutes

9) When the stock has reduced by about one-third and the sauce is moist, but not loose, add the cream and simmer 3 to 5 minutes. Season with salt and pepper to taste.

Per serving (approximate values): 446 Calories; 31g Fat (66.3% calories from fat); 29.7g Protein; 5.7g Carbohydrate; 129mg Cholesterol; 1187mg Sodium.

Mexican Tortilla Lasagna

With the Minnesota culture firmly entrenched in my bones, I love hot dishes (casseroles to the rest of the world). I have included many of them in all their glorious variations, such as this layered dish with a strong Mexican influence.

Makes 6 servings
Prep Time: 45 minutes

1 ½ pounds plum tomatoes, ¼-inch dice
2 whole green onions, sliced thin
1 tablespoon cilantro, chopped
3 cloves garlic
1 ½ teaspoons salt, split
Tabasco sauce, to taste
2 tablespoons olive oil
1 pound boneless skinless chicken breast halves
1 teaspoon chili powder
½ teaspoon cumin
9 ounces frozen corn kernels
5 whole flour tortillas, 9-inch
¾ pound Monterey jack cheese

Preheat oven to 375 degrees. Grease a 9-inch round soufflé dish or casserole that is at least 3 inches deep.

1)   Toss tomatoes, green onions, cilantro, garlic, 1 teaspoon of salt and Tabasco in bowl. Set mixture (salsa) aside.

2)   Heat oil in a large skillet. Cut chicken into ¼-inch strips. Add chicken, spices and remaining ½ teaspoon salt to pan and sauté, stirring often, until chicken is cooked through, about 5 minutes.

3)   Add corn and continue cooking until corn is hot and any liquid in the pan has evaporated, about 3 minutes. Taste for salt and set aside.

4)   Lay a tortilla on bottom of baking dish. Spread ¾ cup chicken and corn over tortilla and cover with ½ cup salsa and ½ cup cheese. Repeat layering of tortillas, chicken, salsa and cheese twice more.

5)   For the last layer, cover tortilla with remaining ½ cup salsa and sprinkle with remaining 1 cup cheese.

6)   Bake lasagna until cheese turns golden brown in spots, about 25 minutes. Remove dish from oven and let lasagna settle for about 10 minutes. Cut into wedges and serve.

Per serving (approximate values): 512 Calories; 25.9g Fat (44.7% calories from fat); 37.3g Protein; 34.9g Carbohydrate; 94mg Cholesterol; 1046mg Sodium.

GREEK LASAGNA

Makes 8 servings
Prep Time: 1 hour

2 tablespoons olive oil
1 medium onion, chopped fine
1 medium carrot, chopped fine
1 ½ pounds ground beef
1 teaspoon cinnamon
½ teaspoon ground nutmeg
1 teaspoon salt
¼ cup white wine
2 cups tomatoes, crushed
<u>White Sauce (Béchamel)</u>
¼ cup butter
¼ cup flour
¼ teaspoon ground nutmeg
½ teaspoon salt
2 cups milk
2 large eggs slightly beaten
18 whole lasagna noodles, cooked
1 ½ cups Parmesan cheese, grated

Preheat oven to 375 degrees. Grease 9x13-inch lasagna baking pan.

Prepare White Sauce (Béchamel):
1) Heat butter over low heat in saucepan until melted.
2) Whisk in flour, salt and nutmeg. Cook over low heat, stirring constantly, until smooth and bubbly. Remove from heat.
3) Gradually stir in milk in a steady stream. Heat to boiling and thick, stirring constantly.
4) Stir a little of the hot mixture into the beaten eggs. Remove milk mixture from heat source and whisk in heated egg mixture to remaining milk mixture.

To assemble Lasagna:
1) Heat oil in a large saucepan. Add the onion and sauté over medium heat until translucent, about 5 minutes.

2) Add the carrot and cook until slightly softened, about 5 minutes. Stir in ground beef and crumble with a fork. Cook until the meat loses its red color.

3) Stir in cinnamon, nutmeg, salt, wine and tomatoes. Bring mixture to a boil, reduce heat and simmer gently until sauce thickens, about 30 minutes. Set aside.

4) Cook and drain noodles according to package instructions.

5) Spread 3 tablespoons béchamel across bottom of baking pan. Line bottom with layer of noodles. Spread ¾ cup meat sauce over noodles. Drizzle with ¼ cup béchamel and sprinkle with 3 tablespoons cheese.

6) Repeat layering of pasta, meat sauce, béchamel and cheese two more times. For the fourth layer, coat noodles with 6 tablespoons béchamel and sprinkle with remaining 6 tablespoons cheese.

7) Bake lasagna until top turns golden brown in spots and sauce is bubbling, about 25 minutes. Remove and let set for about 10 minutes.

Per serving (approximate values): 1267 Calories; 43.3g Fat (31.0% calories from fat); 49.5g Protein; 167.3g Carbohydrate; 85mg Cholesterol; 1853mg Sodium.

MOUSSAKA

To the uninitiated, I call this dish the 'Greek lasagna with layers of eggplant instead of pasta' dish. I have made it for many occasions where I want to serve a group of people something different than an Italian-style lasagna.

Makes 8 servings
Prep Time: 1 hour 30 minutes

<u>Tomato Beef Sauce</u>
2 tablespoons olive oil
1 ½ pounds ground beef, extra lean
1 medium onion, chopped
4 cloves garlic, crushed
29 ounces canned tomatoes, chopped
½ cup water
1 teaspoon salt
1 teaspoon basil leaves
½ teaspoon sugar
¼ teaspoon pepper
1 whole bay leaf, crushed
6 ounces tomato paste
¾ cup red wine
¼ teaspoon ground nutmeg

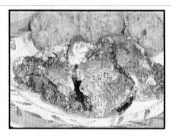

<u>White Sauce</u>
¼ cup butter
¼ cup flour
¼ teaspoon ground nutmeg
½ teaspoon salt
2 cups milk
2 large eggs, slightly beaten
<u>Remaining:</u>
2 pounds eggplant
6 quarts water
1 ½ cups Parmesan cheese, grated
⅔ cup bread crumbs
1 large egg, slightly beaten

Preheat oven to 350 degrees.

Prepare Tomato Beef Sauce:
1) Heat butter in a large skillet over high heat. Add ground beef, onions and garlic. Cook until beef is browned and onion is translucent.
2) Add tomatoes, water, salt, basil, sugar, pepper and bay leaf. Heat to boiling, stirring constantly. Reduce heat. Simmer uncovered until thickened, about 30 minutes. Stir in tomato paste.
3) Add red wine and nutmeg. Adjust for salt and pepper. Continue cooking uncovered for about 20 minutes.
4) Add ½ cup Parmesan cheese and ⅓ cup bread crumbs to mixture and mix well. Remove from heat and set aside.

Prepare Eggplant:
1) Cut eggplant crosswise into 1-inch thick slices. Cook slices in 6 quarts of boiling water until just tender. Drain on paper towels.

Prepare White Sauce:
1) Heat butter over low heat in saucepan until melted. Blend in flour, salt and nutmeg. Cook over low heat, stirring constantly, until smooth and bubbly. Remove from heat.
2) Gradually stir in milk in a steady stream. Heat to boiling and thick, stirring constantly.
3) Stir a little of the hot mixture into the beaten eggs. Remove milk mixture from heat source and whisk heated egg mixture to remaining milk mixture. Stir until well blended.

Assemble Moussaka:
1) Grease deep 13x9-inch baking dish. Sprinkle remaining bread crumbs over bottom of baking dish. Arrange eggplant so it covers bottom. Cover with half of meat mixture. Sprinkle with ½ cup of Parmesan.
2) Top with another layer of eggplant. Cover as much surface as possible. Top with remaining meat mixture. Pour white sauce over. Sprinkle with remaining cheese.
3) Sprinkle top with cinnamon and nutmeg. Cover with aluminum foil. Bake 45 minutes. Remove foil and bake another 15 minutes. Let stand no less than 20 minutes before cutting.

Per serving (approximate values): 558 Calories; 33.3g Fat (54.4% calories from fat); 31g Protein; 31.9g Carbohydrate; 175mg Cholesterol; 1119mg Sodium.

CHILEAN CHICKEN AND CORN POT PIE

Makes 8 servings
Prep Time: 30 minutes

1 medium onion, chopped
2 cloves garlic, minced
2 tablespoons butter
2 tablespoons all-purpose flour
1 cup chicken broth
¾ teaspoon chili powder
3 cups chicken, cooked, cubed or shredded
½ cup black olives, pitted, sliced
¼ cup currants
2 cups corn kernels, frozen or fresh
½ cup milk
1 large egg, beaten
½ teaspoon salt

Preheat oven to 350 degrees. Butter a 2-quart baking dish.

1) In a medium heavy skillet, cook the onion and garlic in 1 tablespoon of the butter over medium heat for 3 to 4 minutes until soft.
2) Stir in 1 tablespoon of the flour, then the chicken broth. Cook, stirring until thickened.
3) Add the chili powder, chicken, olives and currants. Spoon into prepared casserole.
4) Combine the corn, 1 tablespoon melted butter, 1 tablespoon flour, milk, beaten egg and salt. Spoon the custard mixture over the chicken mixture.
5) Bake the pie for 35 minutes or until bubbly and speckled with brown.

Per serving (approximate values): 240 Calories; 13.1 g Fat (48.6% calories from fat); 14.3g Protein; 16.9g Carbohydrate; 75mg Cholesterol; 488mg Sodium.

BOBOTIE

Makes 6 servings
Prep Time: 1 hour

1 ½ pounds ground beef
1 cup soft bread crumbs
1 cup milk
1 large egg
1 medium onion, chopped
¼ cup slivered almonds, chopped
¼ cup raisins
1 tablespoon lemon juice
2 teaspoons curry powder
1 teaspoon salt
¼ teaspoon pepper
Custard:
2 large eggs, beaten
1 cup milk
Dash paprika

Preheat oven to 325 degrees.

1) In large mixing bowl combine ground beef through pepper thoroughly.
2) Spread mixture in 2-quart casserole dish. Cook uncovered for 45 minutes. Remove from oven and drain fat.
3) Mix beaten eggs and 1 cup milk. Pour over hot beef mixture.
4) Place casserole in larger oblong pan, such as a 13x9x2-inch pan. Pour very hot water up to 1-inch in pan. Place all in oven. Bake uncovered until custard is set, about 30 minutes.
5) Remove from oven and let sit for 10 minutes. Serve!

Per serving (approximate values): 517 Calories; 38.3g Fat (66.7% calories from fat); 26.9g Protein; 16.3g Carbohydrate; 215mg Cholesterol; 545mg Sodium.

VEGETARIAN POT PIE

Talk about a lot of ingredients! While at my day job (a Minnesota law firm at the time), I was challenged by a vegetarian co-worker that I couldn't prepare something for them that they hadn't already tried, having run out of new and interesting dishes. This was my response. A man of few words, he took the remaining home with him!

Makes 6 servings
Prep Time: 45 minutes

1 9-inch deep dish pie crust (frozen prepared is fine)
Filling:
1 large onion, chopped
3 tablespoons vegetable oil
1 small eggplant, diced
1 medium potato, diced
½ teaspoon sweet Hungarian paprika
½ teaspoon dried basil
½ teaspoon dried marjoram
½ cup red bell pepper, diced
1 cup mushrooms, sliced
½ cup peas, frozen or fresh
½ cup corn, frozen or fresh
Salt and pepper, to taste
Roux:
2 tablespoons butter or margarine
2 tablespoons all-purpose flour
1 cup milk
1 teaspoon Dijon mustard
¼ teaspoon ground nutmeg
2 cups cheddar cheese, grated
Topping:
1 tablespoon butter or margarine
⅔ cup bread crumbs
¼ teaspoon dried marjoram
¼ teaspoon dried basil
Dash Hungarian sweet paprika

Preheat oven to 400 degrees.

Filling:
1) In a large saucepan, sauté the onions in the oil until soft.
2) Add the eggplant, potatoes, paprika, basil and marjoram. Cover and cook over medium heat, stirring frequently, about 10 minutes.
3) Stir in the bell pepper, mushrooms, peas and corn. Add salt and pepper to taste. Cover and continue to cook until the eggplant is tender, about 5 to 10 minutes.

Roux:
1) In a medium saucepan, melt the butter. Add the flour and stir constantly on low heat for 3 to 5 minutes.
2) Whisk in the milk, mustard and nutmeg. Continue to stir over low heat until the mixture is hot and slightly thickened. Do not let boil. Remove roux from the heat and whisk in the grated cheese until well blended.

Topping:
1) In a small skillet, melt the butter over low heat.
2) Add the bread crumbs and herbs. Stir to coat them with the butter and sauté them for about 3 minutes or until bread crumbs are lightly crisped.
3) Check the sautéed vegetables. Completely drain any accumulated liquid.
4) To assemble the pie, spoon the drained vegetables into the waiting pie crust. Pour the roux over the vegetable filling and poke holes down into the vegetables to encourage the roux to seep in. Sprinkle on the bread crumbs. Bake for about 40 minutes until lightly browned and bubbly.

Per serving (approximate values): 584 Calories; 35.9g Fat (54.4% calories from fat); 18.1 g Protein; 49.7g Carbohydrate; 61 mg Cholesterol; 631 mg Sodium.

Shepherd's Pie with Feta Cheese and Potato Topping

The British created a winner with their various renditions of Shepherd's Pie. This one borrows ingredients from the Middle East to create a spectacular cross-cultural main course!

Makes 8 servings
Prep Time: 45 minutes

1 tablespoon olive oil
4 cloves garlic, minced
1 large onion, chopped
2 pounds ground lamb
2 teaspoons dried mint leaves, crumbled
1 teaspoon cinnamon
1 teaspoon oregano leaves
½ teaspoon ground allspice
6 medium plum tomatoes, chopped
¼ cup Parmesan cheese, freshly grated
Salt and pepper, to taste
<u>Feta Potato Topping:</u>
6 large potatoes, peeled and cubed
2 tablespoons butter
¼ cup Parmesan cheese, freshly grated
2 cups feta cheese, crumbled
Salt and pepper, to taste

Preheat oven to 375 degrees. Butter a 2-quart baking dish.

1) In a large, heavy skillet heat the olive oil. Add the garlic and onion and cook for 1 minute.

2) Add the lamb and cook. Stir until lamb is no longer pink. Drain off any excess fat.

3) Add the mint, cinnamon, oregano, allspice, tomatoes, salt and pepper. Stir in the Parmesan cheese. Turn mixture into baking dish.

4) For the topping put the potatoes into a large saucepan with water to cover. Cook for 15 to 20 minutes or until tender. Drain and reserve

some of the liquid. Beat with an electric mixer (or put through potato ricer). Add the butter, salt, pepper and enough cooking liquid so that the potatoes become fluffy.

5) Blend the Parmesan and feta cheese into the beaten potatoes. Spoon the potato mixture over the lamb mixture in the casserole. Bake for 35 to 40 minutes or until lightly brown.

Per serving (approximate values): 724 Calories; 41.3g Fat (50.8% calories from fat); 33g Protein; 56.9g Carbohydrate; 128mg Cholesterol; 633mg Sodium.

PORK POT PIE WITH GREEN CHILE AND CORN BREAD TOPPING

Makes 6 servings
Prep Time: 45 minutes

1 ½ pounds ground pork
1 cup chopped onion
1 large red bell pepper, chopped
15 ounces tomato sauce
2 tablespoons tomato paste
10 ounces corn kernels, frozen or canned
1 tablespoon cornmeal
1 tablespoon Worcestershire sauce
1 tablespoon ground cumin
1 tablespoon chili powder
1 teaspoon hot pepper sauce
½ teaspoon ground allspice
½ cup chicken broth
<u>Corn Bread Topping:</u>
1 cup all-purpose flour
1 cup yellow cornmeal
3 tablespoons sugar
2 teaspoons baking powder
3 tablespoons butter, melted
¾ cup milk
1 large egg, beaten
½ cup Monterey jack cheese, shredded
4 ounces green chile peppers, drained, chopped

Preheat oven to 375 degrees. Grease 2 ½-quart baking dish.

1) In a large, heavy skillet, brown the pork with the onion and bell pepper until the pork is cooked through.

2) Stir in the tomato sauce, tomato paste, corn, cornmeal, Worcestershire sauce, cumin, chili powder, hot pepper sauce and allspice. Simmer for 30 minutes, stirring occasionally. Spoon the mixture into baking dish.

3) For the crust, stir the flour, cornmeal, sugar and baking powder together in a large mixing bowl.

4) Stir the butter, milk and egg together in another bowl. Add to the dry ingredients. Stir until just blended. Stir in the cheese and chile peppers.

5) Drop large spoonfuls of the crust mixture onto the pork mixture. Bake for 10 minutes. Reduce the oven temperature to 350 degrees and bake for 30 minutes longer or until the filling bubbles and the crust is lightly brown.

Per serving (approximate values): 746 Calories; 35.5g Fat (42.6% calories from fat); 42.4g Protein; 65.3g Carbohydrate; 170mg Cholesterol; 1004mg Sodium.

Low-fat Sausage and Egg Casserole

Makes 8 servings
Prep Time: 30 minutes

1 pound turkey sausage, bulk
3 cups bread cubes
2 cups skim milk
1 ½ cups egg substitute
4 ounces cheddar cheese, reduced fat
1 teaspoon dry mustard

Preheat oven to 350 degrees.

1) Cook sausage in medium skillet until well browned, stirring to crumble. Drain well.
2) Combine sausage and remaining ingredients in mixing bowl. Pour into 9x13-inch baking dish coated with cooking spray.
3) Bake for 45 minutes until knife inserted comes out clean. Cool slightly and serve!

Per serving (approximate values): 163 Calories; 7g Fat (39.3% calories from fat); 12.7g Protein; 11.6g Carbohydrate; 16mg Cholesterol; 300mg Sodium.

HOMINY CASSEROLE

Makes 6 servings
Prep Time: 20 minutes

2 cans hominy, yellow or white, drained, rinsed
1 medium onion, finely chopped
12 ounces cheddar cheese, shredded
4 ounces green chiles, diced
3 medium Roma tomatoes, diced

Preheat oven to 375 degrees. Grease 8x8-inch glass baking dish.

1) Spread half of the hominy in baking dish. Sprinkle with half the onion, then half the tomatoes, then the chiles, then half of the cheese.
2) Layer with remaining hominy, onion, tomato, green chiles and then cheese.
3) Bake uncovered until hot in the center and a nice crust has formed. Garnish with fresh chopped green onions if desired.
4) Remove from oven and let settle for about 10 minutes. Serve immediately!

Per serving (approximate values): 294 Calories; 19.6g Fat (59% calories from fat); 16g Protein; 14.6g Carbohydrate; 59mg Cholesterol; 471mg Sodium.

CAJUN EGGPLANT, CORN AND CHEDDAR CHEESE CASSEROLE

Between a Cajun/Creole cooking phase and a vegetarian cooking phase, I developed this recipe. Perhaps because I like to combine cultures when creating new dishes, whereas they already do it so successfully, I'm not sure. You will find several recipes with this influence. On the other hand, this dish is good as either a side dish or for a nice vegetarian main course.

Makes 6 servings
Prep Time: 1 hour

3 ½ cups eggplant, 1-inch cubes
3 cups water
½ cup butter
1 ½ cups onions, chopped, divided
1 ½ cups frozen corn
2 large eggs, beaten
½ cup green peppers, chopped
1 teaspoon garlic, minced
½ teaspoon salt
½ teaspoon cayenne
¼ teaspoon black pepper
3 cups cheddar cheese, grated
1 ½ cups saltine crackers, crushed

Preheat oven to 350 degrees.

1) Place the eggplant and water in a 3-quart saucepan. Cover pan and bring to a boil. Reduce heat and simmer until eggplant is tender, about 15 minutes. Drain well in a colander with a bowl underneath to catch the liquids. Reserve in separate containers the eggplant and 1 cup of the broth.

2) Heat the butter in a 3-4 quart saucepan over medium heat. Add 1 cup of the onions and sauté until well browned, about 9 minutes. Remove pan from the heat and transfer onions with a slotted spoon to a bowl.

3) Add the corn to the same pan and return to a medium heat. Cook about 4 minutes, stirring frequently, scraping bottom well. Remove

from heat and add the reserved cooked onions, reserved eggplant and the eggs. Mix well.

4) Add the remaining ½ cup onions, green peppers, garlic, salt, cayenne and black pepper, 1 ½ cups of the cheese, 1 cup of the cracker crumbs and the reserved eggplant stock. Mix well.

5) Pour the mixture into an 8x8-inch baking dish. Pat the mixture down evenly. Sprinkle the remaining cheese evenly over the top. Sprinkle the remaining cracker crumbs evenly over the cheese.

6) Bake at 350 degrees until the crumbs are lightly browned, cheese is melted and the mixture bubbles around the edges, about 40 minutes.

7) Remove casserole from oven. Let cool about 10 minutes and serve immediately.

Per serving (approximate values): 711 Calories; 43g Fat (53.7% calories from fat); 24.2g Protein; 59.1 g Carbohydrate; 172mg Cholesterol; 1481 mg Sodium.

TATOR TOT HOT DISH

This was a hot dish (casserole for uninitiated non-Minnesotans) my paternal grand-mother made my brother, sister and I while living with her during my mom's and dad's separation. We got so excited when she made it, we could hardly stand it. It was many years before I scoured old recipe books for something that came close to what I remember. After much experimentation, this dish brings back happy memories.

Makes 6 servings
Prep Time: 30 minutes

1 pound ground beef
2 cloves garlic, minced
1 teaspoon onion powder
1 ⅓ cups cooked rice
5 tablespoons soy sauce
1 can cream of celery soup
1 can cream of chicken soup
2 ½ cups water
1 package tator tot potatoes
Salt and pepper, to taste

Preheat oven to 325 degrees. Grease a 1 ½-quart baking dish.

1) Layer tator tots in bottom of baking dish.
2) In large skillet, brown ground beef with onion powder and garlic. Drain if necessary.
3) Mix in all remaining ingredients. Add salt and pepper as needed. Pour mixture over tator tots.
4) Bake 90 minutes or until all ingredients are hot and bubbling. Remove from oven and let sit 10 minutes. Serve.

Per serving (approximate values): 354 Calories; 22.4g Fat (57.6% calories from fat); 15.8g Protein; 21.4g Carbohydrate; 68mg Cholesterol; 1236mg Sodium.

BAKED TAMALE CASSEROLE

Makes 8 servings
Prep Time: 20 minutes

¾ cup yellow cornmeal
1 cup milk
1 large egg, slightly beaten
1 pound ground beef
2 cloves garlic, crushed
1 teaspoon chili powder
½ teaspoon cumin
1 teaspoon seasoned salt
15 ounces salsa, chunky tomato
16 ounces canned corn, drained
2 ¼ ounces black olives, sliced
4 ounces cheddar cheese, shredded

1) In a medium sauté pan, brown ground beef with garlic until beef no longer shows any pink. Drain fat and let cool slightly.

2) In a large mixing bowl, combine cornmeal, milk and egg until just moistened and no large lumps remain. Stir in meat, chili powder, cumin, salt, salsa, corn and olives until just combined.

3) Pour mixture into slow cooker. Cover and cook on HIGH 2 hours. Sprinkle cheese over top. Cover and cook another 5 minutes.

Per serving (approximate values): 381 Calories; 23.4g Fat (54.1 % calories from fat); 18.4g Protein; 26.2g Carbohydrate; 94mg Cholesterol; 540mg Sodium.

THAI VEGETARIAN CURRY

Makes 6 servings
Prep Time: 40 minutes

10 whole shiitake mushrooms
2 whole green onions
4 cloves garlic, minced
1 tablespoon vegetable oil
1 cup vegetarian bouillon, divided
2 cans coconut milk
3 tablespoons Panang (or red curry) paste
3 tablespoons fish sauce
⅛ teaspoon red pepper flakes
1 tablespoon brown sugar
¾ pound fresh or frozen green beans
1 small can baby corn
2 tablespoons cornstarch
½ cup peanuts, dry-roasted

1) Break off stems of mushrooms. Slice caps into thin strips.
2) Cut roots from green onions. Cut onions into thin slices on the diagonal.
3) In medium saucepan, heat coconut milk to boiling.
4) Reduce heat and add curry paste, fish sauce, brown sugar and red pepper flakes. Stir until curry paste is completely incorporated. Lower heat and keep warm.
5) Heat medium skillet over medium high heat. Add oil and swirl to coat surface. Add garlic and cook for 1 minute.
6) Add green beans and mushrooms. Stir fry for 2 minutes.
7) Add ½ cup of vegetable bouillon and cook until liquid boils. Stir frequently.
8) Cover and reduce heat to low and simmer 8-10 minutes until beans are crisp tender. Add baby corn and stir until hot again.
9) Add vegetables to curry mixture. Increase heat to medium.
10) Combine cornstarch and ½ cup vegetable bouillon in small bowl. When mixture begins to boil, add cornstarch mixture to curry. Stir until thickened.

11) Add peanuts. Serve immediately.

Per serving (approximate values): 400 Calories; 29.4g Fat (61.7% calories from fat); 9.1 g Protein; 32g Carbohydrate; 2mg Cholesterol; 397mg Sodium.

SOUTH ASIAN GROUND BEEF CURRY

This is as close as I come thus far to Indian cooking. It is a cuisine I am just now start-ing to explore more. The country is huge and with many subcultures, so it's an intimi-dating and exciting adventure at the same time!

Makes 6 servings
Prep Time: 45 minutes

1 ½ pounds ground beef
2 medium onions, chopped
2 medium potatoes, diced
1 medium green pepper, chopped
2 tablespoons vegetable oil
2 ½ cups water
½ cup shredded coconut meat
3 tablespoons tomato paste
½ teaspoon ground ginger
1 stick cinnamon
1 whole clove
2 teaspoons salt
1 teaspoon curry powder
1 teaspoon chili powder
½ teaspoon turmeric
½ teaspoon cardamom
3 cups cooked white rice

1) In large skillet, cook and stir ground beef, potatoes, onions and green peppers in the vegetable oil. Cook until beef is brown. Drain fat.

2) Stir in next set of ingredients (water through cardamom). Heat to boil-ing. Cover and reduce heat. Simmer 30 to 40 minutes until vegetables are tender.

3) Uncover and cook until mixture thickens. Remove cinnamon stick and whole clove.

4) Serve over white rice.

Per serving (approximate values): 668 Calories; 37.7g Fat (50.7% calories from fat); 25.3g Protein; 57.2g Carbohydrate; 96mg Cholesterol; 872mg Sodium.

NEPALESE PORK CURRY

Makes 6 servings
Prep Time: 45 minutes

1 teaspoon white vinegar
1 teaspoon cayenne
2 pounds pork, 1-inch cubes
2 cups plain yogurt
1-inch piece fresh ginger root, peeled and grated
1 teaspoon vegetable oil
¼ cup butter
1 teaspoon black pepper
1 teaspoon turmeric
1 cup water
Salt to taste
½ cup cilantro, chopped fine
1 teaspoon ground cumin
1 teaspoon ground nutmeg
½ teaspoon ground cloves
½ teaspoon ground cardamom
3 cups cooked white rice

1) Combine the vinegar and cayenne and toss the pork in the mixture. Add the yogurt and ginger. Marinate the pork covered in the refrigerator for 3 hours.

2) Heat the oil in a large skillet over low heat for 1 minute, then add the butter. Add the pork with its marinade, black pepper, turmeric, water and salt and bring to a rapid boil. Cover and reduce heat and simmer for 40 minutes.

3) Add the cilantro, cumin, nutmeg, cloves, and cardamom and stir for 5 minutes. Serve hot over rice.

Per serving (approximate values): 492 Calories; 36.5g Fat (67.1 % calories from fat); 31.5g Protein; 8.8g Carbohydrate; 135mg Cholesterol; 207mg Sodium.

VIETNAMESE CHICKEN CURRY

Makes 4 servings
Prep Time: 45 minutes

1 teaspoon cayenne
1 teaspoon ground cumin
1 teaspoon ground coriander
¼ teaspoon ground cardamom
¼ teaspoon ground cloves
1 teaspoon black pepper, freshly ground
1 teaspoon sugar
¼ teaspoon salt
2 pounds boneless skinless chicken breasts
⅓ cup vegetable oil
2 cups sweet potatoes, peeled, 1-inch cubes
6 cloves garlic, chopped
1 large onion, finely chopped
4 bay leaves
1 stalk lemon grass, two-inches, including bulb
2 cups coconut milk
1 cup carrots, 1-inch thick
1 cup milk

1) Combine all the dry spices, sugar, and salt and toss with the chicken. Cover and marinate for up to 1 hour.

2) In a large skillet, heat the oil for 1 minute over medium heat. Add the sweet potatoes and fry for about 10 minutes. Remove the sweet potatoes with a slotted spoon and set aside.

3) Using the same oil, fry the garlic and the onion for 3 minutes over low heat. Add the bay leaves and lemon grass. Stir and cook for 1 minute.

4) Add the chicken with its marinade. Stir well. Cook over high heat for 4-5 minutes.

5) Add the coconut milk. Mix well and cook covered for 10 minutes.

6) Add the carrots, sweet potatoes and the milk and cook covered for another 10 minutes.

7) If curry is too fluid, add 1 tablespoon corn starch to 1 tablespoon water and mix into hot cooked mixture. Stir until thickened.

Per serving (approximate values): 850 Calories; 53.3g Fat (55.5% calories from fat); 59.9g Protein; 36.5g Carbohydrate; 140mg Cholesterol; 358mg Sodium.

THAI RED BEEF CURRY

Makes 6 servings
Prep Time: 30 minutes

½ cup canned coconut milk (the thick portion that floats to top of can)
1 tablespoon red curry paste
1 pound lean beef, sliced thin
3 cups canned coconut milk
1 pound sweet potato, peeled and diced
1 pound zucchini, diced
2 tablespoons fish sauce
1 tablespoon brown sugar
¼ cup fresh basil

1) In a medium saucepan, heat thick portion of canned coconut milk to boiling. Lower heat to simmer and simmer about 5 minutes.

2) Add curry paste and stir to dissolve into coconut milk. Continue cooking for about 2 minutes until curry has a pleasing aroma.

3) Add the beef and stir-fry to coat evenly with paste. Increase the heat and add remaining coconut milk.

4) Heat about 2 minutes, then add the diced sweet potato, zucchini, fish sauce and salt. Stir well. Adjust the heat to maintain a simmer and cook for 8-10 minutes. Stir occasionally.

5) When beef is done and vegetables are crisp tender, stir in basil leaves. Remove from heat and transfer to serving bowl. Serve immediately over rice.

Per serving (approximate values): 593 Calories; 45.3g Fat (66.1 % calories from fat); 20.3g Protein; 31.9g Carbohydrate; 47mg Cholesterol; 71 mg Sodium.

TURKEY PICADILLO

This is a variation of a Spanish dish. Sweet spices, fruit and meat are the common ingredients. I use turkey instead of pork or beef and serve it over rice. You could just as well serve it as an appetizer with chips.

Makes 4 servings
Prep Time: 30 minutes

1 pound ground turkey
1 teaspoon cumin
1 teaspoon salt
1 teaspoon pepper
1 tablespoon olive oil
4 cloves garlic
1 small onion, chopped
1 small green pepper, diced
2 medium Roma tomatoes, chopped
½ cup green olives, chopped
¼ cup golden raisins
½ cup white wine
1 tablespoon tomato paste
Salt and pepper, to taste

1) Combine turkey, cumin, salt and pepper and mix well. Let stand for 5 minutes.

2) Heat oil in large skillet over medium heat. Add the garlic, onion and bell pepper and cook until soft but not brown. Stir in tomatoes and cook for about 2 more minutes.

3) Add the turkey mixture and cook until turkey is cooked through, about 5 minutes. Stir in olives and raisins and cook for 2 more minutes.

4) Stir in white wine and tomato paste. Gently simmer for 6 to 8 minutes until most of liquid has been absorbed. The Picadillo should be moist but not soupy. Correct the seasoning with salt and pepper as needed.

Per serving (approximate values): 312 Calories; 15.3g Fat (46.2% calories from fat); 22g Protein; 18.2g Carbohydrate; 90mg Cholesterol; 1089mg Sodium.

CHICKEN CURRY WITH PEAS

Makes 6 servings
Prep Time: 45 minutes

3 tablespoons vegetable oil
2 medium onions, chopped
3 cloves garlic, minced
¼ cup fresh ginger root, peeled, minced
3 tablespoons curry powder
1 teaspoon cumin powder
¼ teaspoon cinnamon
2 tablespoons flour
1 cup plain yogurt
3 tablespoons tomato paste
3 cups chicken broth
1 cup applesauce
3 pounds boneless skinless chicken breast halves, ½-inch pieces
10 ounces frozen peas
½ cup sour cream
½ cup canned coconut milk, unsweetened
Salt and pepper, to taste

1) Heat oil in heavy, large skillet over medium heat. Add onions and garlic until onions are translucent, about 15 minutes. Add ginger. Sauté another minute.

2) Add curry powder, cumin and cinnamon. Sauté another minute.

3) Add flour until all is well combined. Add yogurt and mix continuously until smooth. Mixture will be quite thick.

4) Add tomato paste. Remove pan from heat.

5) In a slow stream, add chicken broth. Stop when necessary to make sure the mixture is combining well.

6) Add applesauce. Return pan to heat and bring to a boil. Reduce heat and simmer until sauce has thickened, stirring occasionally, about 30 minutes.

7) While mixture simmers, sauté chicken in non-stick skillet over medium-high heat until barely cooked through, about 5 minutes.

8) Once the spice mixture is ready, add chicken and peas. Stir until combined and mixture is thoroughly heated.

9) Add sour cream and coconut milk. Reduce heat to it slowest setting or take off the heat. You do not want the mixture to boil once you add the sour cream. Add salt and fresh ground pepper to taste.

10) Serve with rice.

Per serving (approximate values): 591 Calories; 23g Fat (35.1 % calories from fat); 65g Protein; 30.6g Carbohydrate; 147mg Cholesterol; 1093mg Sodium.

VIETNAMESE GROUND BEEF

Makes 6 servings
Prep Time: 25 minutes

2 stalks fresh lemon grass
3 tablespoons vegetable oil
4 stalks green onions, white part, chopped
3 cloves garlic, chopped
1 pound ground beef
4 tablespoons fish sauce
4 tablespoons sesame seeds
2 tablespoons granulated sugar
Fresh ground pepper

1) Discard tough outer leaves of lemon grass and slice very thin. Set aside.
2) Heat oil in a frying pan over medium high heat. Add the green onions and garlic and fry for one minute.
3) Add the lemon grass and cook for another minute. Add ground beef and stir well to break up beef. Turn the heat down to medium and continue cooking until meat is completely cooked.
4) Add the fish sauce, sesame seeds, sugar and black pepper. Stir until meat has absorbed all the liquids.
5) Remove from pan. Serve immediately over white rice.

Per serving (approximate values): 402 Calories; 31.5g Fat (69.3% calories from fat); 15.6g Protein; 15.9g Carbohydrate; 66mg Cholesterol; 57mg Sodium.

THAI PINEAPPLE BASIL CHICKEN

This was the favorite dish of my first class teaching Southeast Asian cuisine. I have made it many times due to people's willingness to try this before other dishes from this region.

Makes 4 servings
Prep Time: 30 minutes

2 small Serrano peppers
2 cloves garlic, minced
8 ounces pineapple chunks in juice
2 teaspoons cornstarch
2 teaspoons peanut oil
1 pound boneless skinless chicken
breasts, cut bite-size
2 stalks green onions, cut into 1-inch
¾ cup cashews
¼ cup fresh basil
1 tablespoon fish sauce
1 tablespoon soy sauce

1) Mince Serrano peppers very fine.
2) Drain pineapple and reserve juice. Combine reserved juice and cornstarch in small bowl. Set aside.
3) Heat medium skillet over high heat until hot. Drizzle oil into pan and heat 30 seconds. Add chicken, peppers, and garlic and stir-fry until chicken is no longer pink. Lower heat as necessary. Add green onions. Stir-fry 1 more minute.
4) Give the cornstarch mixture a quick stir and add to skillet. Cook 1 minute or until thickened.
5) Add pineapple, cashews, basil, fish sauce and soy sauce. Stir until heated through. Serve immediately over rice.

Per serving (approximate values): 381 Calories; 16.7g Fat (38.1 % calories from fat); 33g Protein; 28.1 g Carbohydrate; 66mg Cholesterol; 345mg Sodium.

VIETNAMESE CHICKEN IN GINGER SAUCE

Makes 6 servings
Prep Time: 40 minutes

2 stalks fresh lemon grass
3 tablespoons fresh ginger, peeled and grated
4 tablespoons white vinegar
1 pound chicken thighs without skin
4 tablespoons fish sauce
¼ teaspoon black pepper, fresh ground
2 teaspoons cornstarch
12 tablespoons water
1 teaspoon sugar
2 tablespoons vegetable oil
6 cloves garlic, chopped
1 large yellow onion, peeled and cut into 8 wedges
2 stalks green onions, cut into 4 pieces each

1) Discard tough outer leaves of lemon grass stalks and upper two-thirds of stalk. Slice the remainder paper thin.

2) In a small bowl cover the grated ginger with the vinegar and set aside.

3) Cut chicken into bite-size pieces. Place into medium mixing bowl. Season chicken with 2 tablespoons of fish sauce and black pepper. Add lemon grass and mix well.

4) Combine cornstarch, water, 2 tablespoons fish sauce and sugar in small bowl and set aside.

5) Heat the oil in medium skillet and fry garlic for 1 minute. Add the onion and green onions and sauté for 3-4 minutes.

6) Add chicken and cook, stirring constantly, for 8-10 minutes until chicken is just cooked through.

7) Add the ginger mixture and cornstarch mixture and stir well. Cover for about 5 minutes over a medium-low heat. Uncover and continue cooking until thickened.

8) Serve immediately over rice.

Per serving (approximate values): 178 Calories; 8.7g Fat (42.9% calories from fat); 13.3g Protein; 12.6g Carbohydrate; 51 mg Cholesterol; 57mg Sodium.

FIVE-SPICE BEEF STIR-FRY

Makes 4 servings
Prep Time: 45 minutes

Sauce:
½ cup orange juice
1 tablespoon cornstarch
2 tablespoons soy sauce
2 teaspoons sugar
1 teaspoon five spice powder
½ teaspoon crushed red pepper
Stir-Fry:
12 ounces sirloin steaks, trimmed, thinly sliced
1 medium onion, cut into thin wedges
4 cloves garlic, minced
6 ounces broccoli flowerets
1 medium red bell pepper, cut into strips

1) In a small bowl, combine all sauce ingredients. Mix until well blended. Set aside.

2) Spray large skillet with non-stick cooking spray. Heat over medium-high heat until hot. Add beef and cook until the meat has just a little pink. Remove from pan and set aside.

3) Add onions and garlic to skillet. Sauté until onion is crisp tender. Add broccoli and red bell pepper. Cover and cook until veggies are crisp-tender.

4) Add beef and cook another 3-4 minutes until beef is heated through.

5) Add sauce. Cook and stir until sauce is thickened and bubbly. Serve over hot rice.

Per serving (approximate values): 370 Calories; 5.0g Fat (12.3% calories from fat); 24.7g Protein; 55.4g Carbohydrate; 52mg Cholesterol; 581 mg Sodium.

SPINACH-WALNUT PESTO

The summer of 1996, a summer I'll never forget. I was introduced to another world, that of the internet. I had chance to meet people from all over the country. One of them was from Kansas City. He introduced me to the world of beef brisket preparation for the most delicious bbq recipes ever. He also had a penchant for pesto, funny enough. Thus before I went to visit him for the first time, I had to prepare some pesto he hopefully had never tried, as a gift. He loved it!

Makes 6 servings
Prep Time: 15 minutes

1 ½ cups fresh spinach, stemmed and washed
¾ cup olive oil
1 cup Romano cheese, grated
1 cup walnuts, chopped
4 cloves garlic, minced
2 tablespoons lemon juice
Salt and pepper, to taste
8 ounces cooked linguine or fettuccine pasta

1)   Put all ingredients into a food processor fitted with a metal blade. Pulse the ingredients several times until coarsely chopped. Scrape down the work bowl. Continue processing until the sauce is smooth. If the pesto is too thick, pulse in a little hot water.

2)   Toss with the cooked pasta the moment the pasta has been drained. Serve immediately.

Per serving (approximate values): 444 Calories; 43.9g Fat (85.8%/a calories from fat); 11.6g Protein; 4.8g Carbohydrate; 19mg Cholesterol; 236mg Sodium.

FETTUCCINE ALFREDO

Other than a basic spaghetti sauce, this was the first pasta sauce with which I ever experimented. It has since become a family favorite. It is my niece's number one request!

Makes 4 servings
Prep Time: 30 minutes

8 ounces fettuccine pasta noodles
6 tablespoons butter
1 ½ cups half and half
1 cup Parmesan cheese, freshly grated
Salt and pepper, to taste
Ground nutmeg

1) Prepare pasta noodles per package directions.
2) While noodles are cooking, melt butter in a large skillet over medium heat until butter is golden in color. Add ½ cup of the half and half and boil rapidly until slightly thickened.
3) Reduce heat slightly. Add noodles to sauce and toss gently.
4) Add half of the cheese and half of the remaining half and half. Toss gently and add remaining cheese and half and half.
5) Season with salt and pepper to taste. Sprinkle lightly with nutmeg. Serve immediately.

Per serving (approximate values): 360 Calories; 33.5g Fat (82.6% calories from fat); 11.2g Protein; 4.7g Carbohydrate; 95mg Cholesterol; 583mg Sodium.

QUATTRO CHEESES

Quattro, meaning 'four', can mean any four cheeses for this dish. It's also so very easy to create a completely new dish by simply switching pasta types. This is one of my nephew's favorites!

Makes 6 servings
Prep Time: 40 minutes

8 ounces fettuccine or linguine pasta noodles
1 ½ cups cream
1 cup half and half
¼ pound cheddar cheese, shredded
¼ pound smoked Gouda cheese, shredded
¼ pound Swiss cheese, shredded
½ cup Parmesan cheese, grated
Salt and pepper, to taste

1) Prepare pasta per package directions
2) Pour the cream and half and half into a medium saucepan over moderate heat. Once the cream mixture is hot, but before it begins to boil, stir in the cheeses.
3) Bring the sauce just to a boil, stirring constantly.
4) Reduce the heat and simmer gently until the sauce is thick and creamy, about 5 minutes. Pour over pasta noodles and serve.

Per serving (approximate values): 443 Calories; 38.2g Fat (77.1 % calories from fat); 20.3g Protein; 5.4g Carbohydrate; 131 mg Cholesterol; 484mg Sodium.

PUTTANESCA

Makes 6 servings
Prep Time: 40 minutes

8 ounces your favorite packaged pasta noodles
2 tablespoons olive oil
½ pound bacon, cut into ½-inch pieces
6 cloves garlic, minced
2 medium onions, chopped
2 small Serrano peppers, chopped fine
28 ounces canned whole tomatoes
1 teaspoon dried oregano leaves
1 teaspoon dried basil leaves
½ teaspoon salt
½ teaspoon pepper

1) Prepare pasta per package directions
2) In a large skillet, heat the olive oil over moderate heat. Add the bacon and sauté only until the bacon begins to brown, about 5 to 7 minutes.
3) Add the garlic, onions and Serrano peppers. Sauté until onions are soft, about 4 minutes.
4) Add the tomatoes.
5) Stir in remaining ingredients (oregano through pepper). Gently boil until thick, about 10 to 15 minutes. Serve with pasta noodles.

Per serving (approximate values): 319 Calories; 23.7g Fat (65.5% calories from fat); 14.1 g Protein; 13.9g Carbohydrate; 32mg Cholesterol; 1001 mg Sodium.

LEMON CREAM PASTA WITH CAPERS

Makes 6 servings
Prep Time: 40 minutes

8 ounces fettuccine or linguine pasta noodles
¼ cup butter
1 medium onion
1 pound boneless skinless chicken breasts, cut into ½-inch strips
½ cup lemon juice
2 cups cream
2 tablespoons capers, minced
Salt and pepper, to taste

1) Prepare pasta per package directions
2) In a large skillet, melt butter over moderate heat. Add the onions and sauté until soft, about 5 minutes.
3) Raise the heat slightly and add the chicken pieces. Sauté until they are evenly browned, about 5 minutes.
4) Add the lemon juice. Stir and scrape the bottom of the pan with a wooden spoon to remove any lumps or browned bits. When most of the lemon juice has evaporated, add the cream in a steady stream. Gently boil until thick, about 10 minutes.
5) Stir in the capers and add salt and pepper, to taste. Serve over prepared pasta.

Per serving (approximate values): 362 Calories; 28.8g Fat (70.9% calories from fat); 20g Protein; 6.7g Carbohydrate; 134mg Cholesterol; 185mg Sodium.

BOLOGNESE

Makes 6 servings
Prep Time: 40 minutes

8 ounces spaghetti pasta noodles
4 tablespoons olive oil
6 cloves garlic, minced
1 large onion, chopped fine
1 pound ground beef
28 ounces canned whole tomatoes
1 tablespoon tomato paste, double-strength
1 teaspoon dried oregano leaves
1 teaspoon dried basil leaves
¼ cup milk
Salt and pepper, to taste

1) Prepare pasta per package directions
2) In a large skillet, heat the olive oil over moderate. Add the garlic and onion and sauté until tender, about 4 minutes.
3) Add the beef and raise the heat slightly. Sauté until beef has lost all its pink color, about 6 minutes.
4) Add the tomatoes, breaking them up as you go. Stir and scrape the bottom of the pan with a wooden spoon to dissolve the pan deposits.
5) Stir in the remaining ingredients and gently boil until thick, about 15 minutes.
6) Add milk and reduce until thickened. Serve over pasta.

Per serving (approximate values): 358 Calories; 29.5g Fat (73.4% calories from fat); 14.5g Protein; 9.6g Carbohydrate; 64mg Cholesterol; 290mg Sodium.

Tuna, Green Olive and Tomato Pasta

Tuna, olives and tomatoes combine to make a delicious alternative to a spaghetti sauce. I make this for myself more often than just about anything.

Makes 6 servings
Prep Time: 40 minutes

8 ounces medium shell pasta noodles
3 tablespoons olive oil
3 cloves garlic, minced
28 ounces canned whole tomatoes
1 tablespoon tomato paste, double-strength
1 ½ teaspoons oregano leaves
1 ½ teaspoons basil leaves
10 ounces tuna in water, drained
¾ cup green olives, chopped
Salt and pepper, to taste

1) Prepare pasta per package directions
2) In a large skillet, heat the olive oil over moderate heat. Add the garlic and sauté until golden brown, about 2 to 3 minutes.
3) Add the tomatoes, breaking them up as you go. Stir in the tomato paste, oregano, basil, salt and pepper. Raise the heat slightly and gently boil until fairly thick, about 10 minutes.
4) Stir in the tuna and olives. Simmer until heated through, about 2 minutes. Serve over pasta shells.

Per serving (approximate values): 166 Calories; 9.6g Fat (50.7% calories from fat); 13.8g Protein; 7.2g Carbohydrate; 14mg Cholesterol; 803mg Sodium.

CARBONARA

Makes 6 servings
Prep Time: 40 minutes

8 ounces spaghetti pasta noodles
3 tablespoons butter
½ pound bacon, cut into ½-inch
3 cloves garlic
5 medium egg yolks
1 cup cream
1 cup half and half
1 ½ cups Parmesan cheese, grated
Salt and pepper, to taste

1) Prepare pasta per package directions
2) In a large skillet, melt the butter over moderate heat. Add the bacon and
    sauté until crisp, about 3 to 5 minutes. Drain off all but a thin film of fat.
3) Add the garlic and sauté about 1 more minute.
4) In a medium mixing bowl, beat the egg yolks, cream, half and half and
    1 cup of the Parmesan.
5) Add cooked and drained pasta to the skillet and pour in the cream mix-
    ture. Toss over low heat until the sauce thickens and coats the pasta,
    about 2 to 3 minutes. Serve immediately. Sprinkle generously with
    remaining Parmesan cheese and black pepper.

Per serving (approximate values): 560 Calories; 49.2g Fat (79% calories from fat);
24.5g Protein; 4.9g Carbohydrate; 290mg Cholesterol; 1071 mg Sodium.

TURKEY WITH PEPPERS AND OLIVES

Makes 6 servings
Prep Time: 40 minutes

2 tablespoons olive oil
1 medium green bell pepper, chopped
1 medium red bell pepper, chopped
1 medium onion, finely chopped
2 cloves garlic
1 pound ground turkey
28 ounces canned whole tomatoes
¾ cup black olives, sliced
1 tablespoon tomato paste, 2x concentrate
½ teaspoon dried basil leaves
½ teaspoon dried oregano leaves
¼ teaspoon rosemary leaves, crushed
¼ teaspoon red pepper flakes

1) In a large saucepan, heat the oil over moderate heat. Add the red and green peppers, onion and garlic. Sauté until tender, about 2 to 3 minutes.

2) Add the ground turkey and raise the heat slightly. Sauté the turkey until it has lost its pink color and left a brown glaze in the pan, about 10 minutes.

3) Add the tomatoes, breaking them up as you go. Stir and scrape the bottom of the pan with a wooden spoon to dissolve the pan deposits.

4) Stir in the remaining ingredients and boil gently until thick, about 15 to 20 minutes. Serve over rice or pasta.

Per serving (approximate values): 207 Calories; 11.4g Fat (48.3% calories from fat); 14.1 g Protein; 13.5g Carbohydrate; 41 mg Cholesterol; 220mg Sodium.

TURKEY TETRAZZINI

My entire family are suckers for anything involving cream. This dish I first prepared while living with my dad. He stills raves about it.

Makes 6 servings
Prep Time: 1 hour

6 tablespoons butter
5 tablespoons flour
2 ½ cups chicken broth
1 ¼ cups light cream
½ cup dry white wine
¾ cup Parmesan cheese, freshly grated
¾ pound mushrooms, sliced
12 ounces spaghetti pasta noodles
3 ½ cups cooked turkey, ½-inch pieces
Salt and pepper to taste

Preheat oven to 350 degrees. Grease 2-quart baking dish.

1) In a 2-quart saucepan, melt 3 tablespoons of the butter over medium heat. Mix in flour and cook, stirring until bubbly.
2) Remove from heat and slowly add chicken broth. Once broth is fully incorporated add light cream and wine.
3) Return to heat and cook. Stir until sauce is smooth and thickened.
4) Stir in Parmesan. Remove from heat.
5) Measure out 1 cup of the sauce and reserve both large and small portions.
6) Melt remaining 3 tablespoons butter in a large skillet over medium high heat. Add mushrooms and stir until juices evaporate and mushrooms are tender.
7) Follow package directions for spaghetti.
8) Combine drained spaghetti with the larger portion of sauce, the mushrooms and the turkey. Add salt and pepper to taste. Turn into greased shallow 2-quart baking dish.
9) Spoon the reserved sauce evenly over the top to cover.
10) Bake covered for about 45 minutes until hot and bubbly. Remove from oven and let sit for 10 minutes. Serve immediately.

Per serving (approximate values): 676 Calories; 30.3g Fat (41.5% calories from fat); 43.3g Protein; 53g Carbohydrate; 135mg Cholesterol; 1038mg Sodium.

BRATS IN MUSTARD CREAM

This dish I have made more than just about any other pasta dish, save Fettuccini Alfredo. The German meets French attitude is utterly comforting in combination. The mustard you decide to use is what ultimately will make or break the dish, especially when preparing for family. Any mustard other than French's plain hotdog-style should work, if you don't like those listed here!

Makes 6 servings
Prep Time: 40 minutes

8 ounces your favorite packaged pasta noodles
1 pound bratwurst
Water to cover
2 tablespoons butter
1 tablespoon vegetable oil
1 ½ cups cream
1 ½ cups half and half
2 tablespoons Dijon mustard, or a German-style mustard
1 teaspoon dried sage leaves
¼ cup Parmesan cheese, shredded
Salt and pepper, to taste

1) Prepare pasta per package directions.
2) Put the bratwursts in a large saucepan with enough cold water to cover them. Bring the water to a boil. As soon as the water begins to boil, drain the brats and pat them dry with paper towels.
3) Slice bratwursts in 1-inch pieces. In a large skillet, melt the butter with the oil over moderate heat. Add the sliced bratwurst and sauté until browned on all sides. Remove them from the skillet and set aside.
4) Add the cream and half and half to the skillet. Stir and scrape the bottom of the pan with a wooden spoon to dissolve the pan deposits into the sauce. Gently boil until the cream is reduced by half, about 15 minutes.
5) Stir in the mustard, sage, salt and pepper to taste. Add reserved bratwurst. Reduce the heat.
6) Add the Parmesan and heat through for 2-3 minutes. Serve.

Per serving (approximate values): 541 Calories; 50.2g Fat (83% calories from fat); 15.7g Protein; 7.5g Carbohydrate; 135mg Cholesterol; 1051 mg Sodium.

RISOTTO WITH PROSCIUTTO

The first time I had risotto, I nearly cried. It was so completely comforting, so completely delicious, I couldn't wait to try a recipe out myself. I have since tried many, many variations and include a few of my personal favorites. The funny thing about risotto when dining out is that many restaurants I've ordered it at just don't get it. Arborio rice requires very constant attention in preparation. When reviewing Italian restaurants for <u>Lavender Magazine</u>, an order of risotto led me to review well, or not.

Makes 6 servings
Prep Time: 45 minutes

4 cups chicken broth or stock
½ cup white wine
2 tablespoons butter
1 tablespoon oil
⅓ cup onion, finely chopped
1 ½ cups Arborio rice
¼ pound Prosciutto
¼ cup cream
⅓ cup Parmesan cheese
1 tablespoon parsley, finely chopped

1) Bring the chicken broth or stock to a steady simmer in a large saucepan.

2) Heat the butter and oil in a heavy saucepan over moderate heat. Add the onion and sauté for 1 to 2 minutes until it begins to soften. Be careful not to brown it.

3) Add the rice. Using a wooden spoon stir for 1 minute. Make sure all the grains are well coated. Add the wine and stir until it is completely absorbed.

4) Begin to add simmering broth ½ cup at a time. Stir constantly to prevent sticking. Wait until each addition of broth or stock is almost completely absorbed before adding the next ½ cup.

5) The rice will eventually reach a stage when the rice is tender but still firm, somewhat like al dente pasta. Once it does, add the prosciutto,

cream, Parmesan and parsley. Stir vigorously to combine with the rice. Serve immediately.

Per serving (approximate values): 370 Calories; 13.2g Fat (33.9% calories from fat); 18.3g Protein; 39.5g Carbohydrate; 37mg Cholesterol; 1689mg Sodium.

SUN-DRIED TOMATO RISOTTO WITH SHRIMP

Makes 6 servings
Prep Time: 1 hour

Risotto:
4 tablespoons olive oil
5 tablespoons butter
1 medium onion, chopped
4 cloves garlic, minced
8 whole Roma tomatoes, diced
½ cup white wine
3 cups Arborio rice
9 cups chicken broth or stock
⅓ cup sun-dried tomato paste
1 cup Parmesan cheese, fresh grated
Salt and pepper, to taste
Shrimp:
4 cloves garlic, minced
3 tablespoons olive oil
36 medium shrimp
⅓ cup white wine
1 tablespoon Italian parsley, chopped
10 whole fresh basil leaves
Salt and pepper, to taste

For the Risotto:
1) Bring the chicken broth or stock to a steady simmer in a large saucepan.
2) In a 3-4 quart saucepan, heat the oil and 3 tablespoons of the butter. Add the onion and cook, stirring frequently until soft.
3) Add the garlic and tomatoes and cook until the tomatoes begin to break down and form a sauce, about 10 minutes.
4) Add the wine and stir until bubbly. Add the rice and stir constantly until the rice absorbs all of the juices.

5) Begin to add simmering broth ½ cup at a time. Stir constantly to prevent sticking. Wait until each addition of broth or stock is almost completely absorbed before adding the next ½ cup.

6) When nearly all the stock has been absorbed, add the sun-dried tomato paste.

Shrimp:

1) In a medium skillet, heat the oil and garlic until garlic is quite fragrant. Add the shrimp and cook over medium-high heat for 2-3 minutes.

2) Add the wine and cook until the alcohol evaporates.

3) Lower the heat and add the parsley, basil, salt and pepper. Remove from the heat and set aside.

4) When the rice is al dente, remove saucepan from the heat source. Stir in the remaining butter and the Parmesan cheese.

5) Spoon the Risotto into individual bowls, top with the shrimp and serve immediately.

Per serving (approximate values): 806 Calories; 31.5g Fat (37.3% calories from fat); 31.6g Protein; 87.5g Carbohydrate; 155mg Cholesterol; 3716mg Sodium.

POTATO FAUX RISOTTO IN BACON CREAM

Technically not risotto, the flavors and textures would lead you to believe otherwise. I first tried this out on my friend Cyrus while living downtown Minneapolis. We both licked our plates clean.

Makes 4 servings
Prep Time: 1 hour

<u>Sauce</u>
4 slices bacon, chopped
1 large onion, chopped fine
⅓ cup white wine
¼ cup cider vinegar
1 cup whipping cream
<u>Potato Risotto</u>
2 tablespoons butter
2 cloves garlic, minced
4 large potatoes, peeled, ¼-inch dice
1 cup chicken broth
⅔ cup Parmesan cheese, fresh grated
½ cup mascarpone cheese

<u>Sauce:</u>
1) In a medium skillet, sauté bacon until crisp. Remove with a slotted spoon. Add ½ cup of chopped onions and sauté until soft and translucent. Remove from heat. Add bacon to onions.
2) Return pan to heat. Add wine and vinegar and bring to boil, scraping up any browned bits. Boil until liquid is reduced to about ¼ cup.
3) Add cream to bacon and onion mixture. Simmer until reduced to sauce consistency. Season to taste with salt and pepper. Keep warm.

<u>Potato Risotto:</u>
1) Melt butter in heavy, large saucepan over medium heat. Add remaining chopped onion and sauté until soft.
2) Add garlic and sauté another minute.
3) Add potatoes and sauté about 3 minutes.

4) Mix in chicken stock. Bring mixture to boil. Cover and reduce heat. Cook potatoes until tender and most of the liquid is absorbed, stirring occasionally.
5) Remove from heat. Stir in Parmesan and mascarpone cheese. Season with salt and pepper to taste.
6) Spoon potato risotto onto plates. Drizzle sauce over and serve.

Per serving (approximate values): 750 Calories; 42.5g Fat (50.8% calories from fat); 20.2g Protein; 72.4g Carbohydrate; 133mg Cholesterol; 853mg Sodium.

PORTUGUESE SWORDFISH

I was in a bit of crazy mood for the first dinner for which I prepared this dish. In collusion with my then-roommate Christine Chalstrom, I had an all-women dinner party. It was a success with this dish as its centerpiece.

Makes 6 servings
Prep Time: 45 minutes

6 whole swordfish steaks, 6 ounces each
¼ cup lemon juice
½ teaspoon salt
¼ teaspoon black pepper
1 ½ tablespoons olive oil
1 large yellow onion, chopped
4 cloves garlic, minced
3 large tomatoes, chopped
¾ cup white wine
½ cup sherry
½ cup tomato paste
1 tablespoon brown sugar
½ cup cilantro, chopped
⅛ teaspoon black pepper
1 large lemon

Preheat oven to 375 degrees.

1) Arrange fish in a single layer in a 13x9-inch baking dish. Pour lemon juice over fish. Sprinkle with ¼ teaspoon salt and ¼ teaspoon pepper. Cover and refrigerate.
2) Heat oil in large skillet over medium-high heat. Add onion and garlic. Sauté 10 minutes or until lightly browned, stirring frequently.
3) Stir in tomatoes, wine, sherry, tomato paste and brown sugar. Bring to a boil. Simmer 15 minutes, stirring frequently.
4) Stir in ¼ teaspoon salt, cilantro and ⅛ teaspoon pepper.
5) Pour tomato mixture over fish. Top with lemon slices. Cover and bake for 30 minutes.
6) Remove from oven and serve immediately.

Per serving (approximate values): 348 Calories; 10.7g Fat (30.7% calories from fat); 36.2g Protein; 18.3g Carbohydrate; 66mg Cholesterol; 519mg Sodium.

OVEN-POACHED HALIBUT

Makes 6 servings
Prep Time: 30 minutes

1 cup white wine
6 whole halibut steaks
1 ½ pounds Roma tomatoes
1 large onion, chopped
1 tablespoon dried basil leaves
¼ cup parsley, chopped
2 tablespoons green olives, chopped
1 tablespoon olive oil
½ teaspoon salt
⅛ teaspoon pepper
2 cloves garlic
¼ cup bread crumbs
1 tablespoon Parmesan cheese
1 teaspoon olive oil

Preheat oven to 350 degrees.

1) Coat 9x13-inch baking dish with cooking spray. Pour wine into dish and arrange halibut steaks on top.
2) Combine tomato and next 9 ingredients (through garlic) in a bowl. Stir well, then spoon over steaks. Bake for 35 minutes or until fish flakes easily.
3) Combine bread crumbs, cheese and 1 teaspoon oil in a small bowl. Stir well. Sprinkle over tomato mixture and broil until crumbs are golden. Serve immediately.

Per serving (approximate values): 302 Calories; 8.3g Fat (27.2% calories from fat); 37.9g Protein; 11.98 Carbohydrate; 55mg Cholesterol; 408mg Sodium.

GINGER AND MAPLE-GLAZED ROAST SALMON

I first made this dish for friends at springtime while living downtown Minneapolis. With a simple salad and a slice of cheesecake, it was a hit.

Makes 8 servings
Prep Time: 45 minutes

½ cup fresh ginger, peeled, grated
½ cup rice vinegar
½ cup maple syrup
4 pounds salmon fillet(s)
12 whole shallots, halved lengthwise
1 teaspoon salt
½ teaspoon pepper
½ cup maple syrup

Preheat oven to 450 degrees.

1) Combine ginger, vinegar and ½ cup maple syrup in a small mixing bowl. Use a baking dish or pan that will allow you to place the entire fillet(s) into it with not too much extra room. Pour liquid ingredients into the dish.

2) Add fish, skin side up, to ginger mixture. With your hands, press the fish in mixture to make sure fish has the full effect of the ginger mixture.

3) Cover and marinate fish in the refrigerator for 1 hour.

4) If the dish you used to marinate the fish in is ovenproof, drain the marinade. Turn the fish over so it is skin side down. Place shallots cut-side down evenly around fish.

5) Sprinkle with salt and pepper. With a pastry brush, baste the fillets with maple syrup.

6) Bake salmon for 10 minutes. Baste with additional maple syrup. Bake an additional 7 minutes or until fish flakes easily with a fork.

7) Cut into serving size pieces and serve.

Per serving (approximate values): 400 Calories; 8g Fat (18.1 % calories from fat); 46.3g Protein; 34.8g Carbohydrate; 118mg Cholesterol; 428mg Sodium.

TANGERINE TUNA

Makes 4 servings
Prep Time: 30 minutes

1 ½ pounds fresh tuna, cut into 4 steaks
Marinade:
2 tablespoons soy sauce
¼ cup tangerine juice, fresh
2 teaspoons tangerine zest
3 tablespoons honey
2 tablespoons sesame oil
3 cloves garlic, minced
2 green onions, chopped
1 tablespoon fresh ginger, peeled and grated
3 strips lemon zest
1 tablespoon vegetable oil
Citrus Sour Cream Sauce (recipe follows)

Preheat grill–gas or charcoal—to very hot. Rinse fish steaks and pat dry.

1) Whisk together all of the ingredients for the marinade in a shallow mixing bowl. Place tuna steaks in a non-reactive baking dish and pour marinade on top. Marinate the tuna, covered, in the refrigerator for at least 60 minutes. Turn the steaks once or twice.
2) Drain the tuna steaks and blot dry. Brush the steaks with the oil. Grill the tuna for 2–3 minutes per side or until cooked to taste.
3) Serve with Citrus Sour Cream Sauce.

Per serving (approximate values): 430 Calories; 18.9g Fat (39.4% calories from fat); 42g Protein; 23.4g Carbohydrate; 65mg Cholesterol; 586mg Sodium.

CITRUS SOUR CREAM SAUCE

Makes 6 servings
Prep Time: 30 minutes

½ cup fresh orange juice
¼ cup fresh lemon juice
¼ cup fresh lime juice
1 cup sour cream
Salt and pepper, to taste
Pinch cayenne pepper, to taste

1) Combine juices in heavy non-reactive saucepan. Boil the juice mixture until very reduced, about 2 tablespoons. Cool.
2) Whisk the juice reduction into the sour cream. Season with salt, pepper and cayenne.
3) Serve at room temperature, under and/or over grilled fish.

Per serving (approximate values): 96 Calories; 8.1 g Fat (72.1% calories from fat); 1.5g Protein; 5.6g Carbohydrate; 17mg Cholesterol; 21 mg Sodium.

CHICKEN SMOTHERED IN FRUIT

Makes 8 servings
Prep Time: 1 hour

4 tablespoons olive oil, split
2 pounds boneless skinless chicken breasts
1 large onion, sliced
4 cloves garlic
4 large Roma tomatoes, sliced
10 ounces peas, frozen
1 pound zucchini, sliced
2 medium pears, peeled, cored and sliced
2 medium apples, peeled, cored and sliced
3 cups pineapple chunks in juice, drained
2 medium plantains, peeled and sliced
Salt and pepper, to taste

Preheat oven to 350 degrees.

1) In medium skillet heat 2 tablespoons oil over medium heat. Add chicken and sauté until no longer pink and nicely browned.
2) Brush oil in bottom of ovenproof 4-quart saucepan. Place half of chicken on the bottom.
3) Place half of all remaining ingredients in layers over chicken. Place other half of chicken over fruits and vegetables, then rest of fruits and vegetables. Sprinkle with salt and pepper.
4) Cover saucepan. Place in oven and bake for approximately 1 ½ hours or until heated through. Make sure all fruit and vegetables are fully cooked. Serve over rice.

Per serving (approximate values): 402 Calories; 9.6g Fat (20.7% calories from fat); 30.9g Protein; 51.9g Carbohydrate; 66mg Cholesterol; 128mg Sodium.

SEAFOOD CRÊPE FILLING

After my first viewing of Babette's Feast, I decided to go crazy and create several ethnic-themed menus for my fellow barracks co-habitants. This was one of the main courses for the French night. It was so good, I have made it many times since. Crêpes are such a fun food, especially as an alternative to the now very common tortilla.

Makes 8 servings
Prep Time: 1 hour

8 ounces mushrooms, sliced
2 stalks green onions, chopped
3 tablespoons butter
12 ounces shrimp, small (*not* salad shrimp)
12 ounces scallops, (bay are the best)
12 ounces cream cheese
½ cup heavy cream
3 tablespoons parsley, chopped
2 tablespoons sherry
1 cup Swiss cheese
¼ cup green onion, chopped

1) Melt butter until bubbly. Cook mushrooms and green onions until most of the liquid had cooked out of them. Remove from heat.

2) Stir in seafood, cream cheese, cream and parsley. Place back on stove over low heat. Cook, stirring constantly, until cream cheese is melted. Stir in sherry.

3) In a large baking dish, place your first crêpe (basic crêpe recipe follows). In the center of each crêpe, place ¼ cup filling. Fold one side over filling, then the other side. Continue until baking dish is full. Sprinkle with cheese.

4) Cover and heat in 350 degree oven until crêpes are hot, about 20 minutes. Sprinkle with chopped green onions and serve.

Per serving (approximate values): 399 Calories; 29.8g Fat (66.9% calories from fat); 24.8g Protein; 8.3g Carbohydrate; 170mg Cholesterol; 348mg Sodium.

BASIC CRÊPES

Makes 8 servings
Prep Time: 1 hour

2 ¼ cups flour
¾ teaspoon salt
½ teaspoon baking powder
3 cups milk
3 large eggs
2 tablespoons butter, melted

1)   Mix flour, salt and baking powder in a medium mixing bowl. Stir in milk, eggs and butter. Whisk until smooth.

2)   For each crêpe, brush 8-inch skillet with butter. Heat over medium heat until butter bubbles. Pour ¼ cup batter into skillet. Immediately rotate pan until batter covers the bottom. Cook until top is dry.

3)   Flip crêpe over and cook until just done. Stack crêpes with sheet of wax paper separating each until ready to use.

Per serving (approximate values): 237 Calories; 8.1 g Fat (31.1 % calories from fat); 9g Protein; 31.4g Carbohydrate; 101 mg Cholesterol; 321 mg Sodium.

PAD THAI

A new restaurant had just opened in Minneapolis, not far from where I lived. A friend and I decided to give it a spin and discovered this delicious dish. This is my interpretation of this classic Thai comfort food.

Makes 6 servings
Prep Time: 45 minutes

8 ounces flat rice noodles
¼ cup water
3 tablespoons ketchup
3 tablespoons fish sauce
2 tablespoons brown sugar
1 tablespoon lime juice
2 whole Thai peppers (Serrano peppers can also be used)
1 teaspoon curry powder
2 tablespoons peanut oil, split
1 pound medium shrimp, peeled and deveined
3 cloves garlic, minced
3 large eggs, lightly beaten
1 ½ cups bean sprouts, fresh
⅔ cup peanuts, dry-roasted
3 whole green onions, thin sliced
1 whole lime

1) Place rice noodles in large bowl and cover with hot water. Let stand 10 minutes or until soft and pliable. Drain the water and set aside.

2) To prepare sauce, combine water, ketchup, fish sauce, sugar, lime juice, finely minced Thai peppers and curry powder in medium bowl. Set aside.

3) Heat large skillet over high heat. Add 1 tablespoon oil and swirl to coat. Add shrimp and stir-fry 2 minutes or until shrimp turn pink and opaque. Transfer to bowl with slotted spoon.

4) Reduce heat to medium. Add remaining 1 tablespoon oil and heat 15 seconds. Add garlic and cook until golden.

5) Add eggs and scramble 2 minutes or until eggs are just set. Stir in sauce.

6) Increase heat to high. Add rice noodles and stir to coat with sauce. Cook 2 to 4 minutes, stirring often until noodles are tender. Add water as necessary to ensure noodles do not dry out.

7) Add cooked shrimp, 1 ½ cups bean sprouts, peanuts and green onions. Cook and stir 1 to 2 minutes or until heated through.

8) Cut lime into quarters and squeeze over noodles before eating. Serve immediately.

Per serving (approximate values): 333 Calories; 17.7g Fat (45.9% calories from fat); 24.9g Protein; 22g Carbohydrate; 224mg Cholesterol; 374mg Sodium.

GRILLED GINGER CHICKEN

Makes 4 servings
Prep Time: 30 minutes

2 pounds boneless skinless chicken breasts
4 cloves garlic, crushed
4 ounces fresh ginger, peeled and sliced thin
1 whole lemon peel, grated
½ teaspoon salt
¼ teaspoon ground pepper
½ cup cilantro, leaves
¼ cup lemon juice
2 tablespoons balsamic vinegar
4 teaspoons olive oil

1) In food processor combine garlic and ginger. Mince finely.
2) Add lemon peel, salt, pepper and cilantro. Process until combined.
3) With machine running, add lemon juice, vinegar and then oil.
4) Rub mixture over both sides of chicken. Cover and refrigerate. Let marinate for at least 2 hours.
5) Grease broiler pan and position rack about 4 inches from heat source. Transfer chicken to heated pan. Broil chicken until just tender and deep golden, about 15 minutes on each side. Baste chicken with any remaining marinade when turning over.
6) Transfer chicken to platter. Serve.

Per serving (approximate values): 417 Calories; 10.1 g Fat (21.9% calories from fat); 56.3g Protein; 25.1 g Carbohydrate; 132mg Cholesterol; 439mg Sodium.

CARIBBEAN CHICKEN

Makes 4 servings
Prep Time: 45 minutes

1 ½ tablespoons Caribbean mix (recipe follows)
4 whole boneless skinless chicken breast halves
1 large yellow onion, sliced
½ whole red bell pepper, sliced
½ whole green bell pepper, sliced
4 cloves garlic, crushed
1 bunch green onions, sliced thick
2 tablespoons olive oil

1) In a medium skillet, sauté onions, peppers, garlic and green onions in olive oil until onions are translucent and peppers are soft. At the end of the cooking time, add 1 teaspoon of spice mixture. Set aside.

2) With remaining spice mixture, sprinkle onto the surface of the chicken breasts. Press to evenly distribute it.

3) In a large skillet over medium heat, add 1 tablespoon vegetable oil. Sauté all chicken breasts until nearly cooked through and evenly brown on both sides, about 5-10 minutes per side.

4) Add sautéed vegetables and ½ cup water and cover. Reduce heat and let steam for about 20 minutes or until chicken is completely cooked through. Serve with Caribbean rice!

Per serving (approximate values): 191 Calories; 8.4g Fat (39.5% calories from fat); 21.8g Protein; 7.1 g Carbohydrate; 51 mg Cholesterol; 63mg Sodium.

CARIBBEAN SPICE MIX

Makes 4 servings
Prep Time: 45 minutes

3 teaspoons curry powder
1 ½ teaspoons paprika
1 ½ teaspoons cinnamon
1 teaspoon ground nutmeg
1 teaspoon salt
½ teaspoon cumin
½ teaspoon pepper

1) In a small bowl, combine all ingredients. Use for a dry rub.
2) Makes 3 tablespoons.

Per serving (approximate values): 14 Calories, 0.6g Fat (31.7% calories from fat); 0.5g Protein; 2.6g Carbohydrate; 0mg Cholesterol; 535mg Sodium.

CARIBBEAN RICE WITH FIGS AND DATES

Makes 4 servings
Prep Time: 45 minutes

1 ½ tablespoons Caribbean Spice mix
2 cups chicken broth
1 cup rice, converted long-grain
1 cup figs, Mission or Calimyrna, chopped
¾ cup dates, chopped

1) Bring chicken broth to a boil in medium saucepan. Add all of Spice mix.
2) Add rice, then fruit. Cover and reduce heat. Simmer for 20 minutes.
3) Take off heat and let steam for at least 10 minutes. Fluff and serve with Caribbean Chicken!

Per serving (approximate values): 335 Calories; 1.9g Fat (5% calories from fat); 9.8g Protein; 71.9g Carbohydrate; 1 mg Cholesterol; 786mg Sodium.

GINGER CHICKEN WITH FRUIT

I've always been fascinated with combining fruits and meats. Chicken goes perfectly with so many different fruits, it's hard to narrow down all the possibilities. This recipe has an Asian influence my guests have loved!

Makes 4 servings
Prep Time: 45 minutes

1 pound boneless skinless chicken breasts,
cut into 1-inch chunks
1 teaspoon ground ginger, divided
3 tablespoons soy sauce
1 ½ cups carrot, diced
¾ cup pineapple tidbits, drained
1 cup frozen cherries
1 tablespoon lemon juice
¼ teaspoon black pepper
1 cup cooked white rice
1 tablespoon cornstarch
1 tablespoon water

1) In a small bowl or gallon-size re-sealable bag, combine soy sauce and ginger. Mix well. Add chicken to liquid. Marinate in refrigerator up to 4 hours.

2) In a medium bowl, combine carrots, pineapple, cherries, lemon juice, ½ teaspoon ginger and pepper.

3) In a large saucepan or Dutch oven, brown chicken. When evenly brown and cooked through add fruit mixture.

4) Bring to a boil. Cover and reduce heat to a simmer. Continue to simmer for about 30 minutes.

5) Uncover and add cornstarch and water mixture. Cook until thickened and bubbly. Serve over hot white rice.

Per serving (approximate values): 421 Calories; 2.6g Fat (5.5% calories from fat); 32.1 g Protein; 66.8g Carbohydrate; 66mg Cholesterol; 880mg Sodium.

CORN AND WILD RICE CRÊPES

Makes 6 servings
Prep Time: 30 minutes

6 large eggs, beaten
6 tablespoons butter, melted
1 cup milk
½ cup cornmeal
½ cup all-purpose flour
1 cup wild rice, cooked
4 green onions, sliced thin
1 cup corn, frozen or fresh

1) In a medium bowl, mix together the eggs, 4 tablespoons of the melted butter and the milk.

2) Gradually stir in the cornmeal and flour, stirring constantly. Stir in the cooked wild rice.

3) In a medium skillet, sauté the green onions and corn in the remaining 2 tablespoons butter over medium heat for 2-3 minutes.

4) Add to the batter. Batter should have the consistency of thin pancake batter. Add more milk if needed.

5) Heat a 7-inch nonstick skillet over medium-high heat and brush with oil. Pour in enough of the batter to cover the bottom of the pan, about ¼ cup. Cook 2-3 minutes until the bottom is lightly brown. Turn the crêpe over and cook 1 minute more. Keep warm until all crêpes have been made.

Per serving (approximate values): 363 Calories; 18.5g Fat (44.5% calories from fat); 13.5g Protein; 38.3g Carbohydrate; 252mg Cholesterol; 205mg Sodium.

SPICY CHICKEN Á LA KING

Makes 6 servings
Prep Time: 45 minutes

<u>Seasoning mix:</u>
1 tablespoon salt
1 ½ teaspoons dried basil
1 teaspoon garlic powder
1 teaspoon onion powder
1 teaspoon white pepper
1 teaspoon sweet paprika
1 teaspoon dry mustard
½ teaspoon ground savory
½ teaspoon ground nutmeg
<u>Dish:</u>
2 pounds boneless skinless chicken breasts, cut into 1-inch cube
8 tablespoons butter, softened
5 tablespoons butter, cut into tablespoons
¼ cup all-purpose flour
6 tablespoons dry sherry
1 cup chopped onions
1 cup green bell peppers, chopped
1 cup red bell peppers, chopped
2 cups mushrooms, sliced thin
2 cups heavy cream

1) Combine the seasoning mix ingredients thoroughly in a small bowl. Makes about 3 tablespoons plus 1 ½ teaspoons.
2) Sprinkle 1 tablespoon plus 1 teaspoon of the seasoning mix over the chicken and rub it in well.
3) Combine the 8 tablespoons softened butter with the flour and mash together until the flour disappears into it. Set aside.
4) Place a 5-quart saucepan over high heat. When the pan is hot add the chicken and dot the remaining 5 tablespoons butter evenly over the chicken. Stir until evenly brown.

5)   Add ¼ cup of the sherry, the onions, red and green peppers, mush-rooms and the remaining seasoning mix. Stir well, then cover and cook 5 minutes.

6)   Uncover the pan and add the flour/butter mixture a spoonful at a time. Stir constantly as the mixture dissolves and the sauce thickens.

7)   Stir in cream and stir until sauce thickens.

8)   Remove from heat and stir in the remaining 2 tablespoons sherry. Makes about 8 cups.

9)   Serve over toast or use as filling for crêpes!

Per serving (approximate values): 732 Calories; 57g Fat (70.9% calories from fat); 39g Protein; 13.5g Carbohydrate; 263mg Cholesterol; 1454mg Sodium.

Traditional Chicken Enchiladas

I just knew what Taco Bell® served as an enchilada couldn't be what Mexican's actually dined on. Thus I went in search of an authentic representation of this dish. I found a very old Mexican cookbook, had a friend translate the recipe and updated it. While a fast food enchilada satisfies, this dish enlightens!

Makes 10 servings
Prep Time: 1 hour

1 ½ pounds boneless skinless chicken breasts
2 cups Monterey jack cheese
¾ cup green onions, sliced, including greens
¾ cup sour cream, reduced fat
1 teaspoon salt
¼ teaspoon pepper
24 ounces canned crushed tomatoes
½ whole green pepper, chopped
4 ounces green chiles
1 tablespoon chili powder
¼ teaspoon cumin
4 ounces black olives, sliced
10 whole flour tortilla, 9-inch

Preheat oven to 350 degrees. Have available a 9x13-inch nonstick baking pan.

1) Heat 2 quarts of water to boiling. Add 1 tablespoon onion powder, 1 teaspoon garlic powder, 1 teaspoon salt and ½ teaspoon pepper. Add chicken breasts and cook until thoroughly done, about 30 minutes. DO NOT REMOVE. Leave chicken in broth until water has completely cooled.

2) When cool, remove chicken breasts to drain. With strong tined fork, shred chicken into fine strands into large bowl.

3) To shredded chicken, add 1 ½ cups of cheese, green onion, sour cream, salt and pepper. Cover and set aside in refrigerator.

4) In a medium saucepan, combine crushed tomatoes, green peppers, green chiles, chili powder, cumin and olives. Heat to boiling. Cover, reduce heat and simmer for 30 minutes.

5) Heat tortillas in microwave for 30 seconds. Spoon ¼ cup chicken mixture onto tortilla. Roll tortilla around filling. Continue until all tortillas are filled. Place them seam side down into 9x13-inch baking pan.

6) Pour sauce evenly over enchiladas. Sprinkle evenly with cheese. Bake in oven until bubbly, about 20 minutes.

Per serving (approximate values): 348 Calories; 15.6g Fat (40.2% calories from fat); 26g Protein; 26g Carbohydrate; 67mg Cholesterol; 775mg Sodium.

CHICKEN IN A SPICY SESAME SAUCE

Makes 6 servings
Prep Time: 1 hour

3 pounds chicken, whole, cut up
2 cups water
2 cloves garlic, finely chopped
1 teaspoon salt
½ cup sesame seeds
16 ounces tomato sauce
1 medium onion, chopped
2 teaspoons chili powder
2 teaspoons paprika
¼ teaspoon cinnamon
⅛ teaspoon ground cloves

Preheat oven to 350 degrees.

1) Place chicken, water, garlic and salt in stockpot or Dutch oven. Heat to boiling and reduce heat. Cover and simmer for 35 to 45 minutes until chicken is cooked through. Cool slightly.
2) Remove chicken from broth and set aside.
3) In a large skillet, heat sesame seeds over medium heat until golden brown. Remove from heat.
4) Place sesame seeds in blender with ¼ cup broth from chicken. Cover blender and blend until finely chopped.
5) In 2-quart saucepan, mix together sesame mixture, tomato sauce, onion, chili powder, paprika, cinnamon and cloves.
6) Bring to boil. Reduce heat, stirring constantly until thickened. Add broth from chicken as needed to make sure sauce remains thick and smooth.
7) In a 1 ½-quart baking dish, place chicken pieces in a single layer. Pour sesame mixture over chicken evenly. Cover and bake for 30 minutes.
8) Remove from oven and uncover. Let rest for 10 minutes. Serve over rice.

Per serving (approximate values): 446 Calories; 32.68 Fat (65.7% calories from fat); 26.8g Protein; 11.6g Carbohydrate; 93mg Cholesterol; 920mg Sodium.

CHICKEN BREAST WITH GRAPES

Makes 6 servings
Prep Time: 30 minutes

2 pounds boneless skinless chicken breast halves
½ cup seedless grapes, red or green
3 tablespoons butter
Pinch salt and pepper
1 ½ tablespoons shallots, finely chopped
½ cup dry white wine
1 ½ cups heavy cream

1) Trim chicken of fat. Place breast halves on a flat surface. With a flat mallet, pound them lightly until of even thickness. With a sharp knife, cut the breasts into half-inch strips. There should be about three cups.

2) Heat the butter in a large, heavy skillet. When hot, but not brown, add the chicken breasts. Sprinkle with salt and pepper. Cook over high heat, stirring constantly so that pieces cook evenly. Cook until pieces lose their raw look and are barely cooked through, about 3 to 5 minutes.

3) With a slotted spoon, transfer the chicken to a plate or bowl. Set aside.

4) Add shallots to the skillet. Cook and stir for about 5 minutes. Add the wine. Over high heat, cook the wine mixture until reduced by half. As juices accumulate around the set-aside chicken, drain and add to the wine mixture. Add the cream. Heat to boiling.

5) Add grapes to the sauce. Cook 4 or 5 minutes or until the cream mixture takes on a sauce-like consistency. Add salt and pepper to taste.

6) Spoon the chicken into the sauce and heat through. Serve with curried rice or fettuccine noodles.

Per serving (approximate values): 451 Calories; 30.2g Fat (62.4% calories from fat); 36.6g Protein; 4.3g Carbohydrate; 185mg Cholesterol; 186mg Sodium.

CUMIN PORK TENDERLOIN

Sometimes it's nice to prepare a simple pork dish and this fits the bill. Any tender pork cut will work nicely, but there's nothing like the tenderloin for flavors of this dish to shine through.

Makes 4 servings
Prep Time: 45 minutes

2 tablespoons brown sugar
1 teaspoon cumin
½ teaspoon pepper
2 teaspoons cider vinegar
1 pound pork tenderloin

Preheat oven to 400 degrees.

1) Combine the first 5 ingredients in a shallow dish. Stir well and set aside.
2) Trim fat from the pork. Add entire pork tenderloin to the dish. Turn to coat well. Cover and marinate in refrigerator 30 minutes. Turn pork occasionally.
3) Remove pork from dish. Discard the marinade. Place pork on a broiler pan coated with nonstick spray. Bake at 400 degrees for about 30 minutes. Remove from oven. Let sit for 5 minutes.
4) Cut pork into thin slices.
5) Serve with a good chutney (try the Dried Apricot Chutney!).

Per serving (approximate values): 164 Calories; 4g Fat (22.4% calories from fat); 24g Protein; 7.2g Carbohydrate; 74mg Cholesterol; 60mg Sodium.

PORK MEDALLIONS IN MUSTARD-BEER CREAM

Makes 8 servings
Prep Time: 45 minutes

2 pounds pork tenderloin
3 ½ cups plain bread crumbs
⅓ cup parsley, chopped
½ teaspoon cinnamon
¼ teaspoon ground nutmeg
1 cup flour
3 large eggs, beaten
⅓ cup vegetable oil

Preheat oven to 200 degrees.

1) Thinly slice tenderloin into medallions.
2) Mix breadcrumbs, parsley, cinnamon and nutmeg until well combined. Transfer to a large mixing bowl.
3) Place flour into shallow bowl.
4) Beat eggs in small mixing bowl, set aside.
5) Dredge 1 pork medallion in flour, then eggs, then in the breadcrumb mixture. Place on a plate or baking pan. Repeat with remaining medallions until all are coated.
6) Heat oil in large, heavy skillet over medium-high heat. Add pork in batches and sauté until just cooked through, about 2-3 minutes per side. Add more oil to skillet as needed between batches.
7) Transfer to an ovenproof platter and keep warm in oven until all medallions are cooked. Serve with Mustard-Beer Cream (recipe follows).

Per serving (approximate values): 496 Calories; 18.2g Fat (33.5% calories from fat); 33.6g Protein; 47.5g Carbohydrate; 155mg Cholesterol; 491 mg Sodium.

MUSTARD-BEER CREAM

Makes 8 servings
Prep Time: 1 hour

24 ounces good dark German-style beer
1 cup shallots, chopped
6 cups chicken stock
3 cups whipping cream
½ cup Dijon mustard
4 tablespoons mustard seed
Salt and pepper, to taste

1) Boil beer and shallots in heavy, medium saucepan until beer reduces to ½ cup, about 20 minutes.
2) Add stock and boil until reduced to about 3 cups, about 20 more minutes at a steady boil.
3) Add cream and boil until reduced to about 4 cups, another 20 minutes.
4) Stir in mustard and mustard seeds and cook for 5 minutes. Season to taste with salt and pepper. Keep warm until ready to serve.

Per serving (approximate values): 406 Calories; 35.5g Fat (82.7% calories from fat); 5.2g Protein; 11.5g Carbohydrate; 122mg Cholesterol; 1838mg Sodium.

ROAST PORK WITH BROWN SUGAR SAUCE

Makes 6 servings
Prep Time: 45 minutes

2 pounds pork loin roast, boneless, tied
Paste:
1 cup brown sugar, packed
2 tablespoons dark rum
2 cloves garlic, minced
2 teaspoons ground ginger
1 bay leaf
1 teaspoon salt
½ teaspoon pepper
½ teaspoon ground cloves
Sauce:
½ cup chicken stock
¼ cup light rum
1 tablespoon all-purpose flour
¼ cup fresh lime juice

Preheat oven to 375 degrees. Have ready a roasting pan that can also be used on the stovetop.

1) Place pork in roasting pan. Roast until meat thermometer inserted in the center registers 160 degrees, about 1 ½ hours. Remove roast and set aside.

2) Increase oven to 450 degrees.

3) Mix brown sugar and next 7 ingredients (through cloves) in a medium bowl until paste forms. Cut strings off pork roast and remove. Spread spice paste over pork covering it completely. Place roast back in oven and continue roasting 15 minutes. Transfer roast to platter.

4) Set roasting pan over medium heat. Add chicken stock and ¼ cup light rum and bring to boil, scraping up any brown bits.

5) Sprinkle flour over stock mixture and whisk vigorously to blend. Bring to boil, whisking constantly.

6) Add fresh lime juice and boil until thickened. Continue to whisk vigorously, about two minutes.

7) Slice pork. Serve sauce separately.

Per serving (approximate values): 360 Calories; 7.6g Fat (20.8% calories from fat); 26.4g Protein; 38.9g Carbohydrate; 63mg Cholesterol; 609mg Sodium.

PORK MEDALLIONS WITH MUSHROOMS IN CREAMY COGNAC SAUCE

Makes 4 servings
Prep Time: 45 minutes

1 pound pork tenderloin, cut into ½-inch thick medallions
5 tablespoons butter
⅓ cup cognac
⅓ cup white wine, Riesling (or other sweet white wine)
⅔ cup beef broth
2 ounces Portobello mushrooms
8 ounces button mushrooms, sliced
¼ cup shallots, minced
2 cups cream
Salt and pepper, to taste
2 tablespoons corn starch
2 tablespoons water

Preheat oven to 200 degrees.

1) Brown the pork medallions in 2 tablespoons of the butter in a large, heavy skillet over medium-high heat. Remove cooked medallions to a ovenproof baking dish, cover with foil and keep warm in oven.

2) Once all medallions are finished, add Cognac and wine to the skillet. Heat 1 to 2 minutes, scraping up any brown bits.

3) Add the broth and boil uncovered until reduced by two-thirds.

4) Pour the Cognac mixture over the pork. Cover and set in the oven.

5) Add the remaining 3 tablespoons butter to the skillet.

6) Add the mushrooms and shallots and sauté 8 to 10 minutes until the mushrooms are limp and their juices have evaporated.

7) Stir the pork medallions and all liquids back into the skillet. Add the cream. Boil over low heat for 10 to 15 minutes until the cream reduces by half and is the consistency of a thin white sauce. Season to taste with salt and pepper and serve at once.

Per serving (approximate values): 643 Calories; 48.3g Fat (72.9% calories from fat); 30.5g Protein; 9.8g Carbohydrate; 217mg Cholesterol; 468mg Sodium.

TEQUILA PORK CHOPS

Makes 4 servings
Prep Time: 15 minutes

2 tablespoons tequila
¼ cup jalapeno jelly, melted
2 tablespoons fresh lime juice
¼ teaspoon salt
⅛ teaspoon pepper
4 pieces pork center loin chops, boneless

1) Combine all ingredients except pork in a large sealable plastic bag. Add pork and seal. Marinate in refrigerator at least 8 hours. Remove pork from bag. Reserve marinade.

2) Prepare grill or broiler. Place pork on grill rack or broiler pan covered with non-stick cooking spray. Cook 7 minutes on each side or until pork is done. Baste with reserved marinade. Serve with Mango-Tequila Salsa (recipe follows).

Per serving (approximate values): 371 Calories; 19.2g Fat (49.1 % calories from fat); 30.5g Protein; 14.28 Carbohydrate; 101 mg Cholesterol; 231 mg Sodium.

MANGO-TEQUILA SALSA

Makes 4 servings
Prep Time: 30 minutes

2 cups mango, peeled, diced
⅔ cup red bell pepper, chopped
3 tablespoons tequila
2 tablespoons orange juice
1 tablespoon jalapeno pepper, minced
2 teaspoons fresh mint, chopped
¼ teaspoon salt

1) Combine all ingredients in a small bowl. Stir well.
2) Cover and chill. Good with the Tequila Pork Chops!

Per serving (approximate values): 87 Calories; 0.3g Fat (3.6% calories from fat); 0.7g Protein; 16.2g Carbohydrate; 0mg Cholesterol; 136mg Sodium.

CAPE COD BEEF BRISKET WITH PORTOBELLOS

I recall my first encounter with beef brisket with vivid clarity. The brisket was sliced and marinated in a delicious bbq sauce and was so incredibly tender. The key to a truly successful tender brisket is the long, slow roasting process at a low temperature. Armed with this information, it was a logical step to try it with some of my other favorite ingredients. My bar-owner friends (Doug and Grant) loved it the first time I prepared it!

Makes 8 servings
Prep Time: 4 hours

1 ½ cups red wine
1 ½ cups beef broth
¾ cup cranberry juice cocktail, frozen concentrate
⅓ cup flour
1 large onion, sliced
6 cloves garlic, crushed
2 tablespoons fresh rosemary, chopped
4 pounds beef brisket, flat half
Salt and pepper, to taste
16 ounces Portobello mushrooms, sliced thin
6 ounces dried cranberries

Preheat oven to 300 degrees.

1) Whisk red wine, beef broth, cranberry concentrate and flour to blend in medium bowl. Pour into 15x10x2-inch roasting pan.
2) Mix into pan onions, garlic and rosemary.
3) Sprinkle brisket with salt and pepper. Place brisket fat side up into roasting pan. Spoon some of mixture over top of brisket. Cover pan tightly with heavy-duty foil.
4) Bake brisket until very tender, about 4 hours. Transfer brisket to plate. Cool for no less than 30 minutes.
5) Increase oven temperature to 350 degrees.
6) Thinly slice beef across the grain. Arrange slices in pan with sauce, overlapping slightly.
7) Place mushrooms and cranberries in sauce around brisket. Cover pan with foil. Bake until mushrooms are tender, about 30 minutes.

8)   Remove from oven. Transfer brisket to a serving platter. Pour sauce from baking pan into serving bowl.

Per serving (approximate values): 745 Calories; 53.4g Fat (68% calories from fat); 43.2g Protein; 13.2g Carbohydrate; 157mg Cholesterol; 414mg Sodium.

MOROCCAN MEATBALLS

Makes 6 servings
Prep Time: 20 minutes

1 pound ground lamb
½ cup bread crumbs
½ cup chopped onion
½ cup chopped parsley
½ teaspoon ground coriander
⅛ teaspoon salt
⅛ teaspoon pepper
Dash cinnamon
Dash ground nutmeg

1) Combine all ingredients in a large bowl and stir well.
2) Shape mixture into 1-inch meatballs. Coat a large skillet with non-stick cooking spray. Place over medium-high heat until hot. Add meatballs and cook 8 minutes or until browned. Drain on paper towels.
3) Combine with the Moroccan Tomatoes with Couscous (recipe follows).

Per serving (approximate values): 257 Calories; 18.4g Fat (65.2% calories from fat); 13.9g Protein; 8.1g Carbohydrate; 55mg Cholesterol; 170mg Sodium.

MOROCCAN TOMATOES WITH COUSCOUS

Makes 6 servings
Prep Time: 45 minutes

<u>Tomato Sauce:</u>
½ teaspoon garlic powder
¼ teaspoon salt
¼ teaspoon ground cumin
¼ teaspoon chili powder
¼ teaspoon ground red pepper
29 ounces canned whole tomatoes, chopped with juices
<u>Couscous:</u>
3 ½ cups water
2 ⅔ cups uncooked couscous
¾ cup dried apricot halves, chopped
½ cup dried currants

1) For tomato sauce, combine garlic powder and next five ingredients in 2-quart saucepan over medium-high heat. Bring to a boil. Cover and reduce heat. Simmer for 15 minutes.
2) For couscous, bring water to a boil in a large saucepan. Stir in couscous. Cover and remove from heat. Let stand for 5 minutes. Remove cover and fluff with fork. Stir in apricots and currants.
3) Top couscous with tomatoes.

Per serving (approximate values): 390 Calories; 1.0g Fat (2.2% calories from fat); 12.2g Protein; 84.7g Carbohydrate; 0mg Cholesterol; 328mg Sodium.

MEATBALLS IN BROWN GRAVY

Makes 8 servings
Prep Time: 1 hour

---

3 pounds ground beef
3 slices bread
3 cups green onions, chopped, divided
2 cups onions, chopped, divided
1 cup green peppers, chopped, divided
¼ cup parsley, chopped, divided
1 large egg
2 tablespoons garlic, minced, divided
1 tablespoon Tabasco sauce, divided
2 teaspoons black pepper, divided
2 teaspoons cayenne
½ cup flour
¾ cup vegetable oil
4 cups water, divided
6 cups cooked rice

---

1) Put the meat in a large mixing bowl.
2) Wet the bread under tap water, then squeeze out moisture and add the bread to the meat.
3) Add 1 ½ cups of the green onions, 1 cup of the onions, ½ cup of the green peppers, 2 tablespoons of the parsley, the egg, 2 teaspoons of the garlic, ½ teaspoons salt, 2 teaspoons of the Tabasco, 1 ½ teaspoons black pepper, then the cayenne. Mix thoroughly by hand until the bread disappears into the mixture.
4) Form into 16 meatballs, about 2 inches in diameter.
5) Place the flour in a medium-size bowl and set aside.
6) In a heavy 6 quart saucepan or Dutch oven, heat the oil over medium-high heat for about 3 minutes. Just before browning each batch, dredge meatballs thoroughly in flour, shaking off excess. Brown the meat in two batches. Set aside 2 tablespoons of the flour. Cook each batch in the hot oil until dark brown and crisp on all sides, about 12 to 14 minutes, scraping the pan bottom clean. Reduce heat if oil starts to smoke.

Remove browned meatballs and as many browned bits as possible with a slotted spoon. Set aside.

7) Remove pan from heat and scrape pan bottom again to loosen any sediment. Pout the hot oil into a large glass measuring cup. Return ⅓ cup of the oil to the pan.

8) Combine the remaining 1 ½ cups green onions, 1 cup onions, and 1 tablespoon garlic in a bowl and set aside.

9) Place pan over medium heat (which has the oil in it) and add the remaining 2 tablespoons of the dredging flour and cook about 1 minute, stirring constantly and scraping pan bottom.

10) Add the vegetable mixture and cook about 8 minutes, stirring constantly.

11) Add 1 cup of the water and remaining parsley, scraping until the bottom is clean.

12) Add the remaining 3 cups water and browned meatballs to the pan.

13) Turn heat to medium-high and bring to a strong boil, stirring occasionally. Reduce heat to medium, stirring often, for about 5 minutes.

14) Add the remaining black pepper, 1 teaspoon Tabasco, stirring well. Cover and simmer about 20 minutes more, stirring occasionally.

15) Remove from heat, remove cover and let sit about 15 minutes. Skim as much fat from surface as is possible. Serve 2 meatballs and about ½ cup of gravy over about 1 cup of rice for each serving.

Per serving (approximate values): 995 Calories; 67.48 Fat (61.3% calories from fat); 36.2g Protein; 59.5g Carbohydrate; 171mg Cholesterol; 196mg Sodium.

NEU SAUERBRATEN

You'd think I would have more recipes from Germany! I do have a few and they are some of my very favorites. I love the concept of traditional sauerbraten, but know my family would never go for it. So I tweaked it a bit and this is my result. The family loves it!

Makes 6 servings
Prep Time: 1 hour 40 minutes

Marinade:
4 cups dry red wine
1 cup water
2 ½ teaspoons lemon juice, freshly squeezed
1 small onion, chopped
10 whole peppercorns
2 medium bay leaves.
4 whole cloves

Sauerbraten:
3 pounds top round steak, boneless roast
2 tablespoons parsley, minced
1 teaspoon salt
½ teaspoon pepper
3 tablespoons flour
3 tablespoons butter
2 medium carrots, sliced thin
2 large onions, chopped coarsely
1 tablespoon tomato paste
1 tablespoon sugar
2 tablespoons sherry
½ cup red wine
1 cup raisins
2 tablespoons red currant jelly

1) For the marinade, bring all ingredients to a rapid boil in an uncovered medium, heavy saucepan over moderate heat and cook 5 minutes.
2) For the sauerbraten, place beef in a large, heatproof, nonmetallic bowl. Pour in the hot marinade and cool to room temperature.

3) Add the parsley, turn the beef in the marinade, cover and marinate in the refrigerator for 2 days. Turn the beef in the marinade every 8 hours.

4) On the 3rd day, remove the beef from the marinade and pat it dry. Strain the marinade, reserving both the liquid and solids. Rub the beef with half the salt and pepper, then dredge in flour.

5) Melt 2 tablespoons of the butter in a stockpot or Dutch oven over medium heat. Add the beef and brown well on all sides, about 8-10 minutes. Transfer the beef to a plate, then pour off and discard all pot drippings.

6) Add the remaining 1 tablespoon butter to the pot and melt over moderate heat. Add the carrots, onion and reserved marinade solids. Sauté, stirring often, for 5 minutes.

7) Return the beef to the stockpot and add 2 cups of the reserved marinade and the tomato paste. Bring to a boil over high heat. Adjust the heat so the marinade boils gently and cover the kettle with lid tightly in place. Simmer the sauerbraten 3 ½ to 4 hours, turning occasionally, until tender.

8) As soon as the sauerbraten is tender, remove it to a large plate and cover loosely with foil to keep warm. Strain liquid and discard the solids.

9) Return the marinade to the stockpot and add the remaining reserved marinade. Add the sugar, sherry, red wine and raisins. Bring to a boil, uncovered, over high heat for 5 to 7 minutes, until reduced by half and of good gravy consistency.

10) Taste. If the gravy is too sour, stir in 1 to 2 tablespoons of the jelly. Salt and pepper to taste.

11) To serve, slice the sauerbraten across the grain about ¼ inch thick. Arrange on a large heated platter, overlapping the slices and smother with the gravy.

Per serving (approximate values): 759 Calories; 28.2g Fat (38.7% calories from fat); 52.4g Protein; 48.2g Carbohydrate; 122mg Cholesterol; 693mg Sodium.

OLIVE-STUFFED MEATBALLS

My sister, the olive fiend that she is, fell in love with this dish the first time she had it. It's a pasta dish, it's creamy, it has meat in it and it's stuffed with olives. Yikes!

Makes 4 servings
Prep Time: 45 minutes

¾ pound ground pork
¾ pound ground veal
1 ½ teaspoons onion powder
2 cloves garlic
½ cup bread crumbs
½ cup parsley, chopped fine
1 large egg
1 cup heavy cream
⅛ teaspoon ground nutmeg
Salt and pepper, to taste
Green olives, to stuff with
Black olives, to stuff with
¼ cup vegetable oil
4 tablespoons flour
¾ cup white wine
2 cups chicken broth
1 ½ tablespoons tomato paste
1 tablespoon Dijon mustard

1) Put meat in a large mixing bowl. Add onion powder to meat. Add the bread crumbs, parsley, egg, half of the cream, the nutmeg, salt and pepper to taste.

2) Mix well using hands. Divide the mixture into 18 equal portions. Flatten each into a small patty and place an olive in the center. Bring the edges of the meat together and seal in the olive. Shape into a ball.

3) Heat the oil in two skillets large enough to hold meatballs in one layer. Cook, turning and stirring often so they brown evenly. When nicely browned, remove and keep warm.

4) Pour off all but 4 tablespoons fat. Add flour and thoroughly combine.

5) Add the wine in a thin stream and let cook for one minute, stirring constantly.

6) Whisk in the chicken broth. Stir in the tomato paste. When the sauce is thickened and boiling, add the meatballs. Cover and cook about 10 minutes.

7) Whisk in the remaining ½ cup of cream and mustard into the sauce and serve.

Per serving (approximate values): 892 Calories; 63g Fat (65.9% calories from fat); 50.3g Protein; 22.9g Carbohydrate; 286mg Cholesterol; 1179mg Sodium.

GINGERED BEEF TENDERLOIN WITH MUSHROOMS

Another one of those experiments made while living with my dad, it surprised us both. It sounds like a fairly simple dish, yet the flavors explode.

Makes 4 servings
Prep Time: 45 minutes

2 tablespoons ginger root, peeled, juliennes
½ cup brandy
1 ½ pounds beef tenderloin, trimmed of fat
6 cloves garlic, crushed
½ cup canned condensed beef bouillon
1 tablespoon butter
8 ounces fresh button mushrooms,
2 tablespoons mustard, Dijon *or* Grey Poupon, Spicy Brown-style
Salt and pepper, to taste

Preheat oven to 350 degrees.

1) In a small bowl, combine brandy and ginger. Set aside for 30 minutes for brandy to become infused with ginger flavor.

2) While brandy infuses, take beef tenderloin and rub crushed garlic into it. Let marinate at room temperature for 15 minutes.

3) Roast beef to at least medium rare. Remove from oven. Pour brandy over beef. Ignite with long matchstick. Let flames subside on their own. Remove beef from pan and scrape up any bits from the roasting process. Reduce oven temperature to 200 degrees and place beef in it to keep warmed while completing the following steps.

4) Add beef pan juices to a medium saucepan, add butter and place over high heat. Add mushrooms and let cook until mushrooms have wilted. Add beef bouillon. Cook until mixture is hot and bubbling. Whisk in mustard. Season to taste with salt and pepper.

5) Remove beef from oven and slice. Pour sauce over slices and serve!

Per serving (approximate values): 403 Calories; 85.5g Fat (72.0% calories from fat); 64.5g Protein; 10.4g Carbohydrate; 257mg Cholesterol; 757mg Sodium.

Pepper Lamb Skewers with Red Plum Glaze

Always trying to invent fun dishes to make for my television show, this was created for a spring episode I was taping. Many people are somewhat turned off by the flavor of lamb, yet this preparation helps those persons accept that lamb can be really yummy!

Makes 4 servings
Prep Time: 45 minutes

1 pound lamb, lean, boned
2 tablespoons butter, melted
Fresh coarsely ground pepper
1 tablespoon vegetable oil
1 tablespoon butter
Glaze:
3 large plums
3 tablespoons sugar
½ cup water
2 tablespoons white rum

1) Cut lamb (from either the leg or fillet) into 1-inch cubes. Brush cubes with melted butter. Roll each cube in coarsely ground pepper and place on skewer. Distribute cubes evenly on skewers (about 4 per skewer). Refrigerate to set coating.

2) Peel and halve plums. In medium saucepan, put in plums, water and sugar. Bring mixture to boil. Reduce heat and simmer until fruit is soft.

3) Place mixture through sieve. Add rum. Place mixture back in saucepan over very low heat and keep warm.

4) Remove skewers from refrigerator. Heat butter and oil in large skillet over medium-high heat. Place skewers in pan and cook 2-3 minutes each side until lamb is cooked to at least medium-rare.

5) Place skewers on serving plate. Generously spoon glaze around skewers.

Per serving (approximate values): 439 Calories; 31.4g Fat (66.0% calories from fat); 15.5g Protein; 20.8g Carbohydrate; 86mg Cholesterol; 139mg Sodium.

HOT GREEK LEMON MARINADE FOR POULTRY

Makes 4 servings
Prep Time: 20 minutes

1 cup lemon juice
2 teaspoons garlic, minced
1 tablespoon cinnamon
1 tablespoon tomato paste
2 teaspoons dried oregano leaves
1 whole jalapeno, minced fine
Salt and pepper, to taste
2 pounds chicken breasts without skin, or turkey

1) In a small mixing bowl, combine all ingredients except poultry. Mix well.
2) Place chicken or turkey in a large sealable plastic bag and pour marinade over. Close plastic bag, squeezing out as much air as possible. Place bag in a pan, then in refrigerator for 2 to 3 hours. Turn frequently to ensure even distribution of marinade.
3) Remove chicken and discard marinade. Grill (or broil) chicken over medium heat for 7-9 minutes per side or until the juices run clear. Remove from grill and serve.

Per serving (approximate values): 232 Calories; 2.5g Fat (9.5% calories from fat); 42.8g Protein; 9.6g Carbohydrate; 105mg Cholesterol; 153mg Sodium.

THAI PORK

Makes 4 servings
Prep Time: 20 minutes

½ cup light molasses
½ cup soy sauce
2 tablespoons Thai red curry paste
1 tablespoon fresh ginger, peeled and grated
1 ½ pounds pork tenderloin
Thai Orange and Red Curry Sauce (recipe follows)

Preheat oven to 350 degrees.

1) Mix all ingredients except pork in glass mixing bowl or 2-quart baking dish. Place pork in marinade and turn to coat. Cover and place in refrigerator for at least an hour or up to 4 hours.
2) Remove pork from marinade. Discard marinade. Place pork in baking dish and roast until thermometer inserted into thickest portion registers 160 degrees, about 30 minutes.
3) Remove from oven and let rest at least 10 minutes.
4) Serve with Thai Orange and Red Curry Sauce.

Per serving (approximate values): 318 Calories; 8.4g Fat (23.9% calories from fat); 31.1g Protein; 29.3g Carbohydrate; 70mg Cholesterol; 2130mg Sodium.

THAI ORANGE AND RED CURRY SAUCE

Makes 6 servings
Prep Time: 45 minutes

3 cups orange juice
1 medium carrot, shredded
2 tablespoons cilantro, chopped fine
2 tablespoons ginger, peeled and grated
4 cloves garlic, minced
1 medium jalapeno pepper, minced
2 teaspoons ground cumin
1 tablespoon Thai red curry paste
1 tablespoon cornstarch
1 tablespoon water

1) Combine orange juice, carrot, cilantro, ginger, garlic, jalapeno, cumin and red curry paste in medium saucepan over medium-high heat. Boil mixture until carrot is tender and liquid is reduced by about a third. Stir occasionally, about 10 minutes.

2) Combine 1 tablespoon water with 1 tablespoon cornstarch in a small bowl until cornstarch is dissolved. Pour into hot orange mixture and stir until thick.

3) Serve over sliced Thai Pork tenderloin.

Per serving (approximate values): 78 Calories; 0.7g Fat (7.2% calories from fat); 1.7g Protein; 17.5g Carbohydrate; 0mg Cholesterol; 10mg Sodium.

ORANGE-CORIANDER MARINADE FOR BEEF

Makes 4 servings
Prep Time: 20 minutes

1 teaspoon orange peel, grated
¾ cup orange juice
1 small onion, minced
3 cloves garlic, minced
¼ cup white vinegar
1 ½ tablespoons ground coriander
1 teaspoon black pepper
1 teaspoon basil
2 pounds beef, grilling-favorite cut

1) Combine all marinade ingredients in medium mixing bowl. Mix well. Place beef in plastic sealable bags and pour marinade over. Squeeze air out, seal and refrigerate for up to four hours.

2) Remove meat from marinade and drain. Place on grill over hot fire. Cook, basting with marinade often, until meat is done to your liking.

3) While beef grills, take ½ cup of marinade and heat until hot. Serve to the side of grilled meat.

Per serving (approximate values): 618 Calories; 44.2g Fat (64.8% calories from fat); 42.7g Protein; 11.4g Carbohydrate; 152mg Cholesterol; 130mg Sodium.

GINGER-ORANGE MUSTARD GLAZE

Makes 6 servings
Prep Time: 15 minutes

¼ cup orange juice
¼ cup soy sauce
¼ cup sherry
¼ cup Dijon mustard
2 tablespoons fresh ginger, peeled and grated
2 tablespoons honey

1) Combine all ingredients in a medium mixing bowl. Marinate fish or poultry by placing it in a plastic sealable bag with the marinade.
2) For fish, marinate in the refrigerator for 30 minutes. For poultry, 2-3 hours.
3) Remove from marinade and grill or broil. Place marinade in saucepan and bring to a boil. Serve fish or poultry with hot glaze.

Per serving (approximate values): 55 Calories; 0.5g Fat (9% calories from fat); 1.2g Protein; 9.6g Carbohydrate; 0mg Cholesterol; 812mg Sodium.

DESSERTS

KEY LIME STRAWBERRY PIE

Key limes are a smaller version of the normal limes you find in the produce section of your supermarket. They have a unique flavor that you'll love to highlight in desserts that feature citrus! This dessert is super easy and super yummy!

Makes 6 servings
Prep Time: 30 minutes

1 whole pie crust, vanilla wafer cookie preferably
(pre-prepared)
2 pints fresh strawberries
8 ounces cream cheese, softened
14 ounces sweetened condensed milk
½ cup lime juice, key lime preferably

1) Wash strawberries. Cut off the stem ends of strawberries. Arrange cut side down on crust. Refrigerate.
2) Beat cream cheese until smooth. Add sweetened condensed milk. Beat well. Add lime juice and blend well.
3) Pour over strawberries into prepared crust. Refrigerate until firm, no less than 1 hour.
4) Cover with choice of whipped topping.

Per serving (approximate values): 534 Calories; 30g Fat (49% calories from fat); 9.8g Protein; 60.3g Carbohydrate; 75mg Cholesterol; 349mg Sodium.

ALMOND-BLUEBERRY SOUR CREAM PIE

Something about blueberries and sour cream that people love together. I love the combination, so I set out to again find just the right flavors for a perfect pie. I first served this for a large dinner party for friends involved in politics and have been serving it ever since.

Makes 8 servings
Prep Time: 30 minutes

1 9-inch deep-dish pie crust (frozen)
<u>Filling</u>:
1 cup sour cream
¾ cup granulated sugar
2 ½ tablespoons all-purpose flour
1 large egg, beaten
¾ teaspoon almond extract
¼ teaspoon salt
2 ½ cups fresh blueberries
<u>Topping</u>:
8 tablespoons all-purpose flour
¼ cup butter, chilled, cut into pieces
⅓ cup pecans, chopped
2 tablespoons sugar

Preheat oven to 375 degrees.

<u>Crust:</u>
1) Do not thaw pie crust. Take out of freezer, prick with a fork all over crust and bake until very light brown, about 10 minutes.
2) Let cool 15 minutes.

<u>Filling:</u>
1) Mix first six ingredients (sour cream through salt) in medium bowl to blend.
2) Mix in blueberries. Spoon into crust.
3) Bake until filling is just set, about 25 minutes. Remove from oven.

Topping:

1) Using food processor, pulse flour and butter until small clumps form.
2) Mix in pecans and sugar. Pulse until just blended. Place in small bowl. Mixture should be crumbly. If not, add more flour. Sprinkle over pie.
3) Bake in oven until topping browns lightly, about 15 minutes.
4) Refrigerate pie until ready to serve, at least 4 hours.

Per serving (approximate values): 399 Calories; 21.7g Fat (47.9% calories from fat); 4.8g Protein; 48.3g Carbohydrate; 55mg Cholesterol; 297mg Sodium.

APPLE-CINNAMON TART

Makes 6 servings
Prep Time: 30 minutes

¾ cup red cinnamon candies
2 tablespoons water
2 tablespoons light corn syrup
5 medium green apples, pared, sliced thin
2 tablespoons sugar
1 tablespoon butter
1 whole pie crust (9-inch)

Preheat oven to 375 degrees.

1) Heat candies, water, and corn syrup to boiling over medium heat in a medium saucepan. Reduce heat and simmer uncovered until candies are almost dissolved. Pour into 9-inch round pie pan.

2) Layer half of the apples, overlapping slices on candy mixture. Sprinkle with 1 tablespoon of sugar. Layer with remaining apples, then sprinkle with remaining sugar. Dot with butter.

3) Prepare pastry. Roll out (if not pre-prepared) to 10-inch circle. Carefully place over pan. Trim to fit pan, crimp.

4) Bake until crust is golden brown, 40 to 45 minutes. Cool at least one hour. Invert pie onto plate

Per serving (approximate values): 237 Calories; 10.1 g Fat (37.3% calories from fat); 2.2g Protein; 36g Carbohydrate; 5mg Cholesterol; 221 mg Sodium.

Chocolate Silk Tofu Pie

I was offered a recipe from a friend who insisted I try making a chocolate pie with tofu. Always up for a challenge, I have to admit I didn't at all like my first attempt. But I was intrigued with the concept, thus I continued to work on the recipe until I got it just right.

Makes 8 servings
Prep Time: 45 minutes

2 packages tofu, firm
1 ⅔ cups bittersweet chocolate chips or 1 ⅔ cups carob chips
3 tablespoons honey
1 tablespoon rum
1 teaspoon vanilla
Cinnamon
1 whole pie crust, vanilla wafer cookie preferably (pre-prepared)

1) Beat tofu with mixer at high speed until completely broken up and as smooth as possible, about 5 minutes.
2) Melt chips in microwave and cool slightly.
3) Add chocolate to tofu and blend completely. Add honey, rum and vanilla. Blend until all is completely incorporated.
4) Pour into pie crust and refrigerate for at least an hour.
5) Before serving, sprinkle cinnamon over entire pie until lightly coated.

Per serving (approximate values): 598 Calories; 35g Fat (49.5% calories from fat); 22.8g Protein; 57.5g Carbohydrate; 2mg Cholesterol; 89mg Sodium.

DUTCH APPLE PIE

Makes 6 servings
Prep Time: 45 minutes

Topping:
⅔ cup all-purpose flour
⅓ cup light brown sugar, packed
½ teaspoon cinnamon
⅛ teaspoon ground nutmeg
⅓ cup butter
Filling:
5 large Granny Smith apples, peeled, cored and quartered
2 tablespoons lime juice
¾ cup sugar
3 tablespoons sugar
3 tablespoons flour
1 teaspoon cinnamon
1 whole 9-inch deep-dish pie crust

Heat oven to 350 degrees.

Topping:
1) In medium bowl, combine flour, brown sugar, cinnamon and nutmeg.
2) With fork or pastry blender, cut in butter until mixture resembles coarse cornmeal.

Filling:
1) In a medium bowl, toss with lime juice.
2) In small bowl, combine sugar, flour and cinnamon. Toss gently with apples to combine.
3) Turn apple filling into unbaked pie shell. Spreading apples evenly, making sure there are no gaping holes in pie. Height of filling may seem unusually high, but it will all cook down.
4) Crumble topping evenly over apples. Bake 40 to 45 minutes or until apples are tender. Use a knife through the middle of the pie to determine tenderness. Remove to wire rack to cool.

Per serving (approximate values): 509 Calories; 18.6g Fat (32.1 % calories from fat); 4.1g Protein; 84.3g Carbohydrate; 27mg Cholesterol; 305mg Sodium.

GREEK HONEY AND CHEESE PIE

I have presented this Greek cheesecake as a host/hostess gift more than almost any other dessert. It's easy, it has fun flavors and it travels well.

Makes 8 servings
Prep Time: 45 minutes

<u>Crust:</u>
1 cup flour
⅓ cup butter, softened
1 tablespoon sugar
1 tablespoon sesame seeds, toasted
<u>Filling:</u>
16 ounces cream cheese, softened
2 large eggs
½ cup sugar
½ cup honey
¼ cup whipping cream
¼ teaspoon ground nutmeg

Preheat oven to 450 degrees.

Crust:
1) Place a small sauté pan over a medium heat and add sesame seeds. Stir until seeds are a golden brown color. You'll know they are done by the strong scent they emit as they cook. Make sure they've cooled before adding to other crust ingredients.
2) In a medium bowl, mix all crust ingredients until well blended. Press firmly and evenly against bottom and sides of 9-inch pie plate. Bake for 5 minutes.
3) Lower oven to 350 degrees.

Filling:
1) Beat cream cheese in large mixing bowl on medium speed until creamy. Add eggs at low speed one at a time until just combined.

2)   Add remaining ingredients. Beat until just combined. Pour into baked
     pie shell. Bake until firm, about 40 to 50 minutes. Refrigerate until
     serving time.

Per serving (approximate values): 491 Calories; 32.1 g Fat (57.4% calories from
fat); 7.9g Protein; 45.6g Carbohydrate; 147mg Cholesterol; 265mg Sodium.

PUMPKIN DUTCH APPLE PIE

Makes 8 servings
Prep Time: 45 minutes

Apple Layer:
1 9-inch deep dish pie crust
2 medium Granny Smith apples
¼ cup granulated sugar
2 teaspoons flour
1 teaspoon lime juice
¼ teaspoon cinnamon
Pumpkin Layer:
2 large eggs
1 ½ cups pumpkin, solid packed
1 cup evaporated milk
½ cup granulated sugar
2 tablespoons butter, melted
¾ teaspoon cinnamon
¼ teaspoon salt
⅛ teaspoon ground nutmeg
Crumb topping:
½ cup flour
⅓ cup walnuts, chopped
5 tablespoons granulated sugar

Preheat oven to 375 degrees.

Apple Layer:
1) Combine apples with sugar, flour, lime juice and cinnamon in medium bowl. Place in pie shell.

Pumpkin Layer:
1) Combine eggs, pumpkin, evaporated milk, sugar, butter, cinnamon, salt, and nutmeg in medium bowl. Pour over apples.
2) Bake in oven for 30 minutes.
3) While baking, combine ½ cup flour, ⅓ cup walnuts and 5 tablespoons sugar in medium bowl. Cut in butter until crumbly.

4) Remove pie from oven and sprinkle with crumb topping. Bake for 20 more minutes or until pie is set. Cool and refrigerate.

Per serving (approximate values): 373 Calories; 15.7g Fat (36.9% calories from fat); 7.6g Protein; 52.7g Carbohydrate; 71 mg Cholesterol; 292mg Sodium.

BANANA AND WALNUT PIE

Makes 8 servings
Prep Time: 30 minutes

6 medium bananas, very ripe
¼ cup sugar
1 tablespoon butter, melted
¾ cup walnuts, ground
½ cup raisins, soaked in rum
1 teaspoon ground allspice
¼ teaspoon ground nutmeg
½ teaspoon ground ginger
3 large egg whites, beaten till stiff
1 9-inch pie shell, unbaked

Preheat the oven to 425 degrees.

1) In a medium bowl, mash the bananas until smooth.
2) Add the sugar, butter, walnuts, raisins, allspice, nutmeg, and ginger and mix well. Fold in the egg whites.
3) Transfer the mixture to the pie shell and bake for 30 minutes.
4) Remove from the oven, sprinkle with allspice and cool before serving.

Per serving (approximate values): 321 Calories; 14.6g Fat (38.7% calories from fat); 6.7g Protein; 45.4g Carbohydrate; 4mg Cholesterol; 183mg Sodium.

HAWAIIAN CAKE

Makes 12 servings
Prep Time: 30 minutes

2 cups flour
2 cups sugar
16 ounces crushed pineapple in juice
2 large eggs
1 teaspoon baking soda
1 cup walnuts

Preheat oven to 350 degrees. Spray 9x13-inch baking pan with nonstick cooking spray.

1) In a large mixing bowl, mix all ingredients together. Pour into prepared pan.
2) Bake 35 to 40 minutes or until a toothpick inserted in the middle comes out clean.

Per serving (approximate values): 303 Calories; 7g Fat (20.1 % calories from fat); 5.9g Protein; 56.5g Carbohydrate; 36mg Cholesterol; 117mg Sodium.

GLORIOUSLY CHOCOLATE BUNDT CAKE

This is one of the more stunning desserts I've made for people. As more fun Bundt cake pan shapes appear on the market, the more fun it is to make a dessert like this. I have served this for many catered affairs.

Makes 16 servings
Prep Time: 1 hour 15 minutes

1 cup butter, softened
1 ½ cups sugar
4 large eggs
½ teaspoon baking soda
1 cup buttermilk
2 ½ cups flour
1 ½ cups semisweet chocolate chips, divided
⅓ cup chocolate syrup
8 ounces sweet chocolate squares, melted and cooled
2 teaspoons vanilla
4 ounces white chocolate
2 tablespoons shortening, divided

Preheat oven to 300 degrees. Grease and flour 10-inch Bundt cake pan.

1)   Cream butter in a large mixing bowl.
2)   Gradually add sugar. Beat well on medium speed of an electric mixer.
3)   Add eggs one at a time. Beat after each addition.
4)   In a small bowl, dissolve baking soda in buttermilk. Stir well.
5)   Add to buttermilk mixture to creamed mixture. Alternate additions with flour. Begin and end with flour.
6)   Add 1 cup chips, melted chocolate, chocolate syrup and vanilla. Stir until just blended. Do not over beat.
7)   Spoon batter into Bundt pan. Bake for approximately 70 minutes or until cake springs back when touched. Invert cake immediately onto serving platter and let cool completely.
8)   Combine 4 ounces white chocolate and 1 tablespoon shortening. Microwave until just melted.

9) Drizzle over the top of the cake. Work from the inside of the ring to the outside. Don't worry about the accumulation of chocolate in the center. It will make a fun candy surprise when the cake is finished. Make sure white chocolate has cooled completely before moving to next step.

10) Combine remaining ½ cup chips with 1 tablespoon shortening. Microwave until just melted.

11) Drizzle over white chocolate layer in the same manner, inside to outside. Pour any remaining in the center 'well'.

Per serving (approximate values): 505 Calories; 28.1 g Fat (47.3% calories from fat); 6.1 g Protein; 64.4g Carbohydrate; 85mg Cholesterol; 196mg Sodium.

CHOCOLATE ALMOND TORTE

Makes 16 servings
Prep Time: 30 minutes

Torte:
½ cup butter, melted
8 ounces semisweet chocolate, melted
½ cup powdered sugar
4 large eggs
½ cup almonds, finely ground
¼ cup all-purpose flour
½ cup sour cream
Frosting:
4 ounces semisweet chocolate, melted
2 tablespoons butter, melted
2 tablespoons honey

Heat oven to 350 degrees. Grease 9-inch round cake pan.

Torte:
1) In small saucepan, melt ½ cup butter and 8 ounces chocolate over low heat. Stir constantly until smooth. Set aside.
2) In a large mixing bowl, combine powdered sugar and eggs. Beat at high speed scraping bowl often until light in color and foamy.
3) Add all remaining torte ingredients. Continue beating, scraping bowl often, until well mixed.
4) Add chocolate mixture. Mix well. Spread into prepared pan.
5) Bake for 30 to 35 minutes or until firm to the touch. Do not over bake. Cool on wire rack for 30 minutes. Remove from pan by inverting on serving plate.

Frosting:
1) In small saucepan, melt 4 ounces chocolate, butter and honey over low heat. Stir constantly until smooth. Cool slightly.
2) Frost top and sides of torte with this chocolate mixture. Refrigerate at least one hour or until firm.

Per serving (approximate values): 254 Calories; 18.5g Fat (61.5% calories from fat); 3.9g Protein; 22.3g Carbohydrate; 76mg Cholesterol; 95mg Sodium.

Chocolate Torte with Raspberry Sauce

Makes 12 servings
Prep Time: 45 minutes

<u>Torte:</u>
2 ½ sticks butter
20 ounces semisweet chocolate
1 tablespoon vanilla
6 large eggs, room temperature
<u>Glaze:</u>
⅓ cup heavy cream
⅓ cup semisweet chocolate chips
<u>Raspberry sauce:</u>
24 ounces raspberries, frozen, unsweetened
½ cup sugar
2 tablespoons orange juice

Preheat oven to 400 degrees. Butter the bottom and sides of an 8 ½-inch spring form pan. Wrap the pan tightly in 2 layers of aluminum foil to keep the pan dry in the water bath. Place the spring form pan in a large roasting pan and set aside.

Torte:
1) In a double boiler, melt the butter and the chocolate. Stir until smooth. Remove from the heat and stir in the vanilla.
2) In a medium metal bowl, beat the eggs. Set the bowl over a pan of simmering water and whisk the eggs until they are warm, about 3 minutes.
3) Remove from the heat. Beat the eggs with an electric mixer at high speed until tripled in volume, about 4 to 5 minutes.
4) Transfer the chocolate mixture to a large bowl and add ¼ of the eggs. Mix thoroughly to lighten the chocolate.
5) Gently fold the remaining eggs into the chocolate mixture. Transfer immediately to the prepared spring form pan. Pour hot water into the roasting pan until it reaches halfway up the sides of the pan.
6) Bake for about 18 minutes. The center will not be set when removed from the oven. Remove from the water bath and cool to room temperature.

Glaze:

1) In a small saucepan, bring the cream to a simmer. Remove from the heat and add the chocolate chips.
2) Cover for 15 minutes. Uncover and stir the mixture until smooth. Let cool to room temperature.
3) Pour the glaze over the torte. Refrigerate the torte until firm, about 6-8 hours.

Sauce:

1) Drain the berries in a fine mesh sieve set over a bowl. Press gently on the berries to remove as much juice as possible.
2) Transfer the juice to a small saucepan over medium heat. Bring to a boil and reduce to about ⅓ cup.
3) Return the reduced juice to a medium bowl. Stir in the sugar and orange juice. Cover and refrigerate.
4) Run a knife around the edge of the torte to loosen it, then remove the sides of the spring form pan. Serve the chilled torte with the raspberry sauce.

Per serving (approximate values): 431 Calories; 23.3g Fat (45.0% calories from fat); 5.9g Protein; 58.2g Carbohydrate; 123mg Cholesterol; 65mg Sodium.

CHOCOLATE-CINNAMON BUNDT CAKE

I consider Bundt cakes similar to casseroles. They are a very versatile dish that can be altered in so many different ways. This is one where there is a surprise in the center of this cinnamon-flavored cake.

Makes 12 servings
Prep Time: 45 minutes

<u>Cake:</u>
⅔ cup semisweet chocolate chips
3 cups flour
1 ½ teaspoons baking powder
3 large eggs
2 cups sugar
1 cup vegetable oil
1 cup milk
1 teaspoon vanilla
4 teaspoons cinnamon
<u>Glaze:</u>
⅓ cup heavy cream
¼ cup butter
2 tablespoons light corn syrup
1 cup semisweet chocolate chips

Preheat oven to 325 degrees. Butter 10-inch tube or Bundt pan.

Cake:
1) Place chocolate chips in a microwave-safe container. Microwave about 45 seconds at high to melt. Stir to completely melt all chocolate.
2) Stir together flour and baking powder in medium bowl.
3) In separate large bowl, beat eggs until foamy.
4) Add sugar to eggs and beat until light and fluffy, about 3 minutes. Gradually beat in oil. The consistency will become somewhat like mayonnaise.
5) Beat in milk and vanilla. Add dry ingredients and beat until just blended.
6) Transfer 1 ½ cups batter to small bowl (or large measuring cup). Mix in melted (but slightly cooled) chocolate.

7) Mix cinnamon into remaining batter. Spread half of cinnamon batter into prepared pan. Spoon chocolate batter over. Top with remaining cinnamon batter. Using a knife, swirl batters to marbleize slightly.

8) Bake cake until tester inserted near center comes out clean, about 60 minutes. Cool completely. Remove from pan.

Glaze:

1) Combine cream, butter and corn syrup in heavy, medium saucepan. Stir over medium heat until mixture begins to simmer.

2) Remove from heat and add chocolate. Whisk until chocolate melts and glaze is smooth, about 3 minutes. Let cool until glaze thickens slightly but is still spreadable. Stir occasionally, about 30 minutes.

Presentation:

1) Place cake on platter. Spread or spoon glaze, depending on the consistency of the glaze, over cake.

Per serving (approximate values): 652 Calories; 35.9g Fat (47.7% calories from fat); 7g Protein; 81.6g Carbohydrate; 76mg Cholesterol; 119mg Sodium.

UPSIDE-DOWN CAKE WITH BANANAS AND MACADAMIA NUTS

Upside-down cakes scream comfort! Served warm with a dollop of whipped cream or scoop of ice cream, I have prepared them to finish many of my favorite meals.

Makes 8 servings
Prep Time: 30 minutes

Topping:
1 cup light brown sugar, packed
¼ cup butter, softened
3 tablespoons maple syrup
¼ cup Macadamia nuts, coarsely chopped
4 large bananas, cut diagonally, ¼-inch-thick slice

Cake:
1 cup flour
2 teaspoons baking powder
½ teaspoon cinnamon
¾ cup sugar
6 tablespoons butter, softened
1 large egg
¾ teaspoon vanilla
6 tablespoons milk

Preheat oven to 325 degrees.

Topping:
1) Combine sugar and butter in heavy medium saucepan. Stir over low heat until butter melts and mixture is well blended.
2) Pour into 9-inch cake pan. Spread to coat bottom completely.
3) Pour maple syrup over sugar mixture, then sprinkle nuts over syrup.
4) Place banana slices in a pattern overlapping slightly. Concentric circles are the easiest.

Cake:
1) Beat sugar and butter together in a medium mixing bowl until creamy.
2) Add egg and vanilla. Beat until light and fluffy.

3) In separate bowl, mix together flour, baking powder and cinnamon until well blended.

4) Alternate blending in the flour mixture and milk into the butter-egg mixture beginning and ending with the flour.

5) Spoon batter over bananas. Bake until tester inserted into the center of the cake comes out clean, about 35 minutes.

6) Transfer cake to place to cool down. Cool cake about 20 minutes.

7) Place plate over pan. Invert cake. Let stand about 3 minutes, then gently lift off pan. Serve warm!

Per serving (approximate values): 472 Calories; 17.9g Fat (33% calories from fat); 4.5g Protein; 77.3g Carbohydrate; 66mg Cholesterol; 261 mg Sodium.

UPSIDE-DOWN PLUM CAKE

Makes 8 servings
Prep Time: 40 minutes

Topping:
12 tablespoons butter, room temperature
1 cup light brown sugar, packed
2 tablespoons honey
6 small plums, cut in half; each half then cut into three wedges
Cake:
1 ½ cups all-purpose flour
2 teaspoons baking powder
½ teaspoon cinnamon
1 cup granulated sugar
2 large eggs
¾ teaspoon vanilla
¼ teaspoon almond extract
½ cup milk

Preheat oven to 350 degrees.

Topping:
1) Stir 6 tablespoons butter, brown sugar and honey in heavy medium saucepan over low heat until butter melts and a thick, smooth sauce develops.
2) Pour into a 9-inch cake pan.
3) Arrange plums in pleasant pattern on top of sauce. Set aside.

Cake:
1) Mix flour, baking powder, cinnamon in medium bowl.
2) Using electric mixer, beat remaining 6 tablespoons butter in large bowl until fluffy.
3) Add sugar and beat until creamy.
4) Add eggs and beat until light and fluffy. Beat in extracts.
5) Add dry ingredients alternately with milk, mixing until just blended. Pour batter evenly over plums. Bake cake until golden and toothpick

inserted in the middle comes out clean, about 45 minutes. Transfer to rack to cool for 20 minutes in pan.

6) Using knife, cut around pan sides to loosen cake. Place serving platter over cake pan. Invert cake. Let stand 5 minutes. Gently lift off pan. Serve cake warm or at room temperature.

Per serving (approximate values): 522 Calories; 19.6g Fat (32.9% calories from fat); 5.4g Protein; 84.6g Carbohydrate; 102mg Cholesterol; 366mg Sodium.

HOLIDAY PANETTONE

I first tried this Italian sweet bread while working at Williams-Sonoma. It came packaged in a tin, wrapped in paper. It was light in texture, yet had all the flavors of a fruitcake. It was delightful! This is my humble version.

Makes 6 servings
Prep Time: 30 minutes

3 ½ cups all-purpose flour
⅓ cup sugar
1 tablespoon active dry yeast
1 teaspoon salt
1 cup milk
½ cup butter
¼ cup honey
2 tablespoons orange zest, grated
1 tablespoon lemon zest, grated
½ teaspoon vanilla
¾ cup dried cranberries
¾ cup dried cherries
¾ cup dried apricots, diced

Preheat oven to 350 degrees. Generously butter two 1-lb coffee cans or other large 1-qt molds; or one 2-qt mold.

1) In a large bowl, stir together 1 ½ cups of the flour, sugar, yeast and salt. Set aside.
2) In a small saucepan, combine the milk, butter, honey, orange and lemon zests. Heat, stirring frequently, until a candy thermometer registers 125-130 degrees.
3) Using an electric mixer set on medium speed, gradually beat hot liquid into the flour mixture. Beat for 2 minutes.
4) Add the eggs, vanilla and ½ cup of the remaining flour. Beat on high speed 2 minutes longer.
5) Stir in enough of the remaining 1 ½ cups of flour to form a stiff batter.
6) Cover with plastic wrap and let rise until doubled, about 1 ¼ hours.
7) Stir down the batter, then mix in the cranberries, cherries and apricots.

8) Pour into the mold(s). Cover and let rise in a warm place until doubled, about an hour.

9) Position the rack in the lowest one-third of the oven. Bake until golden brown and a toothpick inserted in the center comes out clean, about 45 minutes for 2 small loaves or 55 minutes for 1 large loaf.

10) Cool in the molds on a rack for 5 minutes. Unmold. Place the bread on their sides on a rack to cool. Store tightly wrapped at room temperature for up to 2 days.

Per serving (approximate values): 557 Calories; 17.4g Fat (27.6% calories from fat); 10.5g Protein; 92g Carbohydrate; 46mg Cholesterol; 534mg Sodium.

SAVARIN

A yeast-leavened cake? Only the Italians could be so creative! The key to this refreshing treat is infusing the cake with syrup while still slightly warm, then chilled completely. With a selection of spring or summer fruits and a little whipped cream, you'll have them scrambling to get a piece!

Makes 10 servings
Prep Time: 1 hour

Cake
1 package dry yeast
½ cup warm water, 105-115 degrees
¾ cup butter
4 large eggs, beaten
2 tablespoons sugar
2 cups flour

Syrup
1 cup sugar
1 cup water
¼ cup orange liqueur
½ cup apricot preserves
2 tablespoons sugar

Preheat oven to 375 degrees.

Cake:
1) Dissolve yeast in warm water in 3-quart bowl.
2) Stir in eggs, butter, 2 tablespoons sugar and 1 cup of flour. Beat until smooth.
3) Stir in remaining flour until smooth. Beat 25 strokes.
4) Spread batter evenly into well-greased 8-cup metal ring mold or 10x4-inch tube pan. Cover and let rise in a warm place until almost double, about 1 hour.
5) Place in oven. Bake until golden brown on top, about 25-30 minutes. If top browns too much, cover loosely with aluminum foil.
6) Remove from oven and cool slightly for 10 minutes. Remove from mold. Cool slightly on wire rack.

Savarin Syrup:

1) Pour water into medium saucepan and add sugar. Heat to boiling, then reduce heat. Simmer uncovered 10 minutes. Cool to lukewarm. Stir in your favorite orange-flavored liqueur (my favorite), rum, or brandy.

2) While cake is still yet warm, take a toothpick and poke into the cake all over. This eases the infusion of syrup.

3) Pour syrup into a container with a spout. Slowly pour syrup over cake. Once all the syrup has been poured, wait about a minute for excess syrup to be absorbed.

4) Pour off syrup into spouted container. Pour over cake one more time.

Apricot Mixture:

1) Press apricot preserves through fine mesh strainer into small saucepan.

2) Heat preserves with 2 tablespoons sugar to boiling. Stir constantly. Reduce heat. Simmer uncovered until slightly thickened, 1 to 2 minutes. Cool 10 minutes.

3) Spread glaze over cake.

Per serving (approximate values): 401 Calories; 16g Fat (36.4% calories from fat); 5.8g Protein; 57g Carbohydrate; 123mg Cholesterol; 173mg Sodium.

MARINATED KEY LIME POUND CAKE

Makes 10 servings
Prep Time: 30 minutes

3 cups all-purpose flour
2 teaspoons baking powder
½ teaspoon salt
1 cup butter
2 cups granulated sugar
5 large eggs
1 cup milk
3 medium limes, zest grated
Glaze:
½ cup lime juice, Key lime juice, if available
½ cup sugar

Preheat oven to 350 degrees. Thoroughly butter a 10-inch tube pan.

1) Mix together flour, baking powder and salt in a medium bowl and set aside.
2) In a large bowl, beat the butter with an electric mixer until creamy. Gradually add sugar and beat until light and fluffy.
3) Beat in eggs one at time.
4) On the lowest speed, alternately add the dry ingredients and the milk to the butter mixture, beginning and ending with the dry ingredients. Beat to mix after each addition.
5) Stir in the grated lime zest. Pour the batter into prepared pan.
6) Bake about 90 minutes or until cake tester inserted near center comes out clean.
7) Remove pan from oven and let cool for 10 to 15 minutes.

Glaze:
1) Stir lime juice and sugar in bowl to mix.
2) Invert cake onto large platter. Using pastry brush, brush glaze all over warm cake until all is completely absorbed. Brush any glaze that drips back onto platter back onto cake.
3) Refrigerate until cold, about 3 hours.

Per serving (approximate values): 553 Calories; 21.9g Fat (34.9% calories from fat); 8.2g Protein; 83.9g Carbohydrate; 160mg Cholesterol; 410mg Sodium.

COCONUT PECAN CAKE WITH BROILED BROWN SUGAR TOPPING

The best way I like to describe this cake sounds a bit bizarre. I think it resembles pancakes and syrup, only in cake form. The crumb is very dense and the topping, while not syrup-like, reminds me of what syrup does after it has a chance to soak into pancakes.

Makes 15 servings
Prep Time: 30 minutes

<u>Cake:</u>
2 cups all-purpose flour
2 cups sugar
1 ½ cups butter, softened
1 cup buttermilk
4 large eggs
1 teaspoon baking soda
1 tablespoon vanilla
2 cups coconut
1 cup pecans, chopped
<u>Frosting:</u>
1 cup brown sugar, firmly packed
1 cup pecans, chopped
⅓ cup butter, melted
¼ cup whipping cream

Heat oven to 350 degrees.

Cake:
1) In large mixing bowl, combine all cake ingredients except coconut and pecans. Beat at low speed, scraping bowl often, until all ingredients are moistened.
2) Stir in coconut and pecans.
3) Pour into greased and floured 13x9-inch baking pan. Bake for 45 to 50 minutes or until cake springs back when lightly touched in the center and edges begin to pull away from sides of pan. Cool at least 15 minutes.

Frosting:

1) Heat broiler.
2) In a small bowl, stir together all frosting ingredients until well mixed. Spread over warm cake.
3) Broil 2 to 4 inches from heat until bubbly (1 to 3 minutes). Serve warm or cool.

Per serving (approximate values): 592 Calories; 38.7g Fat (57.3% calories from fat); 5.7g Protein; 59.2g Carbohydrate; 123mg Cholesterol; 354mg Sodium.

RAISIN CAKE

Makes 8 servings
Prep Time: 30 minutes

¾ cup granulated sugar
½ cup water
1 tablespoon cornstarch
1 cup raisins
½ cup pecans, chopped
½ cup butter
½ cup dark brown sugar
2 large eggs, beaten
2 cups all-purpose flour
1 ½ teaspoons cream of tartar
1 ½ teaspoons baking soda
½ cup milk
1 teaspoon vanilla

Preheat the oven to 350 degrees.

1) Combine ½ cup sugar, water, and cornstarch in a saucepan. Mix well and cook over low heat until mixture thickens, about 5 minutes.
2) Remove from heat. Add the raisins and pecans and set aside.
3) Beat the butter until soft. Add the remaining sugar and the brown sugar and beat until smooth.
4) Add the eggs and beat well.
5) In a medium bowl, sift together the flour, cream of tarter and baking soda. Add to the butter mixture along with the milk and vanilla. Beat until a smooth batter forms.
6) Spoon half of this batter into a greased 8-inch square pan.
7) Spread the raisin-pecan mixture over the batter. Cover with the remaining batter.
8) Bake for 50 minutes or until a dome forms in the middle.

Per serving (approximate values): 437 Calories; 18.1 g Fat (36.4% calories from fat); 6.5g Protein; 64.5g Carbohydrate; 87mg Cholesterol; 379mg Sodium.

PUMPKIN AND APRICOT TRIPLE LAYER CAKE

Makes 12 servings
Prep Time: 1 hour

<u>Apricot Purée</u>
1 ¼ cups apricot nectar
6 ounces dried apricots
6 tablespoons sugar
<u>Cake:</u>
2 cups cake flour
2 teaspoons baking powder
1 ¾ teaspoons cinnamon
½ teaspoon ground allspice
¾ teaspoon baking soda
½ cup Apricot Purée
¾ cup pumpkin, canned
¼ cup buttermilk
¾ cup butter, softened
1 ½ cups sugar
3 large eggs, room temperature
1 ¾ teaspoons vanilla
<u>Frosting:</u>
20 ounces cream cheese, softened
2 ½ cups powdered sugar
½ cup Apricot Purée
⅓ cup pumpkin, canned
½ teaspoon cinnamon
¼ teaspoon ground allspice

Preheat oven to 350 degrees. Grease three 8-inch round cake pans. Dust pans with flour.

Apricot Purée
1) Stir all ingredients in heavy medium saucepan over medium heat until sugar dissolves and mixture simmers.
2) Cover, lower heat and cook until apricots soften, about 6 minutes. Cool.
3) Transfer to a food processor and purée until almost smooth.
4) Refrigerate.

Cake:

1) Sift first 5 ingredients into medium bowl.
2) In a small bowl, blend apricot purée, pumpkin and buttermilk.
3) In a different large bowl, beat butter until fluffy with an electric mixer. Gradually add sugar, beating until well blended.
4) Add eggs one at a time. Beat well after each addition. Mix in vanilla.
5) Mix in dry ingredients, alternately with pumpkin mixture, beginning and ending with dry ingredients.
6) Divide batter equally among prepared pans. Smooth tops. Bake until cake tester comes out clean, about 25 minutes. Cool.

Frosting:

1) Using electric mixer, beat cream cheese and sugar in medium bowl until fluffy.
2) Add apricot purée, pumpkin and spices and beat until blended.

Assembly:

1) Loosen and turn out cakes.
2) Place 1 cake layer on platter. Spread 1 cup frosting over. Top with second layer. Spread 1 cup frosting over. Top with third cake layer. Spread remaining frosting over top and sides of cake. Refrigerate.

Per serving (approximate values): 557 Calories; 29.4g Fat (46.7% calories from fat); 7.2g Protein; 68.4g Carbohydrate; 137mg Cholesterol; 436mg Sodium.

New York Cheesecake

This is the number-one requested recipe of all I have ever prepared. I have several cheese-cakes I make, I have desserts more interesting, yet nothing seems to hit the comfort zone than this cheesecake. I don't know that it's the ingredients, as much as it is the proper preparation of the cheesecake. I have three major rules of thumb in its preparation. All ingredients must be room temperature, I beat the filling ingredients until just combined, no more, and I let the cheesecake cool completely in the oven before I remove it.

Makes 16 servings
Prep Time: 45 minutes

<u>Crust:</u>
1 cup all-purpose flour
¼ cup sugar
½ teaspoon vanilla
1 large egg yolk
¼ cup butter, softened
<u>Filling:</u>
40 ounces cream cheese, softened
1 ¾ cups sugar
3 tablespoons flour
1 teaspoon vanilla
5 large eggs
2 large egg yolks
¼ cup heavy cream

Heat oven to 400 degrees.

Crust:
1)   In a medium bowl, combine all crust ingredients. Blend in with fork until well mixed. Mixture should be like crumbs. If too moist, add additional flour as needed.
2)   Sprinkle ½ of mixture onto bottom of 9-inch spring form pan and pat down evenly. Spread remainder to evenly coat sides completely. Bake 6 minutes. Cool completely.

Filling:

1) In large mixing bowl, blend cheese, sugar, flour and vanilla at high speed until smooth and free of lumps.

2) Beat in eggs and yolks, one at a time, at slowest speed possible. Do not over beat.

3) Beat in cream. Pour into cooled crust.

4) Bake 10 minutes at 400 degrees.

5) Lower oven to 250 degrees and bake one hour longer.

6) Turn oven off and let cheesecake remain in oven for at least one hour or until completely cooled. Remove to rack to cool, about two hours more until room temperature.

7) Refrigerate 8 hours or overnight. Carefully loosen sides of pan. If there is any resistance, run a sharp knife around sides to loosen.

Per serving (approximate values): 451 Calories; 31.6g Fat (62.1% calories from fat); 8.9g Protein; 34.4g Carbohydrate; 198mg Cholesterol; 261 mg Sodium.

CARAMEL APPLE CHEESECAKE

Makes 16 servings
Prep Time: 1 hour

Crust:
3 cups graham cracker crumbs
¼ cup sugar
9 tablespoons butter, melted

Filling:
2 pounds cream cheese, room temperature
2 tablespoons cornstarch
16 ounces sour cream
½ cup orange juice
½ teaspoon vanilla
1 large egg yolk
4 large eggs

Topping:
½ cup butter
1 ½ pounds apples, Granny Smith, peeled cored, cut into ¼-inch-thick wedges
1 cup sugar
1 jar caramel topping

Preheat oven to 325 degrees.

For crust:
1) Combine graham cracker crumbs and sugar in medium bowl. Add melted butter and stir to blend.
2) Press mixture onto bottom and up sides of 10-inch spring form pan. Bake crust 7 minutes. Transfer pan to rack and let cool completely.

For filling:
1) Using electric mixer, beat cream cheese, sugar and cornstarch in large bowl until smooth.
2) Add sour cream, orange juice, and vanilla and beat until well blended.
3) Add eggs 1 at a time, beating until just blended after each.
4) Pour filling into crust. Bake cheesecake until center moves only slightly when shaken, about 70 minutes. Transfer to rack and let cool completely.

Topping:
1) Melt butter in large skillet over medium heat. Add sugar, stir 1 minute.
2) Add ⅓ of apples. Stir gently until apples are al dente. Drain and set on plate. Continue same process with remaining two-thirds apples.

Assembly:
1) Arrange apple wedges in overlapping concentric circles atop cheesecake.
2) Pour prepared caramel over top, spread evenly.
3) Cover with foil very loosely and refrigerate at least four hours.

Per serving (approximate values): 552 Calories; 41.1 g Fat (65.7% calories from fat); 8.3g Protein; 40g Carbohydrate; 175mg Cholesterol; 427mg Sodium.

ORANGE POPPY SEED CHEESECAKE

Makes 16 servings
Prep Time: 1 hour

Crust:
1 ⅔ cups graham cracker crumbs
½ cup almonds, chopped
½ cup butter, melted
Filling:
32 ounces cream cheese, softened
1 ½ cups sugar
3 tablespoons flour
4 large eggs
1 large egg yolk
¼ cup whipping cream
2 ounces marzipan, softened
2 teaspoons orange zest
2 teaspoons almond extract
2 teaspoons orange liqueur
½ cup orange juice, from frozen concentrate
3 tablespoons poppy seeds
Topping:
1 cup sour cream
⅓ cup sugar
2 tablespoons orange liqueur

Preheat oven to 400 degrees.

Crust:
1)   In food processor, chop almonds until finely ground. Add graham cracker crumbs and pulse until just combined.
2)   Add melted butter and pulse until well combined. Pat into the bottom and up the sides of 9-inch spring form pan.

Cheesecake:
1)   In a large mixing bowl, beat cream cheese, flour and sugar until light and fluffy. Beat in eggs at low speed, one at a time, until just combined. Do not over beat!

2) In food processor, purée marzipan, cream and orange zest.

3) Add to the cheese mixture. Mix in almond, orange liqueur, orange juice concentrate and poppy seeds. Mix well.

4) Pour batter into crust. Bake for 15 minutes. Reduce temperature to 225 degrees. Bake for 70 minutes, until set.

5) Mix together sour cream, sugar and liqueur. Spread over hot cheesecake and place back in oven for about 8 minutes.

6) Let cool in oven for 1 hour. Remove and let cool further, about 1 hour. Cover and refrigerate until serving.

Per serving (approximate values): 507 Calories; 35.9g Fat (63.1 % calories from fat); 8.8g Protein; 38.5g Carbohydrate; 156mg Cholesterol; 306mg Sodium.

PUMPKIN CHEESECAKE

I traditionally make this instead of pumpkin pie for Thanksgiving. It serves more and you can freeze the leftovers!

Makes 16 servings
Prep Time: 1 hour

<u>Crust:</u>
1 ½ cups graham cracker crumbs
⅓ cup butter, melted
¼ cup granulated sugar
<u>Cheesecake:</u>
24 ounces cream cheese, softened
1 cup granulated sugar
¼ cup brown sugar, packed
16 ounces pumpkin, solid packed
3 large eggs
1 large egg yolk
⅔ cup evaporated milk
2 tablespoons cornstarch
1 ¼ teaspoons cinnamon
½ teaspoon ground nutmeg
¼ teaspoon ground ginger
¼ teaspoon ground cloves
<u>Topping:</u>
16 ounces sour cream
⅓ cup granulated sugar
1 teaspoon vanilla
½ teaspoon cinnamon
¼ teaspoon ground nutmeg

Preheat oven to 350 degrees.

<u>*Crust:*</u>
1)   Combine graham cracker crumbs, butter and sugar in medium bowl.
2)   Press into bottom and 1 inch up the side of 9-inch spring form pan.
3)   Bake in oven for 8-10 minutes.

Cheesecake:
1) Beat cream cheese, sugar and brown sugar in large mixer bowl until fluffy.
2) Beat in pumpkin, eggs and evaporated milk. Add cornstarch, cinnamon and nutmeg and beat well. Pour into crust.
3) Bake at same temperature for 55 to 60 minutes or until edge is set, but center still moves slightly.

Topping:
1) Combine sour cream, granulated sugar and vanilla in small bowl. Spread over surface of warm cheesecake. Bake at 350 degrees for 8 minutes more.
2) Cool in pan on wire rack. Chill for several hours or overnight.

Per serving (approximate values): 410 Calories; 27.5g Fat (59.1 % calories from fat); 7g Protein; 35.88 Carbohydrate; 126mg Cholesterol; 252mg Sodium.

TROPICAL CHEESECAKE

Makes 12 servings
Prep Time: 30 minutes

Crust:
1 ⅓ cups graham cracker crumbs
¼ cup butter, melted
2 tablespoons sugar
Filling:
1 cup sugar
32 ounces cream cheese, softened
4 large eggs
1 cup sour cream
15 ¼ ounces crushed pineapple in juice, drained
1 cup coconut flakes
Topping:
½ cup coconut, toasted

Heat oven to 325 degrees.

Crust:
1)   In small bowl, stir together all crust ingredients.
2)   Press crumb mixture evenly onto bottom of 9-inch spring form pan.
3)   Bake 7 minutes. Cool.

Filling:
1)   In large mixing bowl, combine 1 cup sugar and cream cheese. Beat at medium speed, scraping bowl often, until light and creamy.
2)   Continue beating, adding eggs 1 at a time, until well mixed. Do not over beat!
3)   Add sour cream, drained pineapple and 1 cup coconut. Continue beating, scraping bowl often, until well mixed.
4)   Spoon filling into prepared crust. Bake for 70 minutes or until set.
5)   Sprinkle top with toasted coconut. Turn oven off, leave cheesecake in oven 2 hours. Refrigerate 8 hours or overnight.

Per serving (approximate values): 540 Calories; 39.8g Fat (64.9% calories from fat); 9.5g Protein; 38.8g Carbohydrate; 173mg Cholesterol; 367mg Sodium.

WHITE CHOCOLATE-DARK CHOCOLATE CHEESECAKE

My poor sister! I served this cheesecake last at the 'Spring Dinner Photo Shoot', when I prepared several dishes from this book for friends and family (find out more at www.thisisdeliciouswhatisit.com). While everyone enjoyed the dinner, this dessert was especially appealing. So much so that when leaving the party, my brother-in-law, Rick, asked to take some home with he and my sister. As they were getting in the car, the leftover piece of cheesecake fell onto the street. Much to my sister's dismay, Rick attempted to recover the now smashed dessert to yet take home with him. Needless to say, my sister had to put her foot down. Now that's true culinary love!

Makes 16 servings
Prep Time: 1 hour

<u>Crust:</u>
3 cups chocolate wafer cookies crumbs
¼ cup sugar
10 tablespoons butter, melted
<u>Filling:</u>
2 ½ pounds cream cheese, softened
1 ¼ cups sugar
¼ cup flour
1 teaspoon vanilla
5 large eggs
2 large egg yolks
¼ cup half and half
8 ounces white chocolate, melted, cooled
<u>Glaze:</u>
¼ cup light corn syrup
3 tablespoons water
2 tablespoons butter
1 cup semisweet chocolate chips

Preheat oven to 400 degrees.

Crust:

1) Mix cookie crumbs and sugar in medium bowl. Add melted butter and stir to blend.
2) Press mixture onto the bottom and up the sides of a 9- or 10-inch spring form pan.
3) Refrigerate while preparing filling.

Filling:

1) Using electric mixer, beat cream cheese in large bowl until smooth.
2) Add sugar, flour and vanilla and beat until well blended.
3) Add eggs and yolks, one at a time, beating until just blended after each addition (Too much beating results in a cracked surface).
4) Stir in half and half. Fold in white chocolate.
5) Pour mixture into crust. Bake for 10 minutes.
6) Lower oven temperature to 300 degrees. Bake 60 minutes longer or until filling is set. Turn oven off and let set in oven an hour longer.
7) Remove from oven. Let cool at room temperature at least an hour, then refrigerate until ready to glaze.

Glaze:

1) Stir corn syrup, water and butter in heavy medium saucepan until butter melts. Bring to a boil.
2) Remove from heat and add chocolate. Whisk until melted and smooth. Cool slightly, about 15 minutes.
3) Pour over top of completely cooled cheesecake. Smooth into a pleasant pattern. Refrigerate until ready to serve.
4) Once ready to serve, wait 15 minutes to soften.

Whatever you do, do not skimp on your white chocolate selection! Buy the best quality you can afford. It makes a huge difference in the texture and taste of the filling. The darker chocolate you need not be so concerned about, although you want to make sure you buy semisweet prepared with vanilla, not vanillin (artificial).

Per serving (approximate values): 783 Calories; 51.2g Fat (56.7% calories from fat); 12.2g Protein; 75.9g Carbohydrate; 197mg Cholesterol; 583mg Sodium.

BANANAS FOSTER CHEESECAKE

Makes 12 servings
Prep Time: 1 hour 30 minutes

Crust:
¼ cup butter
9 whole graham crackers
2 tablespoons sugar
1 package ladyfinger cookies

Bananas Foster Filling:
¼ cup sliced almonds, toasted
¼ cup butter
½ cup dark brown sugar
2 tablespoons banana liqueur
2 tablespoons dark rum
⅛ teaspoon cinnamon
½ teaspoon vanilla
4 medium bananas

Cream Cheese Layers:
5 large eggs
1 ½ pounds cream cheese, softened
1 cup sugar
4 tablespoons banana liqueur
1 teaspoon vanilla

Praline topping:
1 ½ cups pecans, toasted
1 cup butter
1 cup dark brown sugar
1 ½ tablespoons water

Preheat oven to 350 degrees. Butter a 9-inch spring form pan. Wrap outside of entire pan with a large heavy sheet of aluminum foil.

Crust:
1) Melt butter in microwave, cool slightly.
2) In a food processor, finely grind graham crackers with granulated sugar. Add butter, blend until well combined.

3) Press crumb mixture evenly onto the bottom of the spring form pan.
4) Take ladyfingers out of the package. With a sharp knife, cut a small section of one end of the cookies so that a flat, level edge is formed. You are going to place the cookies so that they line the sides of the pan, so do not cut too much off. Place the cookies rounded edge out—it will look wonderful at serving time.

Bananas Foster filling:
1) In a 10 to 12-inch nonstick skillet, melt butter with brown sugar over medium heat, stirring until smooth.
2) Stir in liqueur, rum, cinnamon and vanilla. Whisk until sugar is dissolved. Remove skillet from heat.
3) Traditional Bananas Foster has a very traditional manner of slicing the bananas at an angle. That presentation is lost here when used in a filling. I suggest simply slicing the bananas about ¼-inch thick.
4) Add bananas to butter mix and just barely cook, at the most a minute. Remove from heat, add almonds.

Cream Cheese layers:
1) In a small mixing bowl, whisk eggs until just combined.
2) In a large mixing bowl, beat the cream cheese and the sugar with an electric mixer until smooth.
3) On the mixer's lowest speed, add half the egg mixture until just combined.
4) Add remaining eggs, liqueur and vanilla. Beat again until just combined.

Prepare cheesecake for baking:
1) Pour half of cream cheese filling into spring form pan. Bake in oven for 10 minutes.
2) Remove from oven, cool for 5 minutes.
3) Gently spoon Bananas Foster filling over cream cheese layer. Make sure to evenly distribute bananas over the top.
4) Pour remaining cream cheese filling over the banana filling.
5) Place spring form pan in large roasting pan. Add enough hot water to reach at least an inch on the spring form pan.
6) Bake cheesecake in preheated oven for 50 minutes. Turn oven off, let cheesecake cool in oven for at least an hour. Do not be tempted to open the oven door.
7) Remove cheesecake from oven. Refrigerate until ready to serve.

Praline Topping:
1) In a small to medium heavy saucepan, melt butter with brown sugar over moderate heat, stirring constantly until smooth.
2) Add water. Stir until incorporated.
3) Cool to room temperature.

Final touches:
1) Place pecan halves in decorative pattern on top of cheesecake. Pour Praline Topping to form a even thin layer over the top. Pour too much and the cheesecake will be difficult to cut when chilled.
2) Take any extra pecans and add to the remaining topping.
3) Cover cheesecake and place back in refrigerator for at least 15 minutes to let topping harden.
4) Serve the remaining praline topping on the side or use as a decorative finish to the plate.

Per serving (approximate values): 732 Calories; 56.1g Fat (68.6% calories from fat); 9.6g Protein; 48g Carbohydrate; 217mg Cholesterol; 458mg Sodium.

RHUBARB PUDDING

Nothing reminds me of my childhood more than rhubarb. My relatives in Brainerd (Minnesota—my birthplace) create all sorts of delicious goods based on the tart stalks of the plant. This is a very simple sauce that I love to eat alone or over vanilla ice cream.

Makes 6 servings
Prep Time: 30 minutes

1 ¾ cups water
¾ cup sugar
1 ½ cups rhubarb, cut ½ inch thick
¼ cup cold water
3 tablespoons cornstarch
½ teaspoon vanilla

1) In medium-size saucepan, heat 1 ¾ cups water and ¾ cup sugar to boiling, stirring occasionally.
2) Add rhubarb. Simmer uncovered until rhubarb is tender, 10-15 minutes.
3) In a small bowl, mix ¼ cup water with cornstarch. Stir into rhubarb.
4) Boil and stir 1 minute. Add vanilla. Take off heat and let cool slightly.
5) Pour mixture into container and cover. Place in refrigerator and chill until ready to serve.

Per serving (approximate values): 119 Calories; 0.1 g Fat (0.4% calories from fat); 0.3g Protein; 30.1 g Carbohydrate; 0mg Cholesterol; 4mg Sodium.

STEAMED APPLE PUDDING

This recipe is a variation of the traditional British Plum Pudding. I fell in love with it the first time I tried it! It's like a bread pudding, only prettier to present, due to the use of a steamed pudding mold. This is a special type of mold that comes with a cover. Most cooking specialty stores carry at least one version of this special type of mold.

Makes 12 servings
Prep Time: 30 minutes

⅓ cup granulated sugar
5 tablespoons butter, softened
2 large eggs
⅓ cup light molasses
⅓ cup honey
1 ½ tablespoons lemon rind, grated
¾ cup plain yogurt
1 teaspoon vanilla
2 cups flour
1 ½ teaspoons baking powder
1 teaspoon cinnamon
½ teaspoon baking soda
¼ teaspoon salt
3 medium Granny Smith apples, peeled, cubed into ½-inch pieces

Butter well a 1 ½-quart steamed pudding mold and coat it liberally with sugar. Make sure not to forget the inside of the lid.

1) In a large mixing bowl, cream sugar and butter until light and fluffy.
2) Add eggs, one at a time, beating well after each.
3) Add molasses, honey, lemon rind and mix until well blended. Set aside.
4) In a small bowl, mix yogurt with vanilla.
5) In a medium bowl, sift together flour, baking powder, cinnamon, baking soda and salt.
6) Add flour mixture to butter mixture, alternating with the yogurt, beginning and ending with flour. Stir in apples. Transfer the mixture by spoonfuls to the mold.

7) Cover the mold and secure. Place the mold on a rack or inverted heat-proof plate placed at the bottom of a kettle or stockpot. Add enough boiling water to reach two-thirds of the way up the sides of the mold. Return the water to a boil, cover the kettle or stockpot and steam the pudding over very low heat for 2 hours.

8) Remove the mold from the kettle or stockpot. Remove the lid. Let the pudding cool for 15 minutes.

9) Place serving plate on top of the mold and quickly flip it over. Tap top of mold all around with blunt object to insure a clean unmolding. Slowly and carefully unmold pudding.

10) Serve hot or cover and refrigerate for at least 3 hours. Serve cold.

Per serving (approximate values): 229 Calories; 6.3g Fat (24.3% calories from fat); 3.9g Protein; 40.3g Carbohydrate; 51 mg Cholesterol; 211 mg Sodium.

CHOCOLATE ESPRESSO PUDDING CAKE

Puddings cakes are making a comeback! They are so much fun to make: the cake floats to the top and a delicious chocolate pudding forms at the bottom. Serve it warm with vanilla ice cream. Don't even think of buying the new packaged versions!

Makes 8 servings
Prep Time: 15 minutes

1 cup brown sugar, packed, divided
1 cup all-purpose flour
5 tablespoons unsweetened cocoa powder, divided
1 ½ tablespoons instant coffee powder, divided
1 ½ teaspoons baking powder
½ teaspoon baking soda
½ cup evaporated skim milk
¼ cup vegetable oil
1 teaspoon vanilla
1 cup boiling water

Preheat oven to 350 degrees.

1) Combine ½ cup brown sugar, flour, 2 tablespoons cocoa, 1 tablespoon instant coffee powder, baking powder and baking soda in a medium bowl. Mix well.

2) In separate small bowl, combine milk, oil and vanilla. Add to flour mixture and stir well. Spoon mixture into 8-inch square baking pan.

3) Combine remaining ½ cup brown sugar, 3 tablespoons cocoa and ½ tablespoon instant coffee powder. Stir well. Sprinkle over batter.

4) Pour boiling water over batter, distributing evenly as possible. DO NOT STIR. Bake at 350 degrees for 40 minutes. Cake will be difficult to determine when done. Touch center and if it springs back at all, it should be ready. Serve cake warm!

Per serving (approximate values): 245 Calories; 7.5g Fat (26.4% calories from fat); 3.6g Protein; 43.1 g Carbohydrate; 1mg Cholesterol; 178mg Sodium.

BREAD PUDDING WITH COCONUT AND APRICOTS

Makes 10 servings
Prep Time: 45 minutes

1 pound French bread loaf, cut to 1-inch cubes
1 cup sweetened coconut, shredded
3 ounces dried apricots, sliced thin
3 cups cream of coconut, (Coco Lopez)
2 cups whole milk
½ cup sugar
1 tablespoon vanilla
6 large eggs

Preheat oven to 350 degrees.

1) Arrange bread cubes in a single layer on a baking sheet. Place in oven with door slightly ajar and let bread dry until hard on the outside, but somewhat soft on the inside. Remove from oven.

2) Place half of cubes in 9x13-inch greased glass baking pan. Sprinkle over half the coconut and all of the apricots. Top with remaining bread cubes, then coconut.

3) Combine cream of coconut, milk, sugar and vanilla in medium saucepan. Stir over medium heat until sugar is dissolved and mixture is just warm. Remove from heat.

4) Whisk eggs in large bowl to blend. Pour in warm milk mixture. Pour entire mixture over bread. Using back of spoon, push bread cubes into milk mixture. Make sure each has been soaked. Let stand 15 minutes.

5) Bake until pudding is set and golden brown, about 50 minutes or until knife inserted comes out clean. Transfer to rack and let cool completely. Refrigerate until ready to serve.

Per serving (approximate values): 290 Calories; 8.8g Fat (27.1 % calories from fat); 9.9g Protein; 43.1 g Carbohydrate; 136mg Cholesterol; 341 mg Sodium.

BANANA AND WHITE CHOCOLATE BREAD PUDDING

Makes 12 servings
Prep Time: 45 minutes

16 ounces white chocolate
4 cups light cream
½ cup granulated sugar
8 large eggs, lightly beaten
1 tablespoon vanilla
6 tablespoons butter, softened
¾ pound French bread loaf, ¾-inch slices, dried
2 whole bananas, peeled, sliced
2 teaspoons cinnamon
2 tablespoons brown sugar

Preheat the oven to 350 degrees. Lightly butter a 9x13-inch baking dish.

1) Place the chocolate in a medium bowl. In a large heavy saucepan, bring the cream and granulated sugar to a simmer. Pour the hot cream over the chocolate. Let stand, uncovered, for 5 minutes, then stir until smooth.
2) Beat the eggs and vanilla into the chocolate mixture.
3) Butter the bread slices and then cut into cubes. Layer half the bread into the bottom of the prepared baking dish.
4) Top the bread layer with the banana slices. Top with the remaining bread.
5) Pour in the custard. Press the top of the pudding gently with a spatula to be sure the bread at the top soaks up some of the custard. Cover the dish with aluminum foil.
6) Bake the pudding for 45 minutes or until the custard is set.
7) Meanwhile, in a small bowl, combine the brown sugar and cinnamon.
8) When the pudding is set, remove foil and sprinkle evenly with cinnamon topping. Return to the oven.
9) Increase the oven temperature to 450 degrees and bake for 3 to 4 minutes, until top is browned and caramelized.
10) Cool slightly and serve warm with whipped cream.

Per serving (approximate values): 555 Calories; 38.3g Fat (59.6% calories from fat); 10.6g Protein; 47.9g Carbohydrate; 212mg Cholesterol; 312mg Sodium.

COCONUT DATE PUDDING

Makes 6 servings
Prep Time: 45 minutes

---

5 tablespoons butter
¾ cup sugar
4 ounces dates, finely chopped
1 cup shredded coconut meat
1 cup water
1 teaspoon baking soda
2 large eggs
1 large egg yolk
1 ⅓ cups flour
2 teaspoons baking powder
1 teaspoon vanilla

Preheat oven to 375 degrees. Butter 6 muffin tins, then sprinkle with sugar.

1) Combine the dates, coconut and water in a saucepan over high heat. Bring the mixture to a boil.
2) Remove the pan from the heat. Stir in the baking soda and set aside.
3) Cream 4 tablespoons butter in mixing bowl.
4) Beat in ¾ cup sugar gradually until mixture is light and fluffy.
5) Beat in eggs, one at a time.
6) Stir in baking powder, then flour, alternating with coconut mixture. Add vanilla.
7) Spoon mixture into tins and cover with buttered aluminum foil.
8) Bake the puddings about 20 minutes.
9) Remove from oven. Let the puddings cool for 5 minutes, then unmold onto individual plates. Serve with caramel sauce and sprinkle with toasted macadamia nuts and/or toasted coconut.

Per serving (approximate values): 413 Calories; 16.8g Fat (35.8% calories from fat); 6.3g Protein; 61.6g Carbohydrate; 133mg Cholesterol; 455mg Sodium.

CINNAMON-ENCRUSTED BREAD PUDDING WITH SABAYON

Royalty among comfort foods, bread puddings can comfort in so many different ways! While the pudding portion of this recipe is quite traditional, the sabayon is what makes this dessert my dad's favorite!

Makes 8 servings
Prep Time: 1 hour

1 ¾ cups sugar
½ teaspoon vanilla
2 large eggs
3 large egg yolks
1 cup half and half
1 cup heavy cream
1 whole French bread loaf, ½-inch pieces
2 teaspoons cinnamon
<u>Sabayon</u>
5 large egg yolks
1 cup sugar
½ cup brandy
1 cup heavy cream, chilled

Preheat oven to 350 degrees.

1) In a large bowl, whisk together 1 cup sugar, vanilla, whole eggs, yolks, half and half and cream.

2) Arrange the bread cubes in a well buttered 10-inch round glass baking dish at least 2 inches deep (2 ½ quarts). Pour custard over. Submerge bread cubes in custard and let mixture stand for at least 30 minutes.

3) In a small bowl, combine remaining ¾ cup sugar and cinnamon. Sprinkle evenly over the custard.

4) Place the baking dish in a larger pan. Add enough hot water to reach halfway up the side of the baking dish. Bake the custard for about 45 minutes, until a knife inserted comes out clean.

5) Remove custard and let cool. Refrigerate until well chilled.

Sabayon:

1) In a large stainless steel bowl set over a pan of boiling water, whisk together the yolks, the sugar and the brandy until the mixture is thick and pale and registers 160 degrees on a candy thermometer.

2) In a large chilled stainless or glass bowl, beat the cream until it holds a stiff peak.

3) Add a little of the custard to the whipped cream to soften it. Then add the lightened custard mixture into the whipped cream, making sure to incorporate it gently.

4) Chill the sauce completely.

Per serving (approximate values): 780 Calories; 33.6g Fat (40% calories from fat); 11.5g Protein; 102.1 g Carbohydrate; 359mg Cholesterol; 404mg Sodium.

PEANUT BUTTER PUDDING WITH CHOCOLATE SAUCE

Makes 4 servings
Prep Time: 45 minutes

6 tablespoons water
4 tablespoons sugar
4 ounces bittersweet chocolate, chopped
1 cup peanut butter, creamy
½ cup mascarpone cheese
½ cup sweetened condensed milk
2 tablespoons dark rum
2 ½ cups heavy cream

1) In a medium saucepan, cook water and sugar over moderate heat, stirring until sugar is dissolved.

2) Add chocolate and heat, stirring 1 minute, until smooth and slightly thickened. Cool sauce completely.

3) In a medium bowl, stir together peanut butter, mascarpone, condensed milk, rum and ½ cup cream until smooth.

4) In a chilled metal bowl, with an electric mixer beat remaining two cups of cream until it holds a stiff peak.

5) Fold in 1 ½ cups whipped cream into peanut butter mixture. Reserve remaining whipped cream for topping.

6) In a stemmed glass, layer mousse with chocolate sauce. Garnish with remaining whipped cream and peanuts.

Per serving (approximate values): 1291 Calories; 112.8g Fat (74.9% calories from fat); 25.6g Protein; 59.4g Carbohydrate; 236mg Cholesterol; 426mg Sodium.

RUM-BANANA BAKE

Makes 4 servings
Prep Time: 20 minutes

4 ounces cream cheese
¼ cup packed brown sugar
¼ cup rum
3 tablespoons whipping cream
⅛ teaspoon cinnamon
4 medium bananas
1 tablespoon butter

Preheat oven to 325 degrees.

1) Place cream cheese, brown sugar, rum, cream and cinnamon in blender. Cover and blend on high speed until smooth.
2) Unpeel bananas and slice in half length-wise.
3) Place half the bananas cut side down into 1-quart baking dish. Dot with half of butter, then spread half of cheese mixture evenly over bananas. Place remaining sliced bananas over first layer, then remaining cheese mixture.
4) Bake uncovered until hot and bubbly, about 20-25 minutes.

Per serving (approximate values): 351 Calories; 17.4g Fat (46.7% calories from fat); 3.6g Protein; 41.2g Carbohydrate; 54mg Cholesterol; 124mg Sodium.

RASPBERRY BAVARIAN

Makes 6 servings
Prep Time: 30 minutes

14 ounces raspberries, frozen, in juice
1 package raspberry gelatin powder, sugar-free
1 ¾ cups evaporated milk, reduced fat
1 cup fresh raspberries

1) Drain raspberries over a bowl, reserving juice. Add enough water to juice to make 1 ¼ cups.

2) In a saucepan over medium-low heat, stir in juice mixture and gelatin. Once gelatin is completely dissolved, remove from heat and set aside to cool completely.

3) In a large bowl, beat evaporated milk until thick and frothy.

4) Add raspberries and cooled gelatin mixture in a thin stream, folding so as to fully incorporate into whipped milk.

5) Pour into 2-quart glass serving dish or bowl. Cover and refrigerate until set. Unmold and serve. This is the classic manner in which a Bavarian is prepared.

6) You might also want to pour the mixture into a freezable container, cover and freeze until set. When ready to serve, let warm for about five minutes, scoop and serve.

Per serving (approximate values): 230 Calories; 5.8g Fat (21.8% calories from fat); 6.8g Protein; 39.9g Carbohydrate; 22mg Cholesterol; 114mg Sodium.

TROPICAL TRIFLE

My mom first introduced me to the world of trifles, the quintessential British layered dessert. This was her dessert of choice to bring to pot luck events. It's another dessert that looks pretty and serves many. This version adds a Hawaiian twist.

Makes 6 servings
Prep Time: 45 minutes

15 ounces condensed milk, sweetened
1 ½ cups milk
2 large egg yolks, beaten
3 tablespoons cornstarch
½ teaspoon vanilla
1 whole angel food cake, 9-inch
1 cup pineapple juice
⅓ cup rum
15 ounces crushed pineapple in juice, drained
1 cup coconut flakes
1 cup heavy cream, whipped

1) In a double boiler, combine the condensed milk, milk, egg yolks, cornstarch and vanilla. Cook, stirring constantly, over boiling water until the mixture thickens.

2) Cook for 10 minutes at a simmer without stirring, then remove from the heat and cool.

3) Cut or tear the angel food cake into 2-inch sections and place in a serving bowl.

4) Combine the pineapple juice and rum and sprinkle mixture over the cake squares.

5) Cover with one-half of the custard mixture, then one-half of the pineapple, then one-half of the coconut. Cover with the remaining custard mixture and top with whipped cream.

6) Garnish with remaining coconut and pineapple.

Per serving (approximate values): 846 Calories; 29g Fat (31.2% calories from fat); 16.3g Protein; 127.4g Carbohydrate; 158mg Cholesterol; 911 mg Sodium.

APRICOT PURÉE

Makes 1 serving
Prep Time: 30 minutes

1 ¼ cups apricot nectar
6 ounces dried apricots
6 tablespoons sugar

1) Stir all ingredients in heavy medium saucepan over medium heat until sugar dissolves and mixture simmers.
2) Cover and cook until apricots soften, about 6 minutes. Cool.
3) Transfer to processor and purée until almost smooth. Refrigerate.

Use as a topping for pancakes or waffles.

Per serving (approximate values): 870 Calories; 1.1 g Fat (1% calories from fat); 7.4g Protein; 225.1 g Carbohydrate; 0mg Cholesterol; 27mg Sodium.

RED WINE RED RASPBERRY SAUCE

Makes 8 servings
Prep Time: 1 hour

1 bottle good red wine (3 cups)
12 ounces raspberries, frozen, unsweetened
1 ½ cups sugar
1 whole vanilla beans, split lengthwise, halved
1 tablespoon cornstarch
1 tablespoon water

1) In a heavy non-aluminum saucepan over medium heat, combine the wine, berries, sugar and vanilla bean. Stir until the sugar dissolves, then simmer for 10 minutes.

2) Raise the heat to medium-high and boil until mixture is reduced to 2 ½ cups, about 30 minutes. Remove from the heat.

3) Pour the berry mixture through a sieve into a bowl, pressing on the berries with the back of a wooden spoon to extract as much pulp as possible. Retrieve the vanilla bean and rinse.

4) Return the sauce to the pan, along with the vanilla bean pieces. Bring to a boil.

5) Combine 1 tablespoon cornstarch with water. Add to the sauce. Stir about 1 minute until thickened. Pour into a covered container, ensuring the vanilla bean pieces have been removed. Store in the refrigerator.

Use on pound cake, over ice cream, on pancakes or waffles!

Per serving (approximate values): 172 Calories; 0.2g Fat (1.2% calories from fat); 0.4g Protein; 43.3g Carbohydrate; 0mg Cholesterol; 3mg Sodium.

BRANDIED CHERRIES

Makes 16 servings
Prep Time: 30 minutes

4 pounds cherries, frozen or fresh
1 cup granulated sugar
¼ cup water
4 cups brandy

1) Place cherries in medium saucepan. Add the sugar and water and bring to a boil over medium heat.

2) Reduce heat and cook slowly until a thick syrup forms, about 15 minutes. Remove from heat. Let cool at least 30 minutes.

3) Add brandy, stir thoroughly. Pour cherries and liquid into large container. Cover. Store in a cool dark place for 1 month before using cherries.

4) When ready, ladle cherries with an appropriate amount of brandy into smaller jars for storing or gift giving.

Per serving (approximate values): 236 Calories; 0.5g Fat (3.4% calories from fat); 1.1 g Protein; 30.6g Carbohydrate; 0mg Cholesterol; 2mg Sodium.

Poached Dried Fall Fruits in Wine and Honey

I was desperate to create an elegant fall dessert specifically for my second 'cooking lesson dinner party'. I went and bought every dried fruit I could find, a couple of white wines and experimented until I dropped. You may have a hard time finding certain dried fruits, so feel free to experiment with what you happen to find on your grocery store's shelves.

Makes 6 servings
Prep Time: 45 minutes

1 ½ cups white wine, Gewurztraminer
2 tablespoons honey, or to taste
2 teaspoons aniseed
Zest of 1 lemon
½ pound dried apricots
½ pound dried pears (if you can't find dried pears, try dried mango)
¼ pound dried cherries

1) Pour wine and 2 cups water into a large pot. Stir in 1 tablespoon of honey, aniseed and lemon zest. Bring to a simmer over medium low heat.

2) Add apricots and pears. If necessary, add more water to cover the fruit. Increase heat, bring to a boil, then reduce heat. Cover and simmer for 5 minutes.

3) Add cherries, cover and simmer for another 5–10 minutes or until fruit is tender.

4) Remove as much zest as possible. Add more honey if desired. Serve hot, warm or cold, with the poaching liquid.

Per serving (approximate values): 250 Calories; 0.4g Fat (1.6% calories from fat); 2.2g Protein; 56g Carbohydrate; 0mg Cholesterol; 9mg Sodium.

VIETNAMESE BANANA SOUP

Makes 6 servings
Prep Time: 45 minutes

1 cup sugar
6 whole bananas, peeled, sliced 1-inch
2 tablespoons lime juice
3 cups coconut milk
½ cup water
½ cup rice vermicelli
¼ cup pearl tapioca
¼ cup toasted sesame seeds

1) In a medium mixing bowl, sprinkle lime over bananas, mixing to coat banana slices. Sprinkle sugar over bananas and allow to sit for about 30 minutes.

2) In a medium bowl, break off a section of rice vermicelli (there is typically much more in the package than needed). You'll need about ½ cup. Soak vermicelli in cold water for 15 minutes. Drain.

3) In a 3-quart saucepan, combine the sugared bananas, coconut milk and water. Bring to a boil and simmer, covered, for 15 minutes.

4) Add the rice vermicelli and tapioca and continue cooking, covered, for an additional 10 minutes until tapioca pearls are clear and translucent.

5) Remove from heat and serve immediately. Sprinkle ½ teaspoon sesame seeds over top before serving.

Per serving (approximate values): 563 Calories; 31.7g Fat (47.5% calories from fat); 4.9g Protein; 74.1 g Carbohydrate; 0mg Cholesterol; 21 mg Sodium.

White Hominy Burritos with Strawberry Purée

Makes 4 servings
Prep Time: 30 minutes

---

29 ounces white hominy, canned, drained
2 tablespoons powdered sugar
3 tablespoons whipping cream
1 pint fresh strawberries
2 tablespoons butter
2 tablespoons brown sugar
4 whole flour tortillas

Warm tortillas in microwave (30 seconds at high) or cover and place in 200 degree oven.

---

1) In a food processor, purée the hominy. Add powdered sugar and cream and pulse until combined.
2) Place about ½ cup of mixture in the center of a tortilla. Fold up burrito style.
3) Purée the strawberries. Set aside.
4) Brush non-stick sauté pan with butter. Add 1 tablespoon of brown sugar and over medium heat until sugar melts. Add as many tortillas as will fit in pan comfortably. Sauté for 1 minute. Turn and brown the other side, about 1 minute. Remove to platter. Continue with remaining chimichangas.
5) Spoon purée over burritos and serve!

Per serving (approximate values): 412 Calories; 14.4g Fat (31.2% calories from fat); 6.8g Protein; 64.6g Carbohydrate; 31 mg Cholesterol; 664mg Sodium.

PEACH-ALMOND SORBET

Makes 10 servings
Prep Time: 45 minutes

6 cups fresh peaches, unpeeled, very ripe, diced
1 cup granulated sugar
3 cups water
2 tablespoons lemon juice
2 tablespoons lime juice
½ teaspoon almond extract

1) Combine everything except almond extract in a large saucepan or Dutch oven. Bring to a boil. Cover and reduce heat to medium. Cook until peaches are soft.

2) Remove from stove. Press peach mixture through a medium sieve. Reserve juice mixture and discard solids.

3) Add almond extract to reserved juice mixture and stir well. Pour into a large pan (11x7x2-inch or larger). Cover and freeze until firm. Remove mixture from freezer.

4) If you have a good ice cream scooper, simply scrape across frozen mixture until there is sufficient amount for a serving. Alternatively, break the frozen mixture into chunks. Add chunks to a food processor fitted with a knife blade and process until smooth. Spoon into container, cover and freeze up to a month.

Per serving (approximate values): 123 Calories; 0.1 g Fat (0.6% calories from fat); 0.7g Protein; 31.8g Carbohydrate; 0mg Cholesterol; 2mg Sodium.

TROPICAL FRUIT IN LIME SYRUP

Makes 6 servings
Prep Time: 30 minutes

¾ cup water
½ cup white wine
½ cup sugar
1 whole lime, peel, grated
2 cups pineapple, ¾-inch pieces
3 whole kiwi fruit, peeled, halved crosswise, then quartered
1 whole mango, peeled, ¾-inch pieces
1 ½ tablespoons lime juice
Favorite tropical sorbet, such as mango or passion fruit

Syrup:

1) Combine water, wine, sugar and peel in small saucepan. Bring to a boil, stirring until sugar dissolves. Remove from heat.
2) Pour into container, cover and chill syrup until cold.

Fruit:

1) Combine fruit, lime juice and syrup in large bowl. Mix well. Cover fruit mixture and refrigerate for at least 1 hour or overnight.
2) Scoop ½ cup favorite tropical sorbet into each of 6 compote glasses. Spoon fruit mixture around sorbet. Serve immediately!

Per serving (approximate values): 156 Calories; 0.5g Fat (3% calories from fat); 0.9g Protein; 37.1 g Carbohydrate; 0mg Cholesterol; 6mg Sodium.

PUMPKIN ICE CREAM CAKE

This was a dessert I developed for the TV show, but determined afterwards that it would be impossible to show under hot studio lights. So I brought the concoction into my then current day job and it was gobbled up. It now is my mom's favorite dessert, one that she can safely keep in her freezer until she wants another slice!

Makes 12 servings
Prep Time: 1 hour 40 minutes

Crust:
3 cups pecans, finely chopped
½ cup brown sugar
3 tablespoons butter, melted

Filling:
2 ½ cups whipping cream, chilled
1 cup brown sugar
8 large egg yolks
1 ½ cups pumpkin, canned, solid packed
½ cup light corn syrup
3 tablespoons dark rum
1 ½ teaspoons ground ginger
¾ teaspoon cinnamon
¼ teaspoon ground nutmeg

Topping:
6 ounces pecan halves
12 ounces prepared caramel topping (Kraft)

Preheat oven to 350 degrees.

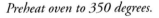

Crust:
1) Finely chop nuts and sugar in processor.

2) Add butter and pulse until moist crumbs form. Sprinkle over the bottom of a 9-inch spring form pan, patting evenly. Freeze 10 minutes.

3) Bake crust until golden, about 10 minutes. Cool completely. Take a sheet of aluminum foil and wrap securely around the outside of pan. Set aside.

Filling:

1) Whisk 1 cup cream, sugar and yolks in medium saucepan. Stir constantly over medium heat until candy thermometer reads 160 degrees, about 10 minutes. Pour into large bowl.

2) Using electric mixer, beat mixture until cool and slightly thickened, about 10 minutes.

3) Beat in pumpkin, corn syrup, rum and spices.

4) Using electric mixer, in a separate large mixing bowl, beat remaining 1 ½ cups cream to stiff peaks.

5) Very slowly whisk a stream of custard into the whipped cream, being careful that the whipped volume of the mixture is as high as possible.

6) Transfer filling to crust. Cover and freeze until firm, preferably at least 8 hours.

Topping:

1) Arrange pecans side by side in a circular pattern atop torte. Drizzle caramel as evenly as possible over top. Spread evenly with a rubber spatula.

2) Freeze again until caramel sets, about three hours.

3) Run a sharp knife completely around pan sides to loosen torte. Release pan sides and serve.

Per serving (approximate values): 735 Calories; 51.8g Fat (61.1 % calories from fat); 6.8g Protein; 67.6g Carbohydrate; 218mg Cholesterol; 173mg Sodium.

TIRAMISU

My first taste of this heavenly dessert was while stationed in Monterey, California. Memory of it haunted me until one quiet weekend I couldn't stand it anymore. I had to recreate that taste sensation. I buckled down and spent an entire weekend attempting to recreate what I has tasted. This was the winner!

Makes 12 servings
Prep Time: 1 hour

¾ cup sugar
6 large egg yolks
16 ounces mascarpone cheese
2 tablespoons Marsala wine
8 ounces heavy whipping cream, whipped
1 ½ cups espresso
3 tablespoons brandy
2 packages ladyfinger cookies
1 ounce bittersweet chocolate, frozen

Spray a 9x13-inch glass baking dish with non-stick coating.

Prepare Cream Mixture:

1) Whisk together yolks and sugar until well blended. Place over (not in) boiling water, and whisk until mixture becomes thick and coats a spoon, 8–10 minutes. A double-boiler is indispensable for this. Be patient. It takes a while to warm the egg yolks to the right consistency. Be sure to constantly whisk the mixture while over the boiling water. It will cook like an over-easy egg if you're not careful! The temperature of the mixture should be between 150 to 160 degrees when it's just right! Cool the mixture completely.

2) Add mascarpone and Marsala. Mix until incorporated. Place covered in the refrigerator while the whipped cream is prepared.

3) Whip the heavy cream to a stiff peak. Fold a little whipped cream into the custard mixture to lighten it. Then add the remaining whipped cream. Make sure to fold gently until fully incorporated. Refrigerate, covered.

4) To prepare espresso mixture, combine espresso and brandy in small mixing bowl.

To assemble:

1) Take basting brush and dip in espresso mixture. Soak the uncut side of ladyfingers. Turn over and place in baking dish, soaked side down and baste the cut side with 2 or 3 good soakings of espresso until the bottom of dish is covered with cookies. Don't soak the fingers until they fall apart. You still want to feel the bite of cake when you eat the dish.

2) Top with one layer of mascarpone mixture. Add another layer of cookies soaked on uncut side only. Coat the cut side once again. Top with a second layer of mascarpone mixture.

3) Grate a square of bittersweet chocolate over top.

4) Cover and refrigerate until ready to serve.

Per serving (approximate values): 343 Calories; 28.5g Fat (75.4% calories from fat); 4.3g Protein; 16.7g Carbohydrate; 191 mg Cholesterol; 37mg Sodium.

ALMOND CUSTARD WITH LITCHIS

My first visit to the big island of Hawaii (while stationed on Oahu), I was introduced to two new taste sensations: Kona coffee and litchi nuts. Litchis are a very strange looking fruit. They are small, round and have a hard prickly exterior. Crack it open, however, and what lies inside is a most delicious fleshy fruit. Canned litchis have a much different flavor and texture, so buy fresh if you can. I see them quite often these days in Denver supermarkets, so odds are they may well be at yours!

Makes 4 servings
Prep Time: 20 minutes

¾ cup water
¼ cup sugar
1 envelope unflavored gelatin
1 cup whole milk
1 teaspoon almond extract
22 ounces canned litchis (or fresh, if you can get them)

1) In small saucepan, heat water, sugar and gelatin to boiling. Stir occasionally until sugar and gelatin are dissolved. Remove from heat.
2) Stir in milk and almond extract. Pour into loaf pan, 9x5x3 inches.
3) Cover and refrigerate until firm, at least 4 hours.
4) Unmold custard. Cut custard into 1-inch diamonds or squares.
5) Place litchis with syrup in serving bowls and arrange custard amongst fruit.

Per serving (approximate values): 126 Calories; 2.1 g Fat (14.5% calories from fat); 12.1 g Protein; 15.3g Carbohydrate; 8mg Cholesterol; 42mg Sodium.

CHOCOLATE RASPBERRY BISCOTTI

Makes 24 servings
Prep Time: 30 minutes

½ cup sugar
¼ cup butter, softened
1 large egg
2 cups flour
⅓ cup cocoa powder
¾ teaspoon baking powder
¾ cup raspberry jam

Preheat oven to 325 degrees. Lightly spray cooking sheet.

1) In a medium bowl, cream together sugar and butter until light and fluffy. Mix in egg.
2) In a small bowl, combine flour, cocoa and baking powder. Add to butter mixture.
3) Stir in jam. Divide dough in half.
4) On a well floured work surface, shape dough into logs. Transfer logs to baking sheet. Bake for about 25 minutes until firm and lightly browned. Cool on rack for at least 5 minutes before cutting.
5) Cut logs on a diagonal into ¾-inch slices. Return slices to baking sheet, leaving plenty of room around each slice. Place back in oven at same temperature for 10 to 15 minutes, turning over once, until desired crispness.

Per serving (approximate values): 100 Calories; 2.4g Fat (20.4% calories from fat); 1.7g Protein; 19.3g Carbohydrate; 14mg Cholesterol; 38mg Sodium.

POLISH RUGELACH

The two years I spent teaching included a yearly Christmas cookie class. It was not much fun for me—I had to make all the dough. It was, however, much fun for the students, who got to prepare and go home with most of their holiday cookies done. This recipe is a bit more complicated than others, but wonderful morsels when all is said and done!

Makes 64 servings
Prep Time: 45 minutes

Dough:
1 cup butter, room temperature
8 ounces cream cheese, room temperature
½ cup sugar
2 ¾ cups flour
½ teaspoon salt

Filling:
¾ cup sugar
⅔ cup dried cranberries, chopped
⅔ cup walnuts, chopped
½ cup butter, melted
2 teaspoons cinnamon
1 teaspoon allspice
1 large egg, beaten sugar

Preheat oven to 350 degrees.

For dough:
1) In large bowl, beat butter and cream cheese until light.
2) Add sugar and beat until fluffy.
3) Mix in flour and salt.
4) Gather into ball and knead until smooth.
5) Divide dough into 4 equal pieces. Flatten into discs. Wrap in plastic wrap and refrigerate about 1 hour.

For filling:
1) Mix all ingredients in a medium bowl until blended. Set aside.

2)   Take out dough. Place one disc on floured work surface. Roll out dough into 8-inch circle.

3)   Spread 3 tablespoons of filling over round. Cut round into 8 wedges.

4)   Starting at wide edge of each wedge, roll up tightly to tip. Place cookies, tip pointing down, on baking sheet and form into crescents.

5)   Brush cookies with egg and sprinkle with sugar. Bake until golden, about 20 minutes. Repeat with remaining discs.

Per serving (approximate values): 94 Calories; 6.4g Fat (59.8% calories from fat); 1.3g Protein; 8.4g Carbohydrate; 19mg Cholesterol; 72mg Sodium.

RUSSIAN TEACAKES

Makes 48 servings
Prep Time: 30 minutes

1 cup butter, softened
½ cup powdered sugar
1 teaspoon vanilla
2 ¼ cups all-purpose flour
¼ teaspoon salt
¾ cup chopped nuts, optional

Heat oven to 350 degrees.

1) Mix butter, powdered sugar and vanilla.
2) Stir in flour, salt and nuts.
3) Shape dough into 1-inch balls. Place on ungreased cookie sheet. Bake until set, but not brown, 8 to 9 minutes.
4) Roll in powdered sugar while warm. Re-roll in powdered sugar when cool, if desired.

Per serving (approximate values): 73 Calories; 5.1 g Fat (61.3% calories from fat); 1g Protein; 6.2g Carbohydrate; 10mg Cholesterol; 50mg Sodium.

BANANA OATMEAL COOKIES

Makes 72 servings
Prep Time: 30 minutes

1 cup sugar
⅔ cup butter or shortening
2 eggs, beaten slightly
¾ cup mashed bananas
½ teaspoon vanilla
½ teaspoon lemon juice
1 ½ cups rolled oats (do not use instant oats)
2 cups flour
¾ teaspoon baking soda
1 teaspoon baking powder
1 teaspoon salt
½ cup nuts (Use pecans, walnuts, or your choice of nuts, chopped)

Preheat oven to 350 degrees.

1) Sift flour, soda, baking powder and salt together.
2) Cream together sugar and shortening. Beat in eggs.
3) Stir in the vanilla, lemon juice and banana.
4) Add rolled oats and nuts to flour mixture, alternately with banana mixture, mixing well after each addition. Stir in nuts.
5) Drop by teaspoonfuls onto greased baking sheet and bake 15 to 18 minutes or until golden.

Per serving (approximate values): 55 Calories; 2.5g Fat (40.5% calories from fat); 1g Protein; 7.4g Carbohydrate; 11 mg Cholesterol; 67mg Sodium.

APPLE PIE BARS

My catering past again appears in this section of the cookbook. Bars are a great way of feeding many with less effort. They are also a great dessert for casual occasions, as you don't need flatware!

Makes 24 servings
Prep Time: 45 minutes

<u>Crumb Topping:</u>
1 ½ cups flour
⅔ cup sugar
10 tablespoons butter
<u>Crust:</u>
2 cups flour
3 tablespoons flour
¾ cup butter
½ cup sugar
1 large egg, beaten
1 teaspoon vanilla
<u>Filling:</u>
2 cups cheddar cheese, shredded
2 teaspoons lemon rind
1 teaspoon cinnamon
½ teaspoon ground nutmeg
6 medium green apples, cored, peeled, grated
2 tablespoons lemon juice

Preheat oven to 375 degrees. Grease a 13x9-inch baking pan.

Crumb topping:
1)   In a medium size bowl, combine flour and sugar.
2)   With pastry blender, strong fork or a food processor, cut in butter until mixture resembles coarse crumbs. Set aside.

Crust:
1)   In a small bowl add 2 cups flour. Set aside.

2) In a large bowl, beat butter and sugar until well combined. Add egg and beat until smooth. Stir in vanilla.

3) Gradually add flour to butter mixture until soft dough forms. With fingers, press dough evenly into prepared pan.

Filling:

1) In a large bowl, combine cheese, remaining ¼ cup sugar, 3 tablespoons flour, lemon rind and spices.

2) Fold in apples and lemon juice.

3) Spoon apple mixture over dough in pan. Sprinkle crumb topping evenly over apple mixture.

4) Bake 45-50 minutes or until golden brown. The golden hue of the topping is what tells you this bar is finished, although if you stick a knife in the center, it should be like slicing butter.

5) Cool completely. Cover and refrigerate until ready to serve.

Per serving (approximate values): 257 Calories; 14g Fat (48.4% calories from fat); 4.8g Protein; 28.8g Carbohydrate; 47mg Cholesterol; 168mg Sodium.

COCONUT MUD BARS

Makes 24 servings
Prep Time: 45 minutes

Crust:
2 cups flour
¾ teaspoon baking powder
Pinch salt
¾ cup brown sugar
¾ cup butter, softened, cut small
Ganache:
10 ounces semisweet chocolate, chopped/chips
¾ cup heavy cream
Topping:
4 tablespoons butter
½ cup sugar
2 teaspoons vanilla
2 large eggs
1 ½ cups coconut, shredded
1 ½ cups pecans, chopped

Preheat the oven to 350 degrees. Lightly butter a 9x13-inch pan.

Crust:
1) In a medium bowl, whisk together the flour, baking powder, salt and brown sugar.
2) With a pastry blender or fork, cut the butter into the dry ingredients until the mixture resembles coarse meal.
3) Press the mixture into the bottom of the prepared pan. Bake for 5 minutes or until the crust is just set. Place the pan on a rack to cool. Leave the oven on.

The Ganache:
1) Place the chocolate in a medium bowl.
2) In a small saucepan, bring the cream to a simmer.
3) Pour the hot cream over the chocolate. Let stand for 5 minutes. Stir until mixture is smooth.

4) Pour the ganache over the crust and refrigerate for about 15 minutes to let the ganache set.

Topping:

1) In a medium bowl, cream the butter. Add the granulated sugar and vanilla. Beat until blended.
2) Beat in the eggs. Stir in the coconut and pecans.
3) Drop the coconut-pecan topping evenly over the ganache and spread gently.
4) Bake for 25 to 30 minutes or until the top is golden brown. Set the pan on a rack to cool. Cut into bars.

Per serving (approximate values): 299 Calories; 20.6g Fat (59.4% calories from fat); 3g Protein; 28.7g Carbohydrate; 49mg Cholesterol; 102mg Sodium.

THREE CHOCOLATE BROWNIES

I couldn't resist including my favorite brownie recipe. These are super dense and super moist. I made these for a local Denver trade show to entice people to visit our booth. While it indeed did the trick, I had to stop my fellow booth-mate Jody Hobbs from eating them all, chocoholic that she is!

Makes 15 servings
Prep Time: 45 minutes

1 cup butter
1 cup brown sugar
⅔ cup granulated sugar
18 ounces semisweet chocolate chips
2 ounces unsweetened chocolate
5 large eggs, room temperature
1 tablespoon vanilla
1 ½ cups flour
2 teaspoons instant coffee powder
¼ teaspoon salt
1 cup walnuts, optional
<u>Glaze frosting:</u>
⅔ cup cream
6 ounces bittersweet chocolate, chopped/chips

Preheat oven to 350 degrees. Butter 13x9-inch pan.

1) In a medium saucepan, combine the butter and sugars. Over medium heat, stir the mixture with a wooden spoon until butter is melted, about 5 minutes. Remove from heat.

2) Add the semisweet (bittersweet is fine) and unsweetened chocolate. Stir until completely melted.

3) Add eggs and vanilla and mix until well combined.

4) Add the flour, instant coffee powder and salt. Mix until all is well combined.

5) Add the walnuts, if desired, and mix until just combined.

6) Scrape the batter into prepared pan and smooth top with spatula. Bake the brownies 25 to 30 minutes or until toothpick inserted 2 inches away from the center comes out slightly moist. Do not over bake the brownies.

7) Cool the brownies completely in the pan.

Glaze Frosting:

1) In a medium saucepan, bring the cream to a gentle boil. Take the pan off the heat and add the chocolate. Let sit for 2-3 minutes.

2) With a wire whisk, stir until mixture is smooth. Cool the glaze 5-10 minutes in the refrigerator, until slightly thickened but still pourable.

3) Pour the glaze over the brownies, spreading as necessary to insure an even coating. Cool completely.

Per serving (approximate values): 588 Calories; 39.8g Fat (56.3% calories from fat); 8.8g Protein; 60.5g Carbohydrate; 114mg Cholesterol; 196mg Sodium.

CRANBERRY-MACADAMIA BARS

Makes 24 servings
Prep Time: 45 minutes

<u>Crust</u>
1 ¼ cups flour
¾ cup sugar
½ cup butter
1 cup macadamia nuts, chopped
<u>Topping</u>
1 ¼ cups sugar
2 large eggs, beaten
2 tablespoons milk
1 teaspoon orange peel, shredded
1 teaspoon vanilla
1 cup cranberries, chopped
½ cup coconut

Preheat the oven to 350 degrees. Have an ungreased 9x13-inch pan ready.

Crust:
1) In a medium bowl, stir together the flour and ¾ cup sugar.
2) Cut in the butter until the mixture resembles coarse crumbs.
3) Stir in ½ cup of the nuts. Press the flour mixture onto the bottom of the pan.
4) Bake for 10 to 15 minutes or until the crust is light brown.

Topping:
1) Combine the 1 ¼ cups sugar, eggs, milk, orange peel and vanilla. Beat until combined. Pour over the hot crust. Sprinkle with the remaining nuts, cranberries and coconuts.
2) Bake for 30–40 minutes or until golden. Cool slightly in the pan. Cut into 24 bars. Cool completely.

Per serving (approximate values): 176 Calories; 9g Fat (44.6% calories from fat); 1.8g Protein; 23.4g Carbohydrate; 28mg Cholesterol; 45mg Sodium.

LEMON CANDY BARS

Pucker up! These bars will totally remind you of those little hard lemon candies found in all good candy stores. This and my plain cheesecake were the most popular items that I offered when catering.

Makes 18 servings
Prep Time: 30 minutes

<u>Crust:</u>
2 cups all-purpose flour
¾ cup butter, cut into pieces
½ cup light brown sugar, firmly packed
<u>Filling:</u>
1 ½ cups granulated sugar
4 large eggs
2 medium lemons, grated peel of
⅔ cup lemon juice, freshly squeezed
1 teaspoon baking powder

Preheat oven to 350 degrees. Lightly butter 9x13-inch baking pan.

<u>Crust:</u>
1) In food processor, combine flour, butter, brown sugar and process until fine crumbs. (If you do not have a food processor, cream butter with sugars until well combined, then add flour and combine until fine crumbs are formed).
2) Press crumb mixture evenly into prepared pan.
3) Bake in oven until lightly browned, about 18-20 minutes.

<u>Filling:</u>
1) In a medium mixing bowl, combine sugar, eggs, lemon peel, lemon juice and baking powder until well mixed. Do this quickly before the crust comes out of the oven.
2) Remove hot crust from oven. Immediately pour over hot crust. Put back into the oven at the same temperature and bake until filling is slightly browned and springy to the touch, about 20-25 minutes. Place on rack to cool.

Per serving (approximate values): 225 Calories; 8.8g Fat (34.4% calories from fat); 3g Protein; 34.9g Carbohydrate; 68mg Cholesterol; 114mg Sodium.

BAKLAVA WITH APPLE FILLING

I love baklava, but it is typically so very sweet. Add apples and the sweetness factor is cut by half. If you can manage the patience in dealing with phyllo dough, this dessert is an awesome treat that will serve many!

Makes 24 servings
Prep Time: 1 hour

3 cups green apples, pared, cored, shredded
1 ½ cups walnuts, chopped
1 cup almonds, chopped
1 cup sugar
½ cup raisins
2 teaspoons lemon peel, grated
2 tablespoons lemon juice
2 teaspoons cinnamon
1 pound phyllo dough
1 pound butter, clarified
½ cup honey

Preheat oven to 350 degrees. Grease 10x15x2-inch baking pan.

1) In a large mixing bowl, combine first 8 ingredients (apples through cinnamon).
2) Sheet by sheet, place 8 sheets of phyllo in buttered pan, trimming phyllo to pan size. Butter each layer generously with pastry brush.
3) Cover these 8 layers with half of apple mixture.
4) Add 6 more phyllo sheets, buttering each sheet as they are added.
5) Spread remaining apple mixture over phyllo.
6) Top with 8 more buttered sheets of phyllo.
7) With a very sharp knife, cut into top layers of phyllo about ½-inch deep, creating a diamond shape.
8) Bake baklava for about 40 minutes until golden brown.
9) While baking, warm honey in microwave until easily pourable. Immediately after removing baklava from oven, pour honey evenly over baklava. Cool completely.

10) Following scores on top with a very sharp knife and a glass of warm water nearby, cut fully to the bottom. Use warm water to loosen bits that cling to knife.

Per serving (approximate values): 344 Calories; 24g Fat (60.5% calories from fat); 4.8g Protein; 30.5g Carbohydrate; 41 mg Cholesterol; 250mg Sodium.

NOTES

All of the photographs in the book have full-color counterparts! You can view them in all their glory on my website:

www.thisisdeliciouswhatisit.com

There you will also find photographs of dinners I conducted in preparation of the cookbook. I prepared four seasonal dinner parties, mostly because I thought I would include photographs of them in the cookbook. They are on the website for now, while I consider a possible theme for a future cookbook that might include them. In the meantime, I wish to thank the following person(s) or companies that helped me with the dinners, particularly because I couldn't include their work in this volume:

Floral Centerpieces:

Fall and Winter Dinner Pictorial:

Veldkamp's
9501 W. Colfax
Lakewood, CO 80215
Toll Free: (800) 247-3730 **24hr:** (800) 247-3730
www.veldkamps.com

Spring Dinner Pictorial:

Urban Wilds
2029 13th Avenue
Denver, CO 80206
(303) 316-4666

Summer Dinner Pictorial:

Sharon Florist & Gift Shop
5 Post Office Square
Sharon, MA 02067

(781) 784-4499
www.ftd.com/sharonflorist

Wine:

Fall, Spring and Winter Dinners:

CORKS
Courtesy of Sommelier Pam Glynn
1620 Platte Street
Denver, CO 80202-6114
(303) 477-5799

Summer Dinner:

Sudbury Wine Merchant
Star Market Plaza
513 Boston Post Rd.
Sudbury, MA 01776
(978) 443-5266
www.sudburywine.com

Dinner Party Hosts:

Fall and Spring Dinners:

Featuring the home of Radleigh Valentine
Denver, Colorado

Summer Dinner:

Featuring the home of Linda Farmer and Kim Matland
Sharon, Massachusetts

Winter Dinner:

Featuring the home of Richard and Susan Malmstein
Parker, Colorado

Shopping, dinner preparation and miscellaneous other help:

Susan Shangle
Susan was helpful in the success of the Summer dinner in Sharon, MA. She also helped with coordination of the Fall dinner in Denver, CO.

Susan and Richard Malmstein
My sister helped in all aspects of the three dinners in Denver. Her sense of style was welcome while setting the table for the Winter dinner. I also want to thank her for the time she spent with me preparing just the right setting for many of the photographs, not dinner-related, but presented in the book. I have Rick to thank for the multitude of errands he selflessly ran, as well as his clean-up duty skills.

Kyle Nelson
Kyle was a huge help with the Fall dinner, my very first.

ABOUT THE AUTHOR

With *Babett's Feast* as inspiration, Robert Meyers-Lussier started cooking while stationed in West Germany. Since leaving the military, Meyers-Lussier has catered *The World on a Platter*, hosted a television show *Talking With Your Mouth Full*, written articles and taught focusing solely on creating comforting culinary experiences for family and friends.

INDEX I: RECIPES IN COOKBOOK ORDER

Desserts

INDEX II: RECIPES IN ALPHABETICAL ORDER

0-595-30505-9

Printed in the United States
20995LVS00004B/1-36